CRIMINAL LAW
FOR THE
LAYMAN

Inbau Law Enforcement Series

SECOND EDITION

CRIMINAL LAW FOR THE LAYMAN
A Citizen's Guide

FRED E. INBAU
John Henry Wigmore Professor of Law Emeritus
Northwestern University

MARVIN E. ASPEN
Judge, Circuit Court of
Cook County (Chicago), Illinois

JEREMY D. MARGOLIS
Assistant United States Attorney
Northern District of Illinois

CHILTON BOOK COMPANY Radnor, Pennsylvania

Copyright © 1977 by Fred E. Inbau,
Marvin E. Aspen, and Jeremy D. Margolis
© 1970 by Fred E. Inbau and Marvin E. Aspen
Second Edition *All rights reserved*
Published in Radnor, Pa., by Chilton Book Company
and simultaneously in Don Mills, Ontario, Canada,
by Nelson Canada Limited
Manufactured in the United States of America

Library of Congress Cataloging in Publication Data

Inbau, Fred E.
   Criminal law for the layman: a citizen's guide

  First ed. by F. E. Inbau, M. E. Aspen
    1. Law, criminal—handbook for laymen
I. Aspen, Marvin. II. Margolis, Jeremy.
III. Title
HF4351.C3832   1977   364.44   77-2478
ISBN 0-8019-6639-6
ISBN 0-8019-6649-3 pb.

4 5 6 7 8 9 0   6 5 4 3 2 1

To Marie and Harriet Christiansen
    from F.E.I.
To Jennifer, Jessica, and Andrew
    from M.E.A.
To Wendy
    from J.D.M.

Preface

The average citizen has always been curious about criminal law and its administration. In spite of this curiosity, however, the available information on the subject has been generally inadequate and frequently distorted, due in large measure to the offerings of novels, movies, television, and other media. In the past, this inadequacy was not disturbing to, or even recognized by, the ordinary viewer or reader; moreover, the general public welfare and safety were themselves little affected by it. But events of the past decade or so have made it imperative that complete and accurate information be made available.

Citizens today are very much concerned about crime and the laws governing criminal conduct. They want to know more about the entire system of criminal justice—about the police, the prosecution and defense lawyers, the criminal courts, and their various functions; about the kinds of activities that come within the scope of the criminal law and their accompanying penalties; about criminal trials and sentencing processes; about paroles and pardons; and, among many other concerns, about the legal safeguards which exist for persons suspected or accused of crime.

Disclosures in recent years of flagrant violations of the law on the part of public officials, high and low, have increased citizen interest in the criminal justice system. Citizen interest is also founded upon the not unreasonable fear that we ourselves, or members of our families, or our close friends, may someday be involved in the criminal justice system, as witnesses, victims, or even as suspects.

Another basis for citizen interest in criminal law is the possibility of a call for jury service in a criminal case, in which event a reasonable acquaintance with the fundamentals of criminal law and its administration will render that civic duty more interesting and more meaningful.

This book was prepared to satisfy the needs of all citizens in general, and students in particular, for easily understood, yet technically accurate, information regarding the criminal law and its application at all levels—on the street, in the police station, in the courts, and throughout the criminal justice system. We trust and believe it measures up to that objective.

FRED E. INBAU
MARVIN E. ASPEN
JEREMY D. MARGOLIS

Supplementing the textual discussion of the law, the authors have reproduced, as an Appendix, those provisions of the Constitution and its amendments which are relevant to the general problems regarding the law of crimes and the procedures by which the criminal law is to be enforced.

In this text, "he" and other masculine pronouns are used generically for the sake of brevity and should be taken to mean both males and females.

Contents

PREFACE — vii

Part I
PARTICIPANTS IN THE CRIMINAL JUSTICE SYSTEM

CHAPTER 1 THE POLICE — 3
  Local Officers — 3
    Municipal Police — 3
    County Sheriff — 4
    State Police — 4
    Other Local Law Enforcement Officers — 4
  Federal Officers — 4
    Federal Bureau of Investigation (FBI) Agents — 4
    Treasury Agents — 5
    Other Federal Civilian Law Enforcement Agents — 5
    Military Law Enforcement Agents — 6
    National Intelligence Agents — 6

CHAPTER 2 THE LAWYERS — 7
  Local Government Lawyers — 7
    Municipal Attorneys — 7
    County or District Attorneys — 7
    Attorney General of the State — 8
    Appointed Defense Attorneys or Public Defenders — 9
  Federal Government Lawyers — 9

Attorney General of the United States	9
Solicitor General	10
United States Attorneys	10
Organized Crime Strike Force Attorneys	10
Defense Attorneys	10
Military Attorneys	10
CHAPTER 3 THE COURTS	11
Local and State Courts	11
Minor Trial Courts	11
Major Trial Courts	12
Juvenile Courts	12
Appellate Courts	12
Federal Courts	13
Magistrate Courts	14
District Courts	14
Courts of Appeal	15
Supreme Court of the United States	15
Military Courts	16
CHAPTER 4 DETENTION AND CORRECTIONAL INSTITUTIONS	17
Local and State Facilities	17
Police Lockups	17
Jails	17
Prisons	18
Juvenile Facilities	18
Federal Facilities	18
Jails	18
Prisons	18

Part II
CRIMES

CHAPTER 5 CRIMES AGAINST THE PERSON	21
Homicide	21
Murder	21
Felony-Murder	22
Degrees of Murder	22
Manslaughter	22
Voluntary Manslaughter	23
Involuntary Manslaughter	23
Federal Homicide Law	24
Modern Murder–Manslaughter Legislation	24
Capital Punishment	25

Contents   xi

    Kidnapping and Unlawful Restraint   26
        Kidnapping   26
        Unlawful Restraint   28
    Assault and Battery   29
        Battery   29
        Assault   29
    Sex Offenses and Related Criminal Conduct   30
        Forcible Rape   30
        Sex Offenses against Children   31
            Statutory Rape   31
            Indecent Liberties and Contributing to Sexual   31
                Delinquency
            Incest   31
        Adultery and Fornication   31
        Bigamy   31
        Deviate Sexual Conduct   32
        Prostitution and Related Offenses   32
        The Federal "White Slave" Act   32
        Exhibitionism   33
        Window Peeping   33
        Anonymous Telephone Calls   34
    Eavesdropping—"Wiretapping" and "Bugging"   34
        Federal Law   35
        State Law   35

CHAPTER 6   CRIMES AGAINST PROPERTY   36
    Theft and Related Offenses   36
        Larceny   36
        Larceny by Bailee and Embezzlement   37
        False Pretenses and Confidence Games   37
        Modern Theft Legislation   38
        Robbery   39
        Burglary   39
        Federal Theft Offenses   40
        Forgery   41
        Credit Card Offenses   42
        Property Damage and Property Intrusions   42
            Arson and Criminal Damage   42
            Trespass   43

CHAPTER 7   OFFENSES AFFECTING PUBLIC MORALS, HEALTH,
                SAFETY, AND WELFARE   44
    Obscenity   44
        Determining Obscenity   44

Abortion	47
Narcotics and Other "Dangerous Substances"	47
Narcotic Addiction Itself	49
Gambling	50
Wagering by Participant	50
Wagering by Bystander	50
Bookmaking	51
Poolselling	51
Lotteries	51
Numbers, Policy, and Bolita	52
Syndicated Gambling	52
Gambling Places	52
Possession of Gambling Devices	53
Federal Prohibitions	53
Miscellaneous Gambling Laws	54
Legalized Off-Track Betting and State-Operated Lotteries	54
The Issue of "Victimless" Crimes	55
The Sale, Possession, and Carrying of Firearms	56
Public Official Corruption	58
Bribery	58
Extortion	59
Conflict of Interest	60
Violations of Civil Rights	60
Election Frauds	61
Annoying and Potentially Dangerous Conduct	62
Disorderly Conduct and Disturbing the Peace	62
Public Intoxication	62
Mob Action, Unlawful Assembly, and Rioting	62
Protest Parades and Marches	63
Restrictions on Residential Picketing	64
CHAPTER 8 "WHITE COLLAR" CRIMES	65
Fraudulent Schemes	65
False Statements	66
Antitrust Activities	67
CHAPTER 9 ORGANIZED CRIME	68
The Nature of Organized Crime	68
Combating Organized Crime	69
CHAPTER 10 MISCELLANEOUS FEDERAL OFFENSES	72
Tax Evasion	72
Immigration Law Violations	73

Contents

Smuggling	73
Counterfeiting	74
Interference with the Mails	74
Espionage and Sabotage	75
Piracy and Other Crimes Committed upon the High Seas	76
Crimes Affecting Aircraft, Motor Vehicles, and Their Auxiliary Facilities	76
Travel Act Violations	77
The Transmission of Threatening Communications	78
Crimes Committed by Military Personnel	78

Chapter 11 Interference with Law Enforcement and Judicial Processes — 80

Interference with Police	80
Obstructing Service of Process	81
Tampering with Evidence	81
Compounding a Crime or Misprision of Felony	81
Unlawful Flight to Avoid or Hamper Prosecutions	82
Harboring Fugitives	83
Prohibited Communications with Jurors and Witnesses	84
Perjury	85
Subornation of Perjury	86
Disobedience of Court Orders and Disruptive Courtroom Behavior	86

Chapter 12 Uncompleted Criminal Conduct and Criminal Combinations — 89

Attempt	89
Solicitation	90
Conspiracy	91

Chapter 13 Accessories to a Crime — 93

Accessory before the Fact	93
Accessory after the Fact	94

Chapter 14 Mental Responsibility — 95

The Defense of Infancy	96
The Defenses of Compulsion and Necessity	96
The Defense of Intoxication	96
The Defense of Entrapment	97
The Defense of Insanity	98
Mental Incompetence	98

Part III
CRIMINAL INVESTIGATIONS AND THE POWERS OF LAW ENFORCEMENT OFFICERS

CHAPTER 15 GENERAL INVESTIGATIVE PROCEDURES   101
  An Overview   101
  Police Investigative Techniques   101
  Investigative Efforts of the Prosecutor and the Grand Jury 102
  Grants of Immunity   103

CHAPTER 16 SPECIFIC POLICE POWERS AND THEIR LIMITATIONS 106
  Arrests without a Warrant   106
    Evidence Required for Probable Cause   107
    Hearsay Evidence and Informers' Tips   107
    Consequences of an Invalid Arrest   108
  Arrests with a Warrant   108
    The Warrant Requirement   109
    The Valid Warrant   110
    Consequences of an Invalid Warrant   110
  Arrests by Federal Officers   111
  Legal Geographic Boundaries for State and Local Police Arrests 112
  Citizen Arrests   112
  Permissible Force in Making Arrests   113
  Post-Arrest Obligations   113
  Legal Alternatives to Arrest   114

CHAPTER 17 EYE-WITNESS IDENTIFICATION PROCEDURES   115

CHAPTER 18 STOP-AND-FRISK   117
  Legal Guidelines and Limitations   117
  Permissible Force   119

CHAPTER 19 SEARCH AND SEIZURE   120
  Search without a Warrant   121
    Search Incident to Arrest   121
    Search Independent of Arrest   122
      Consent Search   122
      Plain View Seizure and Seizure of Abandoned Property 123
      Emergency Search   123
      Vehicle Search   124
      Border Search   124
      "Shocking" Search   124
  Search Warrants   125
    Objects Subject to Seizure   125

Contents   xv

    Form of Complaint for a Search Warrant   125
    Form of the Search Warrant   127
    Issuance and Execution   127
    Warrants for Administrative Agency Search   128
    Court Orders for Procurement of Physical Evidence from
        Suspected Persons upon Less Than Probable Cause   128
    Procedures and Requirements for Having Evidence Rejected   129

CHAPTER 20   INTERROGATIONS AND CONFESSIONS   130
    The Test of Voluntariness   130
    Police Detention   132
    Warnings of Constitutional Rights   132
    General Guideline for Interrogators   134

CHAPTER 21   THE PRIVILEGE AGAINST SELF-INCRIMINATION   135
    History and Policy of the Privilege   135
    Limitations upon the Privilege   136

Part IV
PROCEEDINGS BETWEEN ARREST AND APPEAL

CHAPTER 22   PRE-TRIAL RIGHTS AND PROCEDURES   141
    Right to Counsel   141
    Preliminary Hearing   141
    Habeas Corpus Writ   142
    The Role of Coroner or Medical Examiner   142
    Grand Jury   143
    Bail   144
    Prosecutorial Discretion   146
    Pre-Trial Diversionary Programs   146
    Arraignment and Plea   147
    Pre-Trial Motions   148
        Motion to Quash the Indictment   148
        Motion for a Change of Venue   148
        Motion to Suppress Evidence   149
    Plea Bargaining   149

CHAPTER 23   THE TRIAL   151
    The Law of Evidence—What Can and What Cannot Be Used
        at Trial   151
    Admissibility and Weight of Evidence   151
        Admissibility of Evidence   151
        Rules of Evidence   152
        Weight of Evidence   153

The Exclusionary Rule	154
The Hearsay Rule	154
The Best Evidence Rule	156
Privileges	157
The Opinion Rule	157
Right to a Speedy (Early) Trial	158
Time Limitations for the Initiation of Prosecutions	158
Right to Trial by Jury	159
The Respective Functions of Judge and Jury	159
Composition of the Jury	160
Questioning of Prospective Jurors	160
Opening Statements	161
The Prosecutor's Evidence	162
The Defendant's Evidence	162
Closing Arguments	163
The Court's Instructions to the Jury	163
Jury Deliberation and Verdict	163
The Motion for a New Trial	164
The Ethics of Criminal Law Practitioners	164
CHAPTER 24 SENTENCES	166
Goals of Sentencing	166
Types of Sentences	167
Probation	168
Work-Release	168
CHAPTER 25 PAROLE, PARDONS, AND COMMUTATIONS	170
Parole	170
Pardons and Commutations	170
CHAPTER 26 CURRENT TRENDS IN SENTENCING AND PENOLOGY	172
Rejection of the Concept of Rehabilitation for Prisoners	172
The Determinate Sentence	172
Standardized Sentences	172
Mandatory Sentences	173
Unresolved Problems	173
CHAPTER 27 POST-CONVICTION LEGAL REMEDIES	174
Appeal	174
Collateral Attack	175

Contents

Part V
THE CITIZEN'S DUTY AND HIS PROTECTION FROM POLICE ABUSES

CHAPTER 28 THE CITIZEN AS A COURT WITNESS AND AS A JUROR — 179
  Witness — 179
  Juror — 182

CHAPTER 29 THE CITIZEN'S LEGAL ACTIONS AGAINST THE POLICE AND OTHER LAW ENFORCEMENT OFFICERS — 184
  State Criminal Liability of Police — 184
    Intimidation — 184
    Extortion — 184
    Coercing a Confession — 185
    Assault and Battery — 185
    Electronic Surveillance — 185
    Unauthorized Deadly Weapons — 185
    Aiding Escape — 186
    Perjury and Subornation of Perjury — 186
    Harassing Witnesses or Jurors — 186
    Bribery — 186
    Failure to Report a Bribe — 186
    Tampering with Public Records — 186
    Official Misconduct — 186
    Violating Rights of Accused — 187
  State Civil Liability of Police — 187
    False Arrest and Imprisonment — 187
    Malicious Prosecution — 187
    Action for Negligence — 187
    Indemnification of Police Officers — 188
  Federal Criminal Liability of Police — 188
  Federal Civil Liability of Police — 189
  Prosecutorial Immunity — 191

APPENDIX — 193
GLOSSARY — 197
INDEX — 201

Part I
PARTICIPANTS IN THE CRIMINAL JUSTICE SYSTEM

Chapter 1
The Police

Man's decision to substitute systems of law for the "might makes right" philosophy of our distant ancestors required that certain persons be empowered to enforce laws for our collective security. Unlike some countries in which a single, national police force undertakes the peace-keeping responsibilities for an entire nation, in the United States approximately 400,000 law enforcement officers perform their functions and duties within a wide variety of agencies and governmental entities.

LOCAL OFFICERS

Municipal Police

Municipal police bear the responsibility of enforcing state laws within cities, villages, and towns. In a large metropolis, a high degree of specialization takes place and sharply defined responsibilities are routine. Uniformed officers may be assigned to traffic, patrol, or administrative functions. Detectives may be assigned to the investigation of such crimes as homicides, sex offenses, burglaries, robberies, arson, and auto theft. Special units may be established to combat organized crime, to provide port security, to control vice, to handle juvenile offenders, to track down missing persons, or to utilize special weapons and tactics (SWAT) in sniper and other especially dangerous situations. In smaller communities, however, specialization is both unnecessary and unworkable; during a single day's tour of duty, one police officer or town constable may settle a domestic dispute, write a speeding ticket, find a lost child, investigate a burglary, or arrest a passer of bad checks.

County Sheriff

The county sheriff and his deputies have the authority to enforce state laws anywhere within their county (or the county equivalent, "parish," as in Louisiana). As a rule, though, the sheriff's functions of criminal investigation, patrol, and traffic law enforcement, are confined to the county's unincorporated areas which are unprotected by municipal police. However, where a major crime occurs in a small community, the sheriff's police may provide the local police department with technical services, such as scientific laboratory experts, which cannot be supported at the municipal level.

County sheriffs are also generally responsible for the security and administrative functions of the local court system within the county. Often, the sheriff is also the custodian of the local jail.

Courtroom bailiffs and the servers of subpoenas and other legal documents are generally the deputies of the county sheriff.

State Police

The state police, state troopers, or highway patrol officers usually exercise law enforcement authority anywhere within their respective states. Their primary duty, however, consists of the patrol of roads and highways. While accident prevention and response to accidents are of major concern to these law enforcement agencies, their duties in rural and unincorporated areas are often the same as those that city police perform in the cities. The state police will sometimes have a plainclothes investigative unit to investigate criminal activity from one end of the state to the other. Often, however, such a statewide investigative function is carried out or supplemented by a separate state bureau of investigation. Use of state police facilities, such as a shooting range or a scientific crime detection laboratory, are generally made available to local police departments.

Other Local Law Enforcement Officers

A number of other local law enforcement officers and agencies carry out a variety of functions, most of which relate to particular areas of state concern. For example, state liquor, insurance, revenue, and public aid departments may have their own investigative staffs whose functions are to ferret out wrongdoing related to their respective agencies. In some jurisdictions probation officers or parole officers are empowered by statute to exercise police functions.

FEDERAL OFFICERS

Federal Bureau of Investigation (FBI) Agents

The largest of the federal law enforcement agencies is the Federal Bureau of Investigation, whose 8,500 special agents are stationed throughout the United States. The FBI is responsible for investigating the bulk of crimes committed in violation of the federal criminal law. These crimes include robbery, or burglary of a federally insured bank or business, air piracy, and interstate acts of kidnapping, hijacking, auto theft, transportation of stolen goods, and flight to avoid prosecution. Another important responsibility of the FBI is to insure our security from espionage and other internal threats from foreign powers. Thus the FBI detects and deters spies, traitors, and would-be saboteurs. Close cooperation between federal and local law enforcement is exemplified by local access to the FBI's scientific crime laboratory, to the fingerprint records of the FBI's identification division, and to the National Crime Information Center (NCIC), a computerized source of instant information on stolen cars, stolen merchandise, and fugitives from justice, state as well as federal.

Treasury Agents

The Department of the Treasury maintains a number of law enforcement agencies, each with its own particular area of responsibility. One of these agencies, the United States Secret Service, is best known for the protection it provides the president, the vice-president, their families, and foreign dignitaries. The Secret Service also provides protection for presidential and vice-presidential candidates. The investigative duties of the Secret Service include the detection and apprehension of those who make or pass counterfeit currency and those who steal or forge United States treasury checks.

Special agents of the Internal Revenue Service also are a part of the Treasury Department. Their function is to investigate violations of the tax laws, which include failure to file tax returns, filing false returns, and other forms of tax evasion. Special agents of the Alcohol, Tobacco and Firearms Division of the Treasury Department, often called "revenuers," enforce the federal laws pertaining to untaxed liquor, explosives, and firearms. Agents of the Bureau of Customs patrol our nation's borders and establish checkpoints to prevent the flow of narcotics or other smuggled contraband.

Other Federal Civilian Law Enforcement Agents

There is a host of additional federal civilian law enforcement agencies, in addition to the ones already described, each having a specific area of responsibility. The oldest one, the United States Marshal's Service, is charged with performing a number of functions. It must provide security for the federal courts, transport federal prisoners, serve legal papers such as summonses and subpoenas, and afford protection for and relocate sensitive government witnesses as part of a National Witness Protection Program.

The federal agency with the primary responsibility of investigating and combating illicit traffic in narcotics and dangerous drugs is the Drug

Enforcement Administration. The Postal Inspection Service works to protect the integrity of the United States mails. Its inspectors have the responsibility to detect and apprehend persons who steal from the mails or use the mails to perpetrate fraudulent schemes. The Immigration and Naturalization Service is charged with the responsibility of enforcing the laws governing the entrance and residence of foreign nationals in this country. As such, its special agents track down aliens who have entered the country illegally.

Law enforcement functions on Indian reservations are carried out by the police of the Bureau of Indian Affairs. The security at federal buildings and installations around the country may be provided by either the Federal Protective Service or the guard forces employed by the particular agencies housed in the facilities. Investigative forces are utilized by a number of agencies, such as the Department of State and the Department of Agriculture to insure compliance with the laws promulgated within the particular agency's area of regulatory concern. And even the Supreme Court of the United States has its own protective police force.

Military Law Enforcement Agents

Each branch of the military has a force of individuals who provide "police" protection for military personnel, dependents, their property and that of the government. In addition to such units as the Military Police, Air Police, and Shore Patrol, units of military criminal investigators have been established to perform detective work on military offenses over which civilian law enforcement agencies have no jurisdiction. Units such as the Army's Criminal Investigation Division (CID) or the Navy's Naval Investigative Service (NIS) have no authority, however, over civilians.

National Intelligence Agents

The activities of our nation's intelligence-gathering agencies, such as the Central Intelligence Agency, the National Security Agency, and the Defense Intelligence Agency, have received a great deal of publicity recently. Their functions should be distinguished from those of domestic law enforcement agencies.

Although not the largest of these agencies, the CIA is certainly the most well known. It was established to coordinate the intelligence activities of the other government intelligence agencies, to evaluate and disseminate national security data, and to perform other duties related to intelligence affecting national security as may be directed by the National Security Council. As with the other intelligence agencies, however, the CIA has no police, subpoena, or law enforcement powers and has no internal security functions. These matters are within the jurisdiction of the FBI.

Chapter 2
The Lawyers

The lawyers in the criminal justice system are advocates who prepare cases on behalf of the parties whom they represent and present these cases to the courts. Government lawyers represent the people who make up the various political entities which exist in our representative form of government. Defense lawyers represent the interests of particular clients who have been accused of wrongdoing. Generally speaking, the lawyers enter the picture after the police and before the courts.

LOCAL GOVERNMENT LAWYERS

Municipal Attorneys

The municipal attorney, sometimes known as a city attorney or corporation counsel (one who serves an incorporated government entity), represents in general the interests of the particular city, town, or village. The municipal attorney may also participate in proceedings involving licenses, traffic offenses, and minor ordinance violations. He is usually hired by and generally serves at the pleasure of the mayor or other chief municipal officer.

County or District Attorneys

The county attorney (or prosecutor) has the responsibility for prosecuting practically all violations of state laws (murder, robbery, burglary, rape, etc.) which occur within a particular county. In some states his responsibility may cover several counties which have been combined into a "district."

Depending upon the state in which he functions, the prosecutor for a county may be known variously as county attorney (e.g., Minnesota), or as the commonwealth's attorney (e.g., Kentucky), or as state's attorney (e.g., Illinois), or simply as prosecuting attorney. Where he represents several, usually small, counties combined into a district, he is known understandably as district attorney (e.g., Oklahoma). In some states (e.g., California and New York), although he may only represent a single county, he bears the designation of district attorney.

A state's district attorneys should not be confused with the federal prosecutors, who are sometimes also referred to as district attorneys even though they are officially known as United States attorney for a particular federal district (United States Attorney for the Northern District of Illinois, for example, or United States Attorney for the District of Columbia).

State prosecutors, by whatever titles they are known (e.g., county, or district attorney, etc.), are almost all elected to the office, and, except in a few parts of the country, they select their own assistants. One of the few exceptions is Los Angeles County where the assistants are on civil service status even though the office of district attorney is an elective one.

Prosecutors depend primarily upon local or state police to secure the evidence for criminal prosecutions, although there may be investigators on the prosecutor's staff whose primary purpose is to seek supporting evidence for the actual prosecutions.

In many states the prosecutor also has responsibilities in the civil law field. For instance, he may have to enforce the collection of taxes, or represent his county or district in lawsuits against the county or district, its officials, or other agents.

Attorney General of the State

In most states the attorney general is chosen in a statewide election. In several, however, he is appointed by the governor (for example, Alaska, Hawaii, New Hampshire, New Jersey, Pennsylvania, and Wyoming), or even by the state legislature (Maine) or the state's supreme court. With two exceptions (Alaska and Wyoming) there is no need for legislative confirmation of the appointment.

An attorney general is usually charged with the responsibility of representing the legal interests of the various state agencies. He is frequently called upon to defend those agencies when sued and to enforce the laws which the agencies administer. An additional responsibility of the attorney general is the rendering of legal opinions for units of local government. In the area of law enforcement, his jurisdiction varies from state to state. In most of them he has very little, if any, direct control over the county prosecutors within the state, although there are many occasions involving cooperative efforts.

Some states permit the attorney general to present cases to the local

The Lawyers

grand jury in the same manner as the local prosecutor; however, most do not. A few states are considering creating a statewide grand jury system for dealing with certain types of offenses (e.g., organized crime and political corruption).

One of the recently developed responsibilities of attorneys general is that of protecting the environment by filing suits against industrial facilities which pollute the atmosphere or the waters within the state. Moreover, the state's attorney general may even sue to prevent adjoining states from allowing operations which adversely affect his own state's environment.

Appointed Defense Attorneys or Public Defenders

Every person charged with a criminal offense for which he could go to jail if found guilty is entitled, as a constitutional right, to representation by legal counsel. The earlier practice was for the trial judge to appoint a lawyer to serve in that capacity as a public service without compensation. Subsequently the practice developed to at least partially compensate the appointed lawyers. Later, associations were formed to provide this service, supported either in whole or in part by privately funded sources. Ultimately, in many states the office of public defender was created, at least in the larger counties or districts. Funds for the office come from either the county or the state, or both. A recent development is the creation of a statewide public defender system.

Regardless of the nature or form of the defense that is provided, one thing is certain: no person accused of an offense for which he may be sentenced to a jail or penitentiary will stand trial unrepresented by an attorney.

FEDERAL GOVERNMENT LAWYERS

Most lawyers who work for the federal government are employed by the United States Department of Justice. This department employs thousands of lawyers at its headquarters in Washington, D.C., and throughout the ninety-four federal judicial districts.

Attorney General of the United States

The attorney general of the United States is the nation's chief law enforcement officer. After nomination by the president and confirmation by the Senate, he sits as a member of the cabinet and is in charge of the Department of Justice. The attorney general, therefore, bears the ultimate responsibility for the work of the Justice Department's agencies, including the Federal Bureau of Investigation, the Drug Enforcement Administration, the United States Marshal's Service, the Immigration and Naturalization Service, the Federal Bureau of Prisons as well as the ninety-four offices of United States attorneys.

Solicitor General

The solicitor general, chosen by the attorney general, prepares and presents the government's side of cases brought before the Supreme Court of the United States.

United States Attorneys

Candidates for United States attorney are nominated by the president, traditionally upon the recommendation of a U.S. senator from the nominee's state (usually the senior senator of the president's own party), and confirmed by the Senate. They serve as the chief law enforcement officer in each of the ninety-four federal judicial districts. Each U.S. attorney in turn appoints assistant U.S. attorneys to help investigate criminal activity in violation of federal law and aid in the prosecution of those cases in federal court. United States attorneys enforce civil federal law as well, thus insuring compliance with such federal legislation as the pure food and drug laws, civil rights laws, and pollution laws. In addition, U.S. attorneys defend agencies or agents of the federal government when civil suits are filed against them.

Organized Crime Strike Force Attorneys

In major cities throughout the United States, Department of Justice Strike Forces were established to combat organized crime. These units function under the direction of the Department of Justice in Washington, D.C., and work closely with the full range of federal investigative agencies. Although still directed by the Department of Justice at the time of this book's preparation, proposals have been made to transfer their control to the local United States attorneys themselves.

Defense Attorneys

The defense to which every accused person is entitled is most often provided in federal cases by a privately retained attorney selected and paid by the client. However, in those instances where a defendant is unable to afford the services of a private attorney, one is provided from the staff of a federal defender panel. Some serve full time; others may be private practitioners whose occasional services either are donated free, or are paid for by the government in accordance with fee schedules established by law.

Military Attorneys

In all of the branches of the military (army, navy, marine corps, and the air force), many military personnel who are lawyers serve by command designation either as prosecutors or defense counsel in military trials. They are known as members of the Judge Advocate General Corps (JAGC).

Chapter 3
The Courts

Our judicial branch of government bears the responsibility of conducting fair and impartial trials in determining the guilt or innocence of accused persons. Although the local, state, and federal court systems are similar in that each has a trial function and an appellate function, there are substantial differences between the federal and state systems as well as between those of the various states themselves.

LOCAL AND STATE COURTS

The organizational framework of the court systems within a state will be found in that state's constitution or else in state statutes and in local ordinances.

Minor Trial Courts

The minor trial courts are sometimes called courts of limited jurisdiction. These courts may sit in judgment over matters involving either municipal law or state law. In the municipal courts, cases involving petty state offenses or city ordinance violations may be tried. Other minor state trial courts, such as those presided over by justices of the peace or other local magistrates, will hear matters involving minor violations (such as breaches of the peace, disorderly conduct, and traffic offenses) that are punishable by fine or local jail incarceration for a relatively short period of time. In many case situations, however, the jurisdiction of municipal and state minor trial courts will overlap.

Major Trial Courts

The major trial courts are state courts which have general jurisdiction over criminal prosecutions. Such courts are usually called, depending on the state, circuit courts, district courts, or superior courts. The major trial courts are mainly concerned with the trial of felony offenses—generally those punishable by sentence to a state penitentiary—before a judge or jury. The types of crimes which are heard by such courts range from violent crimes such as murder, rape, and robbery to such nonviolent crimes as check offenses and credit card fraud.

Juvenile Courts

Juvenile courts have been established primarily to aid in reforming delinquent children rather than in "punishing" them. The erection of a judicial framework specifically designed for juveniles is also based upon the belief that children should be detained, processed, adjudicated, and incarcerated separate from adults. Care, education, and protection are seen as the means by which errant youths may be guided toward productive lives. The trend toward informal and nontechnical treatment of juvenile offenders has been limited, however, by rulings of the Supreme Court of the United States which call for procedural uniformity and the application of many constitutional rights and protections which are accorded accused adults.

In certain types of cases juveniles may be prosecuted as adults, where public safety and welfare seem to require it. This is typically the situation regarding major offenses such as murder and armed robbery.

Appellate Courts

After conviction in a trial court, a defendant may seek to have an appellate court review the *record* or *transcript* of the pre-trial and trial court proceedings to determine whether errors occurred which are considered "reversible." Accompanying the record of the proceedings will be *briefs* filed by both the prosecution and the defense attorneys, in which written arguments are presented in support of a reversal or an affirmance of the conviction. Also, oral arguments from both sides are usually heard by the appellate court, which may supplement the hearing with questions asked of the attorneys. There is, however, no presentation of witness testimony or other evidence. The appeal is solely a matter between the attorneys and the court, although in extremely rare instances the defendant himself may be allowed to serve as his own attorney, just as may occur on the trial level. This is known as a *pro se* proceeding.

Many states have both an intermediate appellate court and a supreme court. The former usually consists of three judges (either comprising the entire court or a panel thereof). The supreme courts are composed of either five or seven justices. In many types of cases a decision of the intermediate appellate court is final, but in some instances its decision is appealable to a higher state court. Also, certain cases are appealable to the state supreme court directly from the trial court. Examples of the latter may be death penalty cases or cases involving constitutional issues.

The highest state court is usually known simply as the supreme court of that state. An exception is New York, where the highest court is known as the Court of Appeals of New York. Another exception with respect to New York is that its trial courts are called supreme courts, a rather confusing labeling to many persons outside as well as inside New York.

When an appellate court has reached a decision, it is usually published with an *opinion* giving the reasons in support of the decision. These opinions appear in what are known as *reports*, and they are available for examination in the libraries of courts, bar associations, law schools and in some law office libraries. The opinions serve as guides or *precedents* for future case determinations.

Federal Courts

The Constitution of the United States provides that the judicial power of the nation rests in one Supreme Court and in such other courts as Congress may establish. Pursuant to that authorization Congress has created trial courts known as federal district courts, and Congress divided the nation into ninety-four judicial districts, with a federal district court within each one. Congress also created what are known as circuit courts of appeal. These are courts to which appeals may be taken from a number of district courts from several states.

The lower federal courts were not established as substitutes for state courts, but rather to deal with cases beyond the jurisdiction of state courts, meaning, essentially, those cases involving federal laws and federal legal issues.

In addition to the foregoing courts, in 1968 Congress replaced the federal commissioner system with what are known as magistrate courts, which will be described below.

All federal judges (but not the judicial officers who preside over federal magistrate courts) are appointed for life upon nomination by the president and confirmation by the United States Senate. For years the process of appointment of federal district court judges began quite simply with a recommendation to the president by the senior United States senator from the state in which the particular federal district was located. (Preference was accorded to senators from within the president's own political party, without regard to seniority unless both senators representing a state were of the same party.) Appointments to the intermediate federal courts, the circuit courts of appeals, are made as vacancies occur. They are filled by the process of recommendation by the senator from the state affected by the vacancy.

In 1977 the president issued an executive order which modified somewhat the process of recommendations and nominations of federal district and circuit court judges. Before consideration is to be given to either recommendations or nominations, potential candidates have to be screened by select committees as to their qualifications.

Justices on the Supreme Court of the United States are nominated by the president without reliance upon senatorial recommendations, although they too must receive Senate confirmation. In the traditional selection process, presidents have frequently relied to a considerable degree upon the advice of their own appointed (and confirmed) attorneys general.

Federal judges are subject to removal only upon impeachment by the House of Representatives for "high crimes or misdemeanors," and a finding of guilt by the Senate. The instances of compulsory removal have been exceedingly rare. Voluntary resignations in the face of possible impeachment have occurred but they have also been few in number.

Magistrate Courts

Magistrates must be lawyers (in contrast to the former requirements for the commissioner system which the magistrate courts replaced), and they are appointed by the federal district court judges within the district in which the magistrate court is located. The term of office is set at eight years, but magistrates may be removed by a majority vote of the district court upon grounds of incompetency or misconduct.

One of the functions of a magistrate is to set bail for federal arrestees, and he determines at a preliminary hearing whether there are *reasonable grounds* (or *probable cause*) to support the felony charge or charges that have been filed in the case. A magistrate is also empowered to issue warrants for arrest or for searches and seizures if he or she determines there are reasonable grounds for the issuance. Additionally, he has jurisdiction to try minor federal cases that are the equivalent, generally speaking, of misdemeanors in the state courts. Moreover, with the district courts confronted by an ever increasing caseload, both criminal and civil, magistrates are being entrusted to conduct pretrial hearings as to the admissibility of evidence that the prosecution may plan on using at the trial.

District Courts

The United States is divided into ninety-four judicial districts. A small state may constitute a single district, whereas a larger state may have three or more. A United States district court presides over cases in each of those districts. The number of judges on a district court depends upon the population of each respective district, and Congress decides upon the

The Courts

needed number of judges. Although a district court case is usually assigned to an individual judge, in some rare instances all of the judges comprising the particular district court may consider a case *en banc,* meaning that they hear and resolve the case collectively.

District courts have exclusive jurisdiction over criminal violations defined in the United States Code occurring within their geographic boundaries. District court judges, therefore, preside over criminal trials of federal cases. Following conviction, they have the option of sentencing the defendant to a federal penitentiary or placing him on probation, a feature of our general criminal court system which will be subsequently discussed. Although recently limited, district courts may consider what are known as "habeas corpus" hearings after final adjudications in state offense cases in the state courts. Such hearings, however, must involve allegations of violations of a state-convicted person's federal constitutional rights or privileges.

District Courts do not have separate branches to handle juvenile offenders, but special statutes and procedures are often applicable in those cases.

Courts of Appeal

The United States is divided into ten judicial circuits, each of which has a United States court of appeal, plus there is one for the District of Columbia. A conviction in any one of the district courts within a particular circuit may be appealed to the court of appeal for that circuit. As in state appellate courts, no new evidence is heard; rather, the presence of *reversible error* committed by the trial court is determined from the written transcript of the trial court proceedings, legal briefs, and the oral arguments of counsel. Panels of three judges normally hear and decide the appeals, although the judges of a particular circuit may decide by majority vote to have a case heard by the entire panel of judges. Decisions may be rendered from the bench at the time of oral argument, by memorandum opinion distributed to the parties involved, or in a published opinion in support of the court's decision.

Supreme Court of the United States

The Supreme Court of the United States is the highest court in the land. It is composed of a chief justice and eight associate justices. Any six constitute a quorum.

The Supreme Court has original jurisdiction in a very limited number of situations (such as disputes involving ambassadors), but it is primarily the nation's ultimate appellate court for federal as well as state cases.

Unlike regular federal and state appellate courts, which ordinarily must consider every case presented to them, the Supreme Court exercises broad discretion over what cases it will take under consideration. In a few types of cases, review by the Supreme Court is a matter of right, but the vast majority of cases are accepted only when four or more justices deem review to be warranted. In those cases a *writ of certiorari* is issued to the lower court and the record of that court is then examined and considered in the light of the briefs submitted and the oral arguments presented by counsel from each side. By the very nature of the Supreme Court's position, each of its decisions is of major significance, and each one is normally published in opinion form so that it may serve as a guideline for the conduct of future trials in the courts throughout the land.

In certain cases the Supreme Court will allow citizen organizations, such as the American Civil Liberties Union, the National Association for the Advancement of Colored People, and Americans for Effective Law Enforcement to file *friend of the court* briefs in support of the defense or the prosecution positions.

Military Courts

As previously indicated, the United States military has its own internal system of criminal justice. In general, it parallels its civilian counterpart with the bringing of charges, the holding of trials (called courts-martial), and appellate reviews. The most important point to be made in this regard, however, is that military courts have jurisdiction over military personnel for offenses relating to their military duties only. No military court has jurisdiction over a civilian for any purpose whatsoever.

Chapter 4
Detention and Correctional Institutions

LOCAL AND STATE FACILITIES

Penal institutions run the gamut from overnight "drunk tanks" to computer-controlled maximum security prisons. In an increasing number of prisons, inmates are afforded opportunities to learn trades and to receive other instruction, some even leading to college degrees.

The nature and quality of any penal institution will depend upon a number of factors, the primary ones being the extent of funds available and the existence of a merit system for the selection and retention of administrative personnel.

Police Lockups

Most police stations and sheriffs' offices have some sort of "lockup" that is utilized as no more than a temporary place of detention. The length of time that an arrestee may spend in a lockup may vary from a few hours to a few days, depending upon the nature of the offense, local procedures, and ability to furnish bail. Persons confined in lockups are generally either released on bail or transported to a more permanent facility rather quickly.

Jails

Jails are detention facilities for individuals who are awaiting trial and have either been denied bail (as may be done for murder under certain situations), or have not provided the bail set by a justice of the peace, a judicial magistrate, or a judge. Some jails are also used as penal institutions for convicted persons who are serving short misdemeanor sentences. Institutions serving this latter purpose may have counseling services and educational and recreational opportunities. The quality and quantity of such services, however, vary widely from place to place.

Prisons

Prisons are institutions for the incarceration of persons who have been convicted of serious crimes (felonies) which carry sentences of a year or more.

Depending upon the length of imprisonment and the background of the prisoner, a sentence may be served in a minimum security farm-type institution, which may also allow weekend furloughs, or in a fortress-like maximum security prison which provides total control and regimentation. The availability of rehabilitative resources and special services, such as narcotic drug treatment, varies from jurisdiction to jurisdiction. State penal systems are governed and administered by the state's department of corrections.

Juvenile Facilities

Just as juveniles are treated separately from adults in the law enforcement and judicial systems, they are segregated from adults in the penal system. Special institutions, therefore, house juveniles, and, to varying degrees of success, they seek to deal with the problems of youthful offenders.

Federal Facilities

Jails

Until recent years persons who were being held on federal criminal charges or serving relatively short terms after conviction were detained in local state facilities, for which service the federal government reimbursed the controlling governmental body. In increasing measure, however, the federal government is establishing its own independent quarters for such persons.

Prisons

For persons convicted of serious federal crimes (generally those for which a sentence of a year or more may be given), there are various federally owned and operated prisons. As with the state prisons, the location, nature, and degree of security of the prisons will depend upon the purpose they are designed to serve. Some have been rather cynically described as "country clubs" (for the nonviolent offender), whereas others are of a far less tolerable nature.

Part II
CRIMES

Crimes have traditionally been divided into two categories: 1) conduct which is morally wrong, including acts such as murder, rape, burglary, robbery, and thievery in general; and 2) conduct which is not inherently wrong but which, nevertheless, must be declared unlawful because of its adverse effects upon the public welfare. The latter includes acts such as carrying a concealed weapon or driving a truck carrying a load exceeding a limit and therefore damaging to the public roadways. The first type of conduct is known within the judicial system as *malum in se* (bad in itself); the second, as *malum prohibitum* (bad only because the law has labeled it so).

Similarly, crimes have been differentiated as felonies or misdemeanors. Generally, a felony is a crime of such seriousness that it warrants a penitentiary sentence of one year or more, or possibly, as with murder, capital punishment. A misdemeanor is an offense for which the punishment is generally incarceration for less than a year in a penal institution other than the penitentiary, or perhaps by a monetary fine only, although some statutes provide for either or both forms of penalties.

Very low in the echelon of offenses, both in terms of seriousness and penalties, are violations of county, city, or village ordinances. They are generally considered in the judicial system as "quasi-crimes," meaning wrongful conduct but not quite a crime in the traditional sense. They characteristically are punishable by monetary fine only. However, some business regulatory ordinances may allow for suspension or revocation of licenses which have been issued by a county board, or city or village council through a licensing agency.

English common law was originally the basis for judging and punishing crimes in the American colonies. Common law, which was not codified, was based upon accumulated past court decisions, which relied heavily upon the attitudes and customary habits of the people.

Gradually, legislative enactments replaced much of the common law in the United States, first by separate acts or statutes of the various state legislatures, then by criminal codes. In some state criminal codes (Illinois, for example), the common law has been specifically abolished, so that no conduct in such a state can be considered a crime unless it is declared to be so within the code itself. In the federal system, crimes can only be that conduct which is declared to be such in the United States Code. There have never been, on the federal level, any "common law" crimes, although, to be sure, many of the concepts and even much of the common law language have been perpetuated in Congressional enactments in the field of criminal law.

Chapter 5
Crimes Against the Person

HOMICIDE

Homicide is the killing of one person by another. Not all homicides are criminal, however. For instance, a person who kills another in self-defense has committed no crime; it is considered a *justifiable homicide*. The same is true of a police officer who kills a person to prevent a felony, such as robbery or burglary, and the killing is a necessary preventive measure. It is also justifiable homicide when an officer kills a dangerous felon in order to prevent his escape. Some killings are *excusable homicides,* as when a person accidentally, and without gross negligence, causes death. A killing amounts to a *criminal homicide* when it is committed without lawful justification or excuse. Depending on certain circumstances, it may be considered either murder or manslaughter.

Murder

According to common law, *murder* was a killing with "malice," and the requirement of malice is still found in some statutes and codes. The California Penal Code has retained it and provides, as did common law, that

> ... malice may be express or implied. It is express when there is manifested a deliberate intention to take away the life of a fellow creature. It is implied, when no considerable provocation appears, or when the circumstances attending the killing show an abandoned and malignant heart.

A clear illustration of express malice is the case in which one person intentionally pushes another off a mountainside. An example of implied malice is the case in which a person fires a rifle at a moving passenger train, just to scare the persons aboard or to display his skill at firing a bullet between the cars without hitting anyone. The danger inherent in such conduct would be evidence of malice in any killing that may be reasonably attributed to such conduct. It would indicate, to a California court or jury, "an abandoned and malignant heart."

Felony-Murder

Another example of malice is a killing during the course of a dangerous felony, such as robbery, burglary, or kidnapping. For instance, even though a robber's gun fires accidentally, killing the robbery victim, a bystander, or a police officer, his conduct in committing a felony satisfies the legal requirement of malice, so that the killing becomes punishable as murder and is called a *felony-murder*. A similar line of reasoning by some state supreme courts (California and Illinois, for example) has resulted in holding co-felons guilty of murder when, in the course of an exchange of shots between felons and the police, a police officer is accidentally killed by another officer. Certain other states, Pennsylvania for one, have adopted the position that for the felony-murder doctrine to apply, the killing must have been committed by one of the felons.

Malice may also be attributed to a robber whose partner intentionally kills someone during commission of the robbery or during attempted escape. Malice by all participants is implied in the danger inherent in the robbery itself, and each robber is considered to act as an agent for the others in accomplishing their objective, including the attempt to escape.

The issue of felony-murder stems primarily from the prosecution's interest in seeking the death penalty for killings occurring during the commission of a dangerous felony. In some of the states that have abolished capital punishment (Wisconsin, for example), the legislatures, in order to punish robbers more severely whenever a killing results, have provided that the punishment for such offenses shall be fifteen years greater than that provided for the robbery itself.

Degrees of Murder

Some states have specified varying penalties for murder, depending upon the circumstances of the killing. A "willful, deliberate and premeditated" killing, such as a poisoning or a killing during the commission of a forcible felony, may be labeled first degree murder and punishable by death or long imprisonment. Other forms of murder may be termed second degree, punishable by a lesser penalty. According to common law there were no degrees of murder; any unlawful killing was either murder or manslaughter.

Manslaughter

Manslaughter was defined by common law as an unlawful killing without malice and was classified as either voluntary or involuntary. In our statutes and criminal codes today, the wording may vary, but the same definition usually prevails. Manslaughter, in contrast to murder, is usually punishable by a prison term of one to ten or fourteen years.

Voluntary Manslaughter

An intentional killing after "great provocation" and "in the heat of passion" constitutes the crime of *voluntary manslaughter.* A classic example is the killing of one member of a married couple by the other member who unexpectedly finds his or her spouse in an act of sexual intercourse, or in a situation that indicates impending or concluded adulterous conduct. A killing of the paramour or of the spouse, or both, in such a circumstance would fall within the category of manslaughter because the provocation was great and the killer was in the "heat of passion."

Such a killing is treated less harshly than murder, because the law holds a sympathetic appreciation of the instinctive reaction to kill whenever a husband or a wife is confronted with such a situation. Nevertheless, the view generally prevails that such conduct should be discouraged by criminal sanction, but one with a penalty considerably less than that for murder.

The conviction rate in such killings is quite low, primarily because of the occasional willingness of juries to accept the frequently concocted explanation that the killing occurred in self-defense, as when the paramour attacked the spouse who killed his attacker only in order to keep from being killed himself. Acquittal in such cases is sometimes described in the press to have resulted by reason of "the unwritten law."

In applying the test of whether or not an intentional killing was committed after great provocation and in the heat of passion, a lawyer asks the jury, or the judge in nonjury cases, to consider whether or not the accused reacted as a "reasonable" man. Technically speaking, the particular sensitivity or temper of the killer is not taken into consideration. Instead, an effort is made to determine how a "reasonable" man might have acted under similar circumstances. An apt illustration is a famous English case in which a sexually impotent man felt insulted by the remarks of a prostitute with whom he had tried in vain to have sexual intercourse, and proceeded to kill her. He contended that his sensitivity about his condition should be taken into account in determining whether or not there was serious provocation for his reaction, but the court held that his conduct was to be judged by the standard of an ordinary, normal "reasonable" man.

Involuntary Manslaughter

In general, *involuntary manslaughter* may be described as an unintentional killing resulting from gross negligence, or as a result of dangerous and unlawful conduct. A person may be guilty of manslaughter if he throws a heavy object from an upper floor of a building into an alley frequently used by pedestrians and the object kills someone. Similarly, a motorist who is traveling at an excessive speed may be guilty of manslaughter if he kills a child at a school crossing.

A number of states have created a related crime known as *reckless homicide* or *negligent homicide,* which applies to killings by motorists who were driving in a reckless or grossly negligent manner. Such special homicide legislation was enacted because of the difficulty of convicting motorists for manslaughter, which not only sounded like a horrible crime but also carried a minimum penalty of one year in the penitentiary. It was thought advisable to categorize such conduct with the less revolting label of reckless or negligent homicide and also to permit the imposition of lesser penalties than those prescribed for manslaughter. For the sake of justice, a reasonable number of convictions carrying relatively light penalties is more desirable than few convictions carrying heavy penalties. The permissible range of penalties in reckless or negligent homicide statutes is generally a fine of up to $1,000, or incarceration, other than in a penitentiary, for a period of up to one year, or imprisonment in a penitentiary for up to five years. (When the traffic victim of such conduct does not die, another statutory offense may be invoked, called *reckless conduct.*)

The flexibility of penalties in traffic death cases has had the effect of encouraging pleas of guilty from offenders, and it has resulted in convictions that might not have been secured if a judge or jury had no choice other than a penitentiary sentence or acquittal.

Federal Homicide Law

Only certain homicides are federal offenses, and there is no general federal homicide law. There can be none, in fact, because Congress has no constitutional authority to legislate the subject except in cases involving killings within a federal territory (including the District of Columbia), in federal buildings, or on federal property, or killings of foreign dignitaries, federal officials, federal officers, or other federal personnel.

Examples

1. Without justification or excuse, Jack shoots and kills Frank in a post office. Jack has committed a federal offense of criminal homicide.

2. Hank, a fugitive bank robber about to be apprehended by an FBI agent, shoots and kills the agent. Hank is guilty of a federal crime of murder.

Modern Murder–Manslaughter Legislation

In most states, the statutes covering murder and manslaughter are patterned after common law. The law is slowly becoming more modern, however, as the present Illinois Criminal Code demonstrates. In defining murder, for instance, it avoids such language as "malice" and "abandoned and malignant heart," and uses more precise terminology.

According to the Illinois Code, a person who kills another individual "without lawful excuse" commits murder if he "intended" to kill him or to do great bodily harm; if, without intending to kill, it clearly appears that he "must have known" that his conduct would probably cause death; or if death resulted from "the commission of a very serious crime" like robbery, burglary, or rape.

Capital Punishment

For many years there has been a continuing controversy about how effectively capital punishment serves its intended purpose, that of deterring murder. Nevertheless, a sizeable majority of the people of this country favor its retention as a penalty. In a 1970 referendum in Illinois, the voters favored the death penalty by a two to one margin. A similar result was reached in a California referendum. Moreover, most states have enacted legislation preserving capital punishment for the crime of murder. By 1970, however, because of the rapid decline in executions during the years 1966 to 1968, the issue of capital punishment had become a rather academic one. While there were 199 executions in 1935, there was only one in the entire United States in 1966, two in 1967, and none in 1968 or 1969. Yet in each of those four years, over 500 persons were under sentence of death. Thus, although capital punishment sentences continued to be imposed, there were no executions, due in large measure to court-ordered delays.

Then in 1972 the Supreme Court of the United States delivered a heavy blow to the capital punishment concept. The Court declared that, primarily because of the unevenness and arbitrariness with which most capital punishment statutes were applied by courts and juries (especially through selective application to minority group offenders), such statutes violated the constitutional protection against "cruel and unusual punishment" (Furman v. Georgia, 92 S. Ct. 2726). However, only two of the nine Supreme Court justices felt that no capital punishment statute could be written or applied that would comply with constitutional requirements; in other words, only two justices thought there could be no capital punishment at all. Their two votes, along with the three justices who found unfairness in the administration of the capital punishment statutes, constituted the majority ruling. Four justices dissented.

Immediately after the Supreme Court's 1972 decision on the unconstitutionality of the state statutes which were before it for consideration, a number of state legislatures enacted new death penalty statutes in an effort to meet the Court's objections to the old statutes. Then, in 1976, after a review of five new state statutes, three were found to be in compliance with the Supreme Court ruling, but two were not. The ones in Georgia, Florida, and Texas were upheld (Gregg v. Georgia, 96 S. Ct. 2909; Profitt v. Florida, 96 S. Ct. 2960; Jurek v. Texas, 96 S. Ct. 2950), but the ones from Louisiana and North Carolina (Roberts v. Louisiana, 96 S. Ct. 3001; Woodson v. North Carolina, 96 S. Ct. 2978) were declared invalid. Although the Utah statute was not the subject of a written opinion from the Supreme Court, it was tacitly approved by the Court's refusal to halt an execution there in early 1977.

Even though a few aspects of some of the states' capital punishment statutes still remain in doubt, the basic issue has been resolved. Provided the statute has adequate safeguards against unfairness in the imposition of capital punishment, the Supreme Court will sustain its validity, particularly when it is invoked only in cases where an actual killing is involved. Many legislators and other persons consider capital punishment to be a just penalty for an offense such as a brutal though non-fatal rape, or for an offense like aircraft hijacking where many lives have been endangered even though ultimately no one is killed. In fact, one of the statutes sustained by the Supreme Court in 1976 contained an aircraft hijacking provision, but since the particular case in question did not involve an aircraft hijacking, the Court did not address itself to that particular provision. It should be noted at this point that a federal statute provides for the application of the death penalty in cases of aircraft hijacking, irrespective of whether or not a death has occurred.

KIDNAPPING AND UNLAWFUL RESTRAINT

Kidnapping

A *kidnapping* occurs when a person is unlawfully seized and secretly confined against his will.

Example

Mr. and Mrs. Kay seize Suzie, a six-year-old. They take her in their car to a cottage in the country and make contact with Suzie's parents to demand a ransom payment. The Kays are guilty of the crime of kidnapping.

Kidnapping also occurs when an individual, by deceit, by enticement, by force, or by threat of force, induces another person to go from one place to another with the intent of secretly confining that person against his will.

Example

Joe and Bill meet Joyce at the neighborhood bar. When the bar closes, they promise to drive Joyce home. Instead, they take her to

Joe's home, where they advise her she will be kept prisoner until she obliges them with her sexual favors. At this point, Joe and Bill have committed the offense of kidnapping.

In many jurisdictions, the confinement of a child under the age of thirteen is considered, by law, to be against the will of the child regardless of any purported consent on the child's part. In many states, the penalty for kidnapping a child is greater than that for kidnapping an adult. A greater penalty is frequently provided if a kidnapping is committed while the perpetrator is masked or hooded, or if the victim is seriously harmed physically, or if the kidnapping is for the purpose of obtaining a ransom or any other valuable concession.

Kidnapping becomes a federal crime, as well as a state crime, whenever any elements of the offense occur in more than one state. The constitutional basis for the federal kidnapping law in such situations is the constitutional power of Congress to regulate interstate commerce. The kidnapping of any federal officer or official, or of a foreign government official, is also covered in the federal code.

Example
Joe and Doug kidnap a six-year-old boy in state A and take him to state B, where they hold him pending the delivery of a ransom payment from his father. The federal kidnapping law has been violated because of the interstate scope of the crime. (Joe and Doug can also be prosecuted in state A and in state B for violations of kidnapping laws of those states.)

The federal kidnapping statute was enacted in 1932, shortly after the kidnapping and death of the son of the famous aviator, Charles A. Lindbergh. In 1934, the statute was amended to provide that after the lapse of seven days a presumption arose that the kidnapped person had been taken from one state to another. The purpose of the amendment was to permit the FBI to enter the investigation, which otherwise would have to be conducted exclusively by the state until subsequent events established a crossing of state lines.

In 1956, following inept handling of a kidnapping investigation by local authorities (a newspaper leak resulted in the death of the kidnapped infant), the presumptive period of interstate transportation was reduced to twenty-four hours. Consequently, the FBI may now officially enter the investigation of a kidnapping twenty-four hours after its occurrence. However, as soon as subsequent events establish that there has been no transportation of the kidnapped person outside the state, the FBI authority ceases; the case then becomes one within the exclusive jurisdiction of state and local police agencies.

Unlawful Restraint

An offense of *unlawful restraint* occurs when a person is detained without legal authority, even though there may have been no intent to confine the victim secretly. The penalty for unlawful restraint is less severe than that for kidnapping.

Example
>Bessie, a shopper, observes Tina at the phonograph counter of the ABC Department Store. Bessie is suspicious of Tina and thinks she saw Tina put a record under her coat. Bessie follows Tina to the ladies' room where she refuses to let Tina exit until she confesses to the theft. Bessie has committed the offense of unlawful restraint.

Many states, trying to protect merchants from shoplifting losses, specifically provide that a merchant or an employee who reasonably believes that a person has wrongfully taken, or is about to wrongfully take, merchandise from the merchant's place of business may, without committing the offense of unlawful restraint, detain the suspect for a reasonable time in a reasonable manner for the purpose of determining the ownership of the merchandise.

Example
>A female store detective observes Helen, at the phonograph record counter, place something resembling a record under her coat and walk toward the store exit. In some states, by statute, the detective (or other store employee) may detain Helen and inquire about the object and its ownership.

Despite such statutory authorization, merchants are wary about exercising it for fear of false arrest suits. Generally they do not attempt any detention unless the person's conduct warrants an actual arrest for theft. In other words, unless the person is seen taking and concealing an unpurchased article, no detention is attempted. Some merchants even delay arrest until the taker has left the store; in that way the taker is deprived of any innocent explanation for his conduct. But whenever a person's conduct shows a provable intent to steal, a merchant or his store detective is legally justified in arresting that person as a shoplifter and having him prosecuted for the crime of theft.

As will be discussed later on, a few states (Illinois, for example) have citizen arrest statutes which permit arrests upon "reasonable grounds to believe" that a state offense such as shoplifting (a form of theft) is being committed. Nevertheless, considerable caution must be exercised by store detectives and other private (non-police) individuals who proceed to make an arrest. Establishing "reasonable grounds" to a judge's or jury's satisfaction may at times be difficult.

Crimes Against the Person

Assault and Battery

Although the two offenses of assault and battery are often thought to be one and the same, they actually are separate offenses. Despite their common linkage alphabetically, to understand what constitutes an assault, one must first understand the definition of battery.

Battery

A *battery* is an offense whereby a person knowingly, without legal justification, causes physical harm to an individual or else makes some kind of physical contact with an individual in an insulting or provoking manner.

Examples

1. Harry and Pete arrive in a movie house balcony at the same time from different directions. One seat is available and Harry, in order to stake claim to the seat, aggressively pushes Pete out of the way. Harry has committed a battery.

2. Joe, a student, disagrees with his college instructor's lecture and notes his dissent by spitting in the instructor's face. Joe has committed a battery.

In many jurisdictions, there is an increased penalty for battery when the offender uses a deadly weapon, or is masked or hooded, or selects a member of a particularly designated class of persons as the victim, such as a police officer or a teacher (as in the preceding example). This type of battery is often called *aggravated battery*.

When a person, in the course of a battery, causes permanent disability or disfigurement to a victim, the offense is called *mayhem,* and is more severely punishable.

Another form of battery is *child abuse*. For obvious reasons it, too, is viewed as a more serious offense than ordinary battery. Some state statutes deal with it separately and the prescribed penalties are quite severe.

Assault

Generally speaking, an *assault* is a feigned or actual attempt to commit a battery. It occurs whenever a person, without lawful authority, does anything that places another in reasonable apprehension of being physically harmed. It does not require actual contact; a reasonably interpreted threat is sufficient.

Examples

1. Jim, a husky six-footer, got into an argument at a party with another guest, jockey-sized Ron. Jim took a punch at Ron, but be-

cause of his myopia (of which Ron was not aware) he missed by a foot. Other guests restrained Jim from any further action. Jim is guilty of assault. Had he hit Ron, he would have committed a battery.

2. Joe, enraged at Bill, backed him against a wall and fired a loaded pistol at him. The pistol jammed and did not fire. Joe is guilty of attempted murder, as discussed in another section of this book. But he is also guilty of assault because he put Bill in reasonable apprehension of receiving a battery.

As in the case of battery, an assault by a masked or hooded offender, or by one who uses a deadly weapon, or an assault against a member of a particular class of persons, often calls for a greater penalty than simple assault. This type of assault is often termed *aggravated assault*.

SEX OFFENSES AND RELATED CRIMINAL CONDUCT

Forcible Rape

Rape was originally defined as unlawful sexual intercourse with a female "by force and against her will." Although many earlier cases held that a woman was required to resist "to the utmost," submission out of fear of violence is now generally held to constitute rape.

An early statute in England declared that intercourse with a child under ten years of age was also rape, regardless of "consent." What about a case in which a female is so drunk that she is incapable of consenting? In such a situation, the act is presumed to be without her consent and therefore rape. Modern statutes generally provide that rape is committed whenever the victim is unconscious (as from drink or drugs), or is so mentally deranged or deficient that she cannot effectively give consent to the act of intercourse.

Since the crime of rape requires that the sexual act be unlawful, a married man could not be found guilty of "raping" his wife. Marriage rendered the act lawful. It is interesting to note, however, that if a married man compelled his wife to have intercourse with another man, the husband could be found guilty of rape. His conduct renders him an accessory to the rape and therefore guilty of the crime itself. Under a similar line of reasoning, a woman might be convicted of raping another woman.

Intercourse, within the meaning of rape, consists of any penetration, however slight, of the female sex organ by the male sex organ, regardless of whether or not the organ was erect. Thus, impotency is no defense for rape. Moreover, an emission is not required as an element of the crime.

Sex Offenses Against Children

Statutory Rape

In an effort to protect children from sexual conduct involving older persons, various legislatures have enacted separate child sex offense statutes. One is the crime of *statutory rape*, which consists of sexual intercourse with a *female* under a certain age, usually sixteen, regardless of whether or not she consents. Believing that a girl is over the specified age is generally not a defense, regardless of the reasonableness of the belief. But there are a few court decisions and statutory provisions to the contrary.

Indecent Liberties and Contributing to Sexual Delinquency

Modern legislation, in a further effort to protect the young, has established several additional sex offenses. One is *indecent liberties with a child;* another is *contributing to the sexual delinquency of a child.* The two offenses consist essentially of any lewd fondling for the purpose of arousing the sexual desires of either the male or the female under the specified age, which is usually sixteen.

Incest

Another offense, also defined for the protection of the young, is *incest.* The classic example is sexual intercourse of a father with his daughter. The offense has long been extended to include mothers and sons, brothers and sisters, and, in some states, certain other blood relationships.

Adultery and Fornication

Adultery is sexual intercourse between one married person and another person other than his or her spouse. For divorce purposes, one "sneak" experience is sufficient. In most jurisdictions, however, in order for the act to constitute a crime, the parties' behavior must be well known to others; that is, the adulterous conduct must be "open and notorious."

Fornication generally consists of cohabitation of or sexual intercourse between unmarried persons under circumstances in which their behavior is well known to others or, in other words, is "open and notorious." The penalty for fornication is less than that for adultery. In some states, Louisiana for one, there are no such crimes as adultery and fornication. The same is also generally true in foreign countries.

Bigamy

A married person who marries a second person commits *bigamy.* The crime can also be committed by a single person if he or she marries someone he or she knows to be still married to another. In some states, a defense to a charge of bigamy is that the accused reasonably believed the prior marriage had been legally dissolved or that the previous spouse was dead.

Deviate Sexual Conduct

In the past, almost any sexual gratification derived from heterosexual intimacies other than the one with the potential of reproduction (organ-to-organ intercourse) was considered a crime. Any oral-genital contact, even between husband and wife in the privacy of their home, was unlawful. So was sexual activity between members of the same sex (homosexuality). And, most certainly, any human-animal sexual contact was prohibited and severely punishable.

The trend in recent years, however, has been to remove the stigma of criminality from all forms of sexual conduct performed in privacy between consenting adults. Homosexuality, for instance, has been removed from the criminal statutes in at least two states (California and Illinois), but only when the conduct is mutually consented to, is done in private, and does not involve a young person with an older one. Forcible homosexuality is, of course, a criminal offense.

Prostitution and Related Offenses

Prostitution was not considered a crime under common law, although keeping a house of prostitution was. The keeping of a bawdy house was thought to corrupt public morals, but the act of prostitution was not viewed as seriously. Today, however, both kinds of conduct are generally unlawful. In only a very few states (e.g., parts of Nevada) is prostitution permitted by law.

Some states have made it an offense to solicit or to patronize a prostitute. Outlawed, too, are certain kinds of related conduct, involving a third party who lives off the proceeds of prostitution such as *solicitation for a prostitute, pandering* or *pimping*. Such related offenses commonly involve organized crime and are labeled *commercialized vice*. And in recent years the operation of certain types of "massage" parlors has become practically synonymous with organized crime (hoodlum-controlled) prostitution establishments.

The enforcement of prostitution laws often is directly related to the amount of community support and expectations. Where prostitutes serve as decoys for robbers and pickpockets, enforcement is more energetic.

The Federal "White Slave" Act

A federal statute, passed by Congress in 1910, but amended to some extent thereafter, makes it a crime

> to knowingly transport in interstate or foreign commerce, or in the District of Columbia or in any Territory or Possession of the United States, any woman

or girl for the purpose of prostitution or debauchery, or for any other immoral purpose, or with the intent and purpose to induce, entice, or compel her to become a prostitute or to give herself up to debauchery, or to engage in any other immoral practice.

The "White Slave" Act, also known as the Mann Act because it was introduced as a bill by Congressman James R. Mann, was intended to discourage the "commercial vice" of traffic in women for monetary gain. It has been interpreted, however, to cover the transportation of a woman across a state line for the purpose of becoming the concubine or mistress of the transporter; so, as interpreted by the courts, the transportation need not be for commercial gain. All that is required is transportation for an "immoral purpose" or an "immoral practice," depending upon how those terms may be interpreted in any given situation. As a practical matter, however, the law is generally enforced only in cases of an aggravated nature. Such cases include commercialized vice, the transportation of juveniles, or those instances where physical force is used against the victims. Occasionally the law is also used against an individual who is known to be involved in other forms of criminal activity, such as a person who has numerous convictions for armed robbery or is an organized crime figure.

Exhibitionism

According to common law, any "obscene" or "indecent" act of a public nature was punishable as a crime because of its injurious effect upon "public morality." Under that principle, a person could be punished criminally for "indecently" exposing his or her sexual organs in public, the usual motivation being the sexual gratification of the exhibitor. Today, such conduct is made criminal by specific ordinances or statutes. Prosecutions for such conduct may also be initiated under some general ordinance or statute, such as that prohibiting *disorderly conduct*. Disorderly conduct is usually defined in legislative enactments as conduct that alarms or disturbs another person and thus provokes a breach of the peace.

Window Peeping

Common law prosecutions were attempted against window peepers or peeping Toms when their actions affected "public morality," but the courts were reluctant to classify such conduct within that category. On the other hand, there has been considerable difficulty whenever attempts have been made to draft legislation dealing specifically with conduct of that nature. Constitutional due process guarantees against legislative vagueness or indefiniteness have presented problems of an almost insurmountable nature.

If window peeping were done in such a way as to provoke a "breach of the peace," disorderly conduct might be involved. But, ordinarily, a window peeper indulges in his conduct in secrecy and darkness.

About as far as legislators can go is to make it an offense to enter upon the property of another and to look into a dwelling for a "lewd and unlawful purpose." But, here again, it is difficult to prove that purpose. In any event, the individual who enters upon the property of another without authority is subject to another and more easily established offense—trespass.

Because of the frequent attempts by homeowners to shoot and kill window peepers, it is important to stress that there is no legal justification for using lethal force to discourage such conduct or to apprehend the offender, even when the peeping may involve trespass. Lethal force is justifiable only to prevent a serious felony (for example, burglary) or to apprehend a felon of that type.

Anonymous Telephone Calls

One of the most annoying, though generally harmless, acts of misconduct is the anonymous telephone call that is usually motivated by the need for sexual gratification. The caller may do no more than telephone a female for the purpose of hearing her voice, without saying anything himself. But such a caller often uses obscene language or makes lewd proposals to her.

The legal problem of anonymous telephone calls is usually dealt with in state statutes governing the general use of telephones, rather than in state criminal law provisions. Such statutes generally prohibit, among other things, the use of language that is "obscene, lewd or immoral, with the intent to offend another person." A federal statute also makes it an offense to use the telephone in that manner. Telephone companies are very cooperative in the investigation of such calls and willingly take the necessary measures to protect the recipient from further annoyance.

Some of the foregoing offenses covered within this chapter, and particularly prostitution, are viewed by many persons as "victimless" crimes that consequently should be decriminalized. This issue will be the subject of discussion in chapter 7 under the title of "Offenses Affecting the Public Morals, Health, Safety, and Welfare."

Eavesdropping—"Wiretapping" and "Bugging"

Although eavesdropping by means of tapping telephones or the planting of hidden microphones in places where oral conversations occur are under some circumstances legitimate, lawful practices, there are certain conditions under which such activities may constitute a criminal offense.

There are statutes in a number of states and one Congressional enactment which delineate between the lawful and the unlawful.

Federal Law

It is a federal offense, punishable criminally (and also the basis for a civil suit) for anyone without proper authorization to employ an electronic, mechanical, or other device to tap a telephone or to intercept other oral conversations on the premises of any business engaged in interstate or foreign commerce, or elsewhere than on the premises if done for the purpose of obtaining information regarding the operations of that business. "Proper authorization" means, essentially, a court order obtained by designated law enforcement officials which embodies the safeguards against abuse prescribed by Congress. An important exception exists, however: the tap or other form of interception is permissible to both law enforcement officers and civilians whenever there is the consent of any one person involved in the conversation.

State Law

Several states have statutes which place an absolute ban on all electronic eavesdropping; they make no exception even for law enforcement officers. On the other hand, in some states there are no statutory provisions at all upon the subject. Within these two extremes there are states which permit electronic eavesdropping when *all* parties to the conversation have given their consent, or when merely *one* party has consented. A number of states permit law enforcement officers to conduct electronic eavesdropping without the consent of any participant in either emergency situations (for instance, trying to locate a kidnapped child) or upon a court order which provides for specific restrictions and conditions. In fact, the state laws of that nature must conform very closely to the federal statute which embodies safeguards that the Supreme Court considers necessary because of the Fourth Amendment's guarantee against "unreasonable searches and seizures."

Just as with violations of the federal law, eavesdropping activities which do not conform to the state laws are punishable criminally and may also be the basis for a civil suit filed by an aggrieved party.

Chapter 6
Crimes Against Property

Theft and Related Offenses

Larceny

The earliest crime established by common law to discourage theft was *larceny*. It consisted of "taking and carrying away" of "personal property" of another, with "intent to steal" (i.e., to "permanently deprive" another of his property). If any of these elements was missing in a particular case, the accused could not be found guilty of larceny.

One of the early difficulties in larceny prosecutions occurred when the owner of the property had relinquished possession to another person who proceeded to convert it to his own use, or otherwise to dispose of it. For instance, if John asked Sam to lend him his horse to go to town, and on the way John sold the horse, there could be no larceny because the element of "taking" was not present.

Another problem in early larceny cases was establishing the required element of "carrying away." For instance, assuming a person picked up a piece of personal property belonging to someone else, with the express intent to steal it, how far did he have to go with it for his action to amount to "carrying away"? An additional difficulty, and one that is inherently a part of larceny cases, centered around proving an "intent to steal."

The entire issue can best be illustrated, perhaps, by the following hypothetical case, based upon a shoplifting situation:

> While in a department store, Jane picks up a pair of hose. Instead of walking toward the sales person on duty, she walks to the opposite end of the counter and in the direction of the store exit.

Meanwhile, she is carrying the hose folded in her hand. As she nears the exit, a store detective arrests her for theft (or larceny, depending upon the category into which shoplifting falls in the particular state).

Have the required elements been established? Although the "taking" and "the carrying away" of personal property of another (the store) may seem clear enough, the store may be hard pressed to prove the "intent to steal." Jane may claim she was only taking and carrying away the hose so she could examine them in the daylight near the exit. What proof could the store offer to establish a different intent?

Now consider a slightly different situation:

On the windowed and well-lighted second floor of a department store, Joyce picks up a sweater. Although several sales persons are nearby to handle a sales transaction, Joyce walks to a stairway and heads for the alley exit. A store detective catches her. In this case, there is good reason to believe that Joyce intended to steal the sweater.

As previously pointed out, store detectives generally wait until a person has put some object into a purse or otherwise concealed it before taking any action; or else they wait until the unpaid merchandise has been taken outside the store. But such delayed action is only a precaution to nullify a possible false explanation of innocent purpose. In short, if ample evidence of "intent to steal" exists while the taker is still on the premises, there is no legal need to wait for the taker's departure from the store before detaining or arresting him.

Larceny by Bailee and Embezzlement

In an effort to plug up a loophole in the original common law crime of larceny, and in order to be able to successfully prosecute the person who converts personal property to his own use after having received possession or control of it from the owner, the English Parliament and early American legislatures created the new crimes of *larceny by bailee* and *embezzlement*.

Examples

1. Bill is given a package of merchandise to deliver to Ed. Bill, considered the "bailee," sells it to Leo, and pockets the proceeds. Bill has committed the crime of larceny by bailee.

2. Art, a bank teller, pockets $500 which he received for deposit. He has committed the crime of embezzlement.

False Pretenses and Confidence Games

Another early effort to amend the deficiency in the original definition of larceny was the creation of the offense of obtaining money or property under *false pretenses* or by means of a *confidence game*. The former was usually a misdemeanor; the latter was usually a felony.

Examples

1. Jerry shows Ann a diamond ring which he says is solid gold. He offers to sell it for $300. Ann buys it and later discovers that the ring is gold-plated and that the alleged "diamond" is nothing but a piece of ordinary glass. At the time of the transaction, Jerry knew, of course, that his representation was false. He is guilty of the crime of false pretenses.

2. Henry meets a rich widow, dates her several times, then tells her he knows how he can double her money within sixty days by investing it in an oil drilling operation in Alaska. He induces her to make a large check payable to him in order to simplify the investment transaction. But Henry actually has made no arrangements for such an investment. He leaves town several days after cashing the check, buys a boat with the money, and leaves for South America. Henry is guilty of a confidence game. He fooled his victim after having gained her confidence.

Modern Theft Legislation

Present legislation is doing away with the various theft crimes that in the past have had a variety of labels and created problems of interpretation. The Illinois Criminal Code exemplifies such new legislation.

At one time there were seventy-four separate provisions in the Illinois statutes dealing with theft. Most of them were enacted over many years for the purpose of plugging the loopholes in preceding statutes; now there is one provision for *theft* that covers almost all of the situations which were the basis for the multitude of earlier enactments, including the crime of *receiving stolen property*. The Illinois Code simply states that a person commits theft when he knowingly obtains or exerts unauthorized control over another person's property or obtains control by deception or threats, or when he receives stolen property or receives such property under circumstances which would reasonably indicate it was stolen, when he intends to deprive the owner permanently of the use or benefit of the property.

The punishment for the theft under common law larceny was usually of two grades, based upon the monetary value of the object taken. Any larceny under $15 was labeled *petit larceny;* over that amount it was termed *grand larceny*. Petit larceny was considered a misdemeanor, punishable by a jail sentence of up to one year. Grand larceny was considered a felony, punishable by a penitentiary sentence of one year or more. Today, the dividing line between petit larceny and grand larceny is usually set at a larger amount, such as $100 or $150, which merely reflects monetary inflation.

Another punishment applies when the theft is from the person of another without his knowledge, i.e., pickpocketing. In such instances, in deference to possible physical danger to the victim, the statutory penalty is generally more severe than in stealing other than from the person.

Robbery

Robbery is generally defined as the taking of money or personal property from the person of another by force or by threat of force. The act may occur on the street, in one's home, or in a place of business such as a bank.

Example
Moe grabs Jack around the neck and removes his wallet.

Robbery committed while the offender is armed is called *armed robbery* in some states. Even if not given that designation, however, the penalty for robbery while armed is greater than for ordinary *strong-arm* robbery.

Example
Using a gun, Phil demands and receives Bonnie's wallet.

Burglary

Burglary under common law consisted of "breaking and entering" into the "dwelling house" of another "in the night time" with the "intent to steal." Many early cases created the question of what constitutes "breaking." Suppose a door were slightly ajar and the would-be thief merely shoved it far enough to squeeze his body through. Suppose he hid in a trunk that was labeled for delivery into a home, and gained entry in that way. Would such cases constitute "breaking"?

The meaning of "dwelling house" also presented a problem. Suppose the building were a summer home or cottage and the breaking and entering occurred in the winter, when it was unoccupied and boarded up. Would such a building be considered a "dwelling house"? Even the meaning of "night time" caused trouble when the act occurred at twilight.

Those and similar problems are gradually being resolved by legislation which simply states that a person commits burglary when, without authority, he knowingly enters, or without authority remains within, a building, house-trailer, watercraft, aircraft, railroad car, or any part of such places, with intent to commit a felony or theft. Such legislation eliminates the controversies over the meanings of "breaking and entering," "dwelling house," and "night time."

The difficulty of establishing in all cases the element of "intent" remains, but it has been and will continue to be a problem as long as we adhere to the fundamentally desirable concept that no one should be punished for an offense as serious as burglary unless he *intended* to do wrong. Otherwise, any person who entered a building or any other structure by mistake could be convicted of burglary.

Because of its danger to life and limb, burglary, like robbery, carries a stiffer penalty than theft unaccompanied by dangerous circumstances.

Federal Theft Offenses

In addition to the state statutes that may be violated when a person steals or embezzles from a company, or when a bank, savings and loan association, or other business establishment is burglarized or robbed (by threatening its employees for the procurement of money), the same conduct may violate federal law if the establishment is insured by the Federal Deposit Insurance Corporation or is a member of the Federal Reserve System. Although the federal penalty for such theft offenses is considerable, it is even greater whenever a weapon is used or the establishment's personnel are otherwise placed in danger of life or limb.

Several federal statutes also prohibit and prescribe punishment for the theft of property being transported from one state to another, or for the interstate transportation of stolen property. The authorization for such federal legislation is derived from the constitutional power of Congress to regulate interstate commerce.

Examples

1. Bob steals an automobile in State A and drives it into State B where he is arrested. In addition to violating the theft statute of State A and the possession of stolen property statute of State B, Bob has also committed the federal crime of interstate transportation of a stolen motor vehicle. (Generally speaking, however, violations of this federal law, which is known as the Dyer Act, are prosecuted only when multiple vehicles are involved, or when an offender has a prior criminal record.)

2. One or more persons invade and ransack a dwelling in California and flee to Arizona with jewelry, furs, and other valuables. If the value of goods is $5,000 or more, the federal offense of interstate transportation of stolen goods has been committed. (However, if the goods transported across state lines are forged or counterfeit securities, bonds, or checks, no minimum amount need be present in order for the federal statute to be applicable.)

3. A trailer or railroad flatcar is loaded with color television sets in New York for shipment to Illinois. As the shipment passes through Indiana it is hijacked. The hijackers have committed a theft from an interstate shipment in violation of federal law. (If, however, the hijackers had waited until the shipment had arrived at its ultimate destination before stealing it, the television sets

Crimes Against Property

would no longer have been in the stream of interstate commerce and no federal offense would have been committed. This is because the statute only prohibits thefts of goods which are in interstate shipment at the time of the theft rather than the theft of goods which sometime in the past had traveled interstate. But, regardless of the status of the shipment at the time of the theft, local state prosecution is always available.)

Although the theft of property belonging to the United States government may be punished by the state within which it occurs, as well as by the federal government, the state authorities usually relinquish the right to prosecute. This is also true when federal government property is embezzled, or when stolen federal government property is possessed, concealed, or sold.

Forgery

Forgery occurs when a person knowingly makes, alters, issues, delivers, or possesses with intent to issue or to deliver any document capable of defrauding and designed to defraud another person.

Examples

1. John wrote a check payable to himself and signed it with a fictitious name. He endorsed the check and cashed it at the local tavern. John is guilty of forgery.

2. Ann owed Pete $90 and sent him a $9 check in partial payment. Pete knew Ann had plenty in the bank so he added an extra zero and changed the "nine" to "ninety" before cashing it. Pete is guilty of forgery.

3. Harry is planning a business trip abroad. His friend Tom, a bank official, issues a letter of credit from his bank stating that Harry has $100,000 credit with the bank, when in fact he has no such credit. Harry carries Tom's letter with him to use in case he comes across a favorable business deal requiring a showing of his financial responsibilities. Under some state laws, both Harry and Tom are guilty of forgery.

4. Diane went on a Hawaiian vacation and left her checkbook with Sharon who was instructed to pay all Diane's bills. Sharon signed Diane's name to checks in payment of Diane's rent and clothing bills. Although Diane's name was signed by Sharon, it was signed with Diane's authority and was not done with the intent to defraud. Therefore, neither Diane nor Sharon has committed forgery.

A separate federal statute makes it a crime to forge any instrument with intent to defraud the United States. The statute is used most frequently in connection with Social Security tax refunds and other U.S. Treasury checks.

Credit Card Offenses

The credit card explosion of recent years has resulted in the widespread circulation of hundreds of millions of plastic cards which can be used to obtain instant cash, instant goods, and instant services. Not unexpectedly, a wave of credit card theft and fraud has followed this credit expansion. In order to combat the growing credit card crime problem, specific state and federal statutes have been enacted.

State statutes make it unlawful to possess, use, or sell stolen, lost, or counterfeit credit cards. It is also unlawful to use such a card to assist in the procurement of other credit or the cashing of a check.

In order to supplant the protection afforded by state statutes, a new federal statute has been enacted which makes it unlawful to transport or sell in interstate commerce any stolen, lost, counterfeit, altered, or fraudulently obtained credit card. The federal statute is also violated if an individual uses a credit card to purchase goods valued at greater than $1,000 in a transaction affecting interstate commerce or if the goods are transported interstate.

Examples

1. Bert obtains a BankAmericard in a burglary and uses it to buy hot dogs the next day. The local deceptive practice or credit card statute has been violated.

2. Lew steals a gasoline credit card in Cleveland, Ohio, and takes it with him on a trip to visit a friend in Milwaukee, Wisconsin. While in Milwaukee, Lew uses the card to purchase $1,500 in replacement parts for his expensive but poorly running European car. He then returns to his home in Chicago with the parts. Lew violated the federal credit card statute when he transported the card from one state to another, when he purchased over $1,000 in parts, and also when he transported the auto parts to Chicago.

Property Damage and Property Intrusions

Arson and Criminal Damage

Of all the acts directed at damage to property, the most serious is the crime of *arson*. A modern version of the definition of arson (as in Illinois) provides that a person commits arson when, by fire or explosion, he knowingly damages any real property, or any personal property having a value of $150 or more, of another person without his consent; or, with intent to defraud an insurer, damages any property or any personal property having a value of $150 or more.

Crimes Against Property

Property of another, under that definition of arson, means a building or other property, whether real or personal, in which a person other than the offender has an interest which the offender has no authority to defeat or impair, even though the offender may also have an interest in the building or property. This provision avoids the uncertainties of the old, common law definition of arson. There is now no need to determine if "burning" occurred; it is sufficient if "damage" has been caused by either explosion or fire. The provision also covers the burning of one's own property when the purpose is to defraud an insurer. Under common law, the property had to be another person's dwelling.

The figure of $150 mentioned in the definition of arson, regardless of whether the statute involves one's own property or that of someone else, could be set at any figure selected by the legislature. The monetary specification only draws the line between the penalty designations for felony and misdemeanor.

Generally, the penalty for arson is a severe one. If death occurs because of arson—or, rather, if death can be considered to be a result of the act and the circumstances surrounding it—the offender is guilty of felony-murder.

Other kinds of intentional, criminal damage to another person's property are also punishable, but less severely than is arson. Even when fire or explosion is used to damage personal property other than a building, the conduct may be considered a misdemeanor, subject to appropriate punishment, if the value of the property is under the specified statutory amount. And the offense of criminal damage to personal property may include injuries to domestic animals. Some legislatures have described lesser forms of criminal damage to property as *malicious mischief*. Presently, though, a number of legislatures have made it a felony to intentionally damage school property by fire or explosive.

Trespass

A person who enters upon the land of another, immediately after receiving notice from the owner or occupant that entry is forbidden, commits the offense of *trespass*. A trespass is also committed whenever a person remains on the land of another after receiving notice to depart. The required notice may be oral or in writing. If in writing, it must be conspicuously posted or exhibited, and particularly at the main entrance or at points where access seems available.

The victim of a property offense, and particularly embezzlement, is sometimes offered or seeks restitution, in whole or in part, in return for a promise not to report the offense or to file a criminal complaint. The risks in any such deal are discussed subsequently in chapter 11 under the subtitle, "Compounding a Crime or Misprision of Felony."

Chapter 7
Offenses Affecting Public Morals, Health, Safety, and Welfare

OBSCENITY

The First Amendment to the Constitution of the United States guarantees freedom of speech and freedom of the press, but both freedoms have been held by the courts not to include the protection of obscenity. Because obscenity is not constitutionally protected, the various legislatures may make it a crime to sell, publish, disseminate, or possess with intent to disseminate, any obscene picture or writing. Similarly, it is a crime to perform, direct, produce, or promote an obscene act or performance. But no one can be criminally liable for permitting obscenity within the privacy of his home: the Supreme Court of the United States has held that a person has a constitutional right to possess, read, or look at whatever he desires.

Determining Obscenity

To determine whether or not a particular picture, writing, or performance is obscene, and thus subject to legal prohibitions, the following tests must be applied:

(a) Does the material, considered in its entirety ("taken as a whole"), appeal to a morbid or shameful ("prurient") interest in nudity, sex, or excretion?

(b) Does the material, again taken in its entirety, lack serious literary, artistic, political, or scientific value?

(c) In answering the question in point (a), the material must be examined from the viewpoint of an "average person" based upon "contemporary community standards," which are generally statewide standards, but in some instances the standards may be local ones (of a city, county, etc.).

Offenses Affecting Public Morals

(d) In answering the question in point (b), the standard for determining "serious value" is a national one.

Here are some illustrations of the application of these guidelines for testing obscenity:

Examples

1. A motion picture used for the education of a class of future parents is seized by the police. It contains numerous scenes of nude women. Although the film may appeal to an interest in sex or nudity, that interest is neither shameful nor morbid and is therefore not obscene.

2. A local bookstore is selling an 18th-century English novel detailing the sex life of a prominent female. The book may not be obscene. Although the primary interest of the book is a morbid interest in sex, it may contain redeeming historical or literary merit. The book may be well-written and it may accurately elucidate the morality of a segment of society in an historical period in England.

3. Publisher X reproduces the report of a presidential commission which had been appointed to make a study of the obscenity problem. The report is a public document and therefore can be lawfully reproduced. Publisher X copiously illustrates the various findings of the commission. X also publishes a foldout illustrated brochure advertising the book. The book "taken as a whole" has literary and scientific value (as do many of the so-called sex magazines that are found on newsstands) and is not considered within the obscenity prohibition. However, the brochure does not possess that saving attribute.

4. The police seize a photograph that a man is offering for sale to a youth. The photograph shows a man and woman in the nude in an act of oral-genital contact (cunnilingus or fellatio), which is specifically prohibited by state law. The photograph is considered obscene. It appeals to a morbid or shameful interest in sex and nudity and has no redeeming merit.

In order to convict a person of the offense of obscenity, it must be shown that he knew the nature of the obscene material. Showing such knowledge is called proof of *scienter*. It is rarely proved directly—that is, by an admission of the charged person that he knew the nature of the obscene material. Most often, scienter is shown circumstantially from the facts involved in the case.

Examples

1. A bookseller keeps a substantial stock of obscene books in a separate section of his store. The books were supplied by a wholesale firm that deals exclusively in obscene books. The bookseller

had visited the wholesale firm on many occasions and had purchased its books. Such circumstances establish his knowledge that the books were obscene.

2. Hugh was the managing partner of an enterprise that specialized in books of a salacious character. He prepared the newspaper advertising for the books. He admitted that he knew they could not be sent through the mails because of the nature of their subject matter. Proof of knowledge of the obscene nature of the books is thereby established.

3. The books in question were printed on cheap paper and contained obscene cover pictures. They were also priced high and an excessive profit resulted. Knowledge of the obscene character of the books is thereby established.

4. The sales price of the small paperback books was $4.50 each. The books were kept by the defendant next to the cash register. The covers of the books were themselves "obscene and offensive," and bore the warning "Adults Only." Here, too, the required element of knowledge is present.

Usually an arrest for obscenity is made only after the publication or performance of the alleged obscene material. The exception is pre-release censorship, or *prior restraint,* on motion pictures. Thus the legal procedures for determining whether or not a motion picture is obscene differ from those relating to books and art. Only motion pictures may be subjected to prior restraint as a condition to being licensed for showing. This principle has been approved by the Supreme Court of the United States.

A governmental body may therefore require submission of motion pictures in advance of exhibition before licensing the film for showing, but the Supreme Court has stated that prior restraint procedures must be accompanied by certain safeguards: (a) the burden of proving a film obscene rests upon the governmental agency; (b) the government may not finally determine that a film is obscene without court approval which is received by obtaining an injunction against the showing of the film; and (c) both the government's administrative procedures and the court's judicial procedures must allow for a speedy final determination about whether or not the showing of the film may be prohibited on the ground of obscenity.

When and where a motion picture is licensed by a governmental board, the motion picture, its distributor, and its exhibitor are all protected from prosecution under the criminal law for obscenity, and the police department may not make an arrest based upon its independent judgment that the motion picture is obscene.

Following the suggestion of some members of the Supreme Court, a few jurisdictions have abandoned full censorship of films in favor of a limited form of prior restraint, often referred to as *classification* of films. Under a classification procedure, only those films which are to be shown to audiences that include children need to be licensed. The procedural safeguard requirements are the same as those for full censorship. It is not to be confused, however, with the self-regulation labeling of films by the Motion Picture Association of America.

It is difficult to draft obscenity laws which will comply with the Supreme Court's interpretation of the First Amendment. Thus criminal prosecutions, though often successful in jury trials, are rarely supported by the appellate courts, which carefully scrutinize the laws and the particular facts of any given case. This practical impediment has led many legal authorities and others to the conclusion that obscenity laws should be confined in their scope to the protection of youthful persons, and that there should be no restrictions with respect to adults. Even the most liberal-minded judges have indicated that the strong societal interest with respect to youths outweighs First Amendment considerations.

ABORTION

In recent years some states had revised their abortion laws to permit abortions under some circumstances beyond the traditional one of preserving the life of the pregnant woman. But in 1973 the Supreme Court held unconstitutional any abortion law that prohibited a woman from having an abortion during the first three months of her pregnancy (Roe v. Wade, 410 U.S. 113). This decision was based upon a woman's constitutional right to privacy—the right to determine whether to bear a child or not, even after pregnancy. The Court did hold, however, that with regard to the second three-month period the state legislatures could regulate abortion procedures in ways reasonably related to maternal health, and that they could prohibit abortions altogether during the final three-month period, except when necessary for the preservation of the pregnant woman's life or health.

NARCOTICS AND OTHER "DANGEROUS SUBSTANCES"

The seeds of the modern day narcotic problem were planted thousands of years ago when the opium poppy was first used by the Babylonians, Persians, and Egyptians and later by the Greeks, Romans, Chinese, and Indians as a cure for minor ailments and as an appetite depressant in time of famine.

The opium poppy, grown principally in Turkey, China, India, and Mexico, is the source of several addictive derivatives (heroin, morphine, and codeine), of which heroin is the principal one insofar as crime and law enforcement are concerned. The use of heroin is a highly addictive "habit" that is very costly to sustain. Since it produces a euphoric and sleep-like effect, almost all addicts are rendered incapable of maintaining legitimate employment, and since they generally have no other legal source of income, their only recourse is to crime for monetary gain, although it is a fact that most addicts were criminals *before* they became users.

Contrary to what some persons believe, heroin, as well as other true narcotics, does not accelerate the sex drive but in fact diminishes it; sex offenses, therefore, are less likely to be committed by addicts than by non-users.

There are other dangerous substances, some addictive, some not, which are derivatives of natural vegetation (e.g., cocaine from coca leaves) or of synthetic origin (e.g., barbiturates, amphetamines, and LSD), but even though they are banned their relationship to criminal conduct is far less serious than heroin. The most harmful consequences are to the user himself.

Although marijuana, a euphoria-inducing substance of natural plant origin, is not a narcotic, legal restrictions upon its use and distribution have usually been based upon a consideration of it as a substance harmful to the user and one that can produce undesirable social consequences. This view has been widely challenged, however. While its sale and distribution are generally prohibited by state laws, and somewhat severely punished, the use of it by an individual is now generally treated as a minor offense. Moreover, as will be subsequently discussed, there is a strong movement afoot to decriminalize its private usage completely.

In addition to the various state laws regarding narcotics and other "controlled dangerous substances," there are strict federal laws dealing with the importation and interstate transportation of such items. Even mere possession of a controlled substance which cannot be legally imported into the country and that cannot be grown or produced here, can be a federal offense. In other words federal jurisdiction is based upon the importation factor.

The penalties imposed for federal violations depend upon the substance involved. In the case of heroin and cocaine, a first offender is subject to imprisonment for up to fifteen years, to be followed by a mandatory special parole term of at least three years, and a possible fine imposed up to $25,000. A second offender is subject to imprisonment for up to thirty years, to be followed by a special parole term of at least six years, and a fine of $50,000 also may be imposed. Penalties in the case of LSD range from a five-year sentence and a $15,000 maximum for first offenders to a ten-year term and a $30,000 maximum fine for repeaters. Substances such as barbiturates and amphetamines carry lesser penalties.

Other federal offenses may accrue from carrying a prohibited substance on a vessel of the United States while engaged on a foreign voyage,

Offenses Affecting Public Morals

using a communications facility (e.g., a telephone) in an unlawful transaction, and participating in a conspiracy to violate any relevant federal law.

Although relatively minor in terms of number of occurrences, glue sniffing and the sale of glue substance for that purpose is prohibited by law in some states. The protection of youthful persons is the chief motivating factor for such statutes.

Example

The parents of Sam, a high school drop-out, have warned Rose, the proprietor of a hobby shop, that Sam is an addicted glue sniffer and that Rose should not sell him any glue. In spite of the warning, Rose sells Sam twelve tubes of airplane glue. Later, Sam is arrested while weaving up and down Main Street sniffing the fumes of the airplane glue. Rose is also arrested. Both Rose and Sam are guilty of a criminal offense in those states which have laws prohibiting glue sniffing.

Restrictions upon the issuance of medical or dental prescriptions and the possession of hypodermic equipment supplement the laws governing narcotics and other dangerous substances. Physicians and druggists are required to keep records of prescriptions issued to guard against abuses. Furthermore, physicians may issue prescriptions only for legitimate purposes. Hypodermic equipment may only be sold or possessed for medical purposes.

Narcotics Addiction Itself

The Supreme Court of the United States has held that since narcotic addiction is an illness, an addict cannot be criminally prosecuted for being an addict. To do so, said the Court, is a violation of the constitutional prohibition against "cruel and unusual punishment." The Court's ruling does not mean, though, that an addict is immune from the law prohibiting *possession* or *use* of narcotics. Nor does it mean that an addict is immune from punishment for offenses he may commit in order to support his addiction.

Examples

1. Bill and Bob are arrested while "high" on heroin. Both admit they are addicts. A tin-foil packet containing narcotics is found on Bob's person. No drugs are found on Bill. Bill is guilty of no offense. Bob has violated the law because he possessed narcotics, not because he was addicted to or under the influence of them. If either Bill or Bob had been arrested while driving a car under the influence of a narcotic, they both, of course, could be prosecuted for that act.

2. Jack, a narcotics addict, is caught committing a burglary. At his trial, he contends that his addiction compelled him to steal in order to secure the money needed to buy narcotics. His defense is invalid.

Narcotic addicts may, of course, be subjected to civil commitment to an institution for treatment and attempted cure. The underlying objective of such a commitment is rehabilitation rather than punishment. One form of treatment, either in a place of confinement or in a non-confinement center, is the administration of a synthetic substance called methadone as a substitute for heroin. Although methadone is itself addictive in nature, it does not have the same potential for organic damage as heroin does, and dependency upon methadone is easier to break than is dependency upon heroin.

GAMBLING

Gambling is a game of chance or skill played for money or for other things of value. In all but a few states, many different types of conduct constitute the offense of gambling. The most common are described below.

Wagering by Participant

Anyone who takes part in a game of chance played for money or something of value commits the offense of wagering by participant.

Example

Several people play poker for stakes of $1.00 limit every Friday night at a local club. Their conduct constitutes unlawful gambling. However, when it is a simple social event, not involving profit for the sponsoring individual or for the club itself, rarely is there any police interference.

Many states provide for an exemption from their gambling laws for the awarding of prizes or compensation to the actual contestants in a bona fide contest of skill, speed, strength, or endurance.

Example

A country club stages a professional golf tournament. The winner is to receive $10,000. Other professional golfers who finish high in the tournament standings are to receive lesser sums as compensation. The tournament is not a gambling activity.

Wagering by Bystander

It is gambling for a person to make a wager on any game, contest, or other event involving persons other than himself.

Offenses Affecting Public Morals

Example
> Several baseball fans sitting in the bleachers at a ball park bet on various aspects of the baseball game, that is, on whether the next pitch will be a ball or a strike, on whether or not the batter will get on base, on whether or not the pitcher will complete the game. Such betting is unlawful gambling activity.

Exempted from the prohibition against bystander gambling are insurance agreements to compensate for losses that result from fire, storms, and death. Another usual exemption is the awarding of prizes or compensation to owners of animals or vehicles that are entered in a bona fide contest for the determination of skill, speed, strength, or endurance. By a considerable stretch of judicial reasoning, pari-mutuel betting at race tracks has been held valid even in states whose constitutions prohibit gambling.

Bookmaking

The offense of gambling occurs when a person owns or has any book, instrument, or apparatus that records or registers bets or wagers, or when a person knowingly holds any money that he has received as the result of a bet or wager. Such activity is called *bookmaking*.

Example
> Sam, the proprietor of Sam's Cigar Store, takes wagers at his store for the gambling syndicate. Sam records these wagers in a ledger. He is guilty of gambling.

Poolselling

The offense of gambling also occurs when a person sells pools on the result of any game or contest of skill or chance, political nomination, appointment, or election.

Example
> Members of the steno pool at an office each contribute $1.00 to the Kentucky Derby pot. Each employee draws a slip of paper from a bowl, containing the names of all the horses entered in the race. The employee who has the slip with the name of the winning horse on it wins the money in the pot. All the employees have committed the offense of gambling. Such an infraction of the law, however, is rarely, if ever, prosecuted.

Lotteries

The offense of gambling also occurs when a person sets up or promotes any lottery, or sells, offers to sell, or transfers any ticket or share in any lottery. A *lottery* is any scheme or procedure in which one or more prizes are distributed by chance among persons who have paid or promised consideration for a chance to win the prizes, regardless of whether the scheme or procedure is a raffle, gift, or sale, or is called by some other name. Supermarket and gas station promotional games are usually exempted by statute or court decision on the theory that a purchase of goods is not required in order for a person to obtain a chance or ticket.

Examples

1. A church runs a bingo game, selling bingo cards for $1.00 each per game. Valuable prizes are awarded to the winner. The profits from the game go toward missionary and other charitable work. The activity is unlawful gambling in most states.

2. A supermarket gives a stamp containing a picture of a baseball player to each customer and person who comes in the store and asks for one. When the recipient collects five stamps bearing the pictures of five different players, he receives $100 in cash. In most jurisdictions, it would not be considered an unlawful lottery.

As will be subsequently discussed, there are now in existence a number of state-operated lotteries, obviously legal by reason of state legislative authorization.

Numbers, Policy, and Bolita

Numbers, policy, and *bolita* are illegal because they involve the payment of a sum of money for the chance to win a greater sum of money.

Example

Bill sells tickets containing four numbers each for the "Wheel of Fortune" game. After the tickets are sold, Bill spins his roulette-type wheel four times. The holder of the ticket containing the four numbers selected by the wheel is awarded one half of the total funds collected by Bill from the sale of the tickets. It is an unlawful gambling activity.

Syndicated Gambling

In a special effort to suppress gambling that is controlled by organized crime syndicates, a few states have enacted *syndicated gambling* laws that prescribe a considerably greater penalty whenever the nature of the gambling clearly indicates a large-scale operation, usually determined by the amount and the number of the bets.

Gambling Places

The offense of *keeping a gambling place* occurs when a person knowingly permits any premises or property owned or occupied by him or under his control to be used as a gambling place. A common statutory

Offenses Affecting Public Morals

definition of a gambling place includes any real estate, vehicle, boat, or any other property that is used for the purpose of gambling.

Some states, in addition to penalizing a keeper of a gambling place, move against the gambling place itself as a *nuisance* under state law. If declared by a court to be a nuisance, the building in which gambling has occurred may be ordered closed ("padlocked") for a period of time, perhaps as long as a year. Some states also provide for the forfeiture of the liquor licenses of a tavern where gambling occurs and for the court sale of a gambling place to pay any unsatisfied fine.

Possession of Gambling Devices

A gambling offense occurs in most states when a person operates, keeps, owns, uses, purchases, exhibits, rents, sells, bargains for the sale or lease of, manufactures, or distributes any gambling device. A common statutory definition of a gambling device is any clock, tape machine, slot machine, or other machine or device for the reception of money or other thing of value on chance or skill or upon the action of which money or other thing of value is staked, hazarded, bet, won, or lost; or any mechanism, furniture, fixture, equipment, or other device designed primarily for use in a gambling place. A gambling device does not ordinarily include:

(a) a coin-operated mechanical device played for amusement that rewards the player with the right to replay and that is constructed or devised to make the operation of the device depend, in part, on the skill of the player, and that does not return to the player money, property, or the right to receive money or property; and

(b) vending machines that return full and adequate value for the money invested, with no element of chance or hazard.

Examples

1. A country club has several slot machines. The proceeds from these machines are used to purchase gifts for veterans at the local VA Hospital. However worthy the cause may be, the machines are gambling devices, prohibited by law.

2. A country club has a mechanical bowling machine and a candy bar vending machine (which sometimes malfunctions and gives two candy bars for the price of one). The machines are not gambling devices.

Federal Prohibitions

One of the early actions of Congress with respect to gambling (Title 15, §1172 U.S.C.) was a prohibition upon the transportation of any gambling device into any state unless the state into which it is transported has legalized its usage (e.g., slot machines into Nevada). Another relevant federal statute (Title 18, §1953) prohibits the transportation of tickets, records, slips, writings, "paraphernalia," etc., which may be used in bookmaking, wagering pools on sporting events, policy, numbers, and so on. Exceptions are made, however, for such items as pari-mutuel tickets acquired legally in some state or which may be used legally in the state into which they have been transported. Also specifically exempted in the statute are newspapers or other publications.

Miscellaneous Gambling Laws

Most jurisdictions have statutory provisions that provide for the forfeiture of gambling funds confiscated in a lawful search and seizure. The gambling funds that are seized are usually authorized by statute to be forfeited to the treasury of the state, county, or municipality, and the gambling devices that are seized are usually authorized to be destroyed by the local law enforcement authorities. Motor vehicles used in gambling operations are also subject to confiscation.

Example
>Acting with a proper search warrant, the police raid the back room of Joe's Cigar Store. A poker game is in progress and two slot machines are being played. After Joe's conviction for being the keeper of a gambling place, the money used in the poker game and in the slot machines is forfeited to the county treasury and the machines are destroyed.

Gambling agreements are not enforceable by court proceedings, since they are considered "contracts contrary to public policy."

Example
>Sam places a bet with Jill, a bookmaker, on a football game. Sam wins, but Jill does not pay off. Sam cannot sue Jill for the money due him.

Legalized Off-Track Betting and State-Operated Lotteries

Some states have legalized off-track betting and established state-operated lotteries. Their main motivation is to raise needed revenues and relieve the general citizen tax burden. The secondary motivation is the belief that by legalizing such operations the organized criminal element will be driven out of the gambling business. Despite the fact that such operations are legislatively approved, some scholarly studies and reports indicate that the supposed benefits are more illusory than real. (For references to such reports see the article by Hickman, "Should Gambling Be Legalized for the Major Sport Events," *Journal of Police Science and Administration* vol. 4 (1976), pp. 203–213.) Also, some critics of state-operated lotteries feel that since various state and federal statutes have been enacted to require stores, banks, and other private businesses to tell the truth about installment payments, interest on loans, and the quality of merchandise, the state governments are guilty of hypocrisy when they make no disclosure on lottery tickets or in advertisements about the extremely low odds on big winnings.

The Issue of "Victimless" Crimes

Because the volume of cases being processed has overburdened our criminal justice system, it has been urged that we determine which antisocial conduct is most deserving of our limited law enforcement energies and resources. The prosecution of the so-called victimless crimes of prostitution and those discussed in the preceding four sections ("Obscenity," "Abortion," "Narcotics and Other 'Dangerous Substances,'" and "Gambling") would be given low priority.

Here are some of the arguments offered in support of either eliminating "victimless" crimes from the criminal law or, if not decriminalized completely, treating them as quasi-criminal or civil violations (with fines and other civil remedies used for enforcement):

(1) By eliminating the prosecution of "victimless" crimes the police and courts would be free to concentrate their resources on dealing with violent crime.

(2) Government should not attempt to regulate public morality: e.g., sexual conduct, even of a "deviate" nature, between consenting adults under conditions of privacy.

(3) The State has little interest in prosecuting these offenses since they do not involve a victim in the traditional sense.

(4) The law prohibiting these offenses is generally violated, or at best not respected, by a majority of the citizenry: e.g., playing cards for money, and gambling in general.

(5) Enforcement of the "victimless" crime laws actually increases crime. Thus, it is argued, if the drug addict were given narcotics by the State, he would not commit crimes to obtain the funds to purchase narcotics illicitly.

Those opposing the decriminalization of "victimless" crimes would respond:

(1) The State does have an interest in fostering a moral tone in the community, without which the quality of life as we know it would be eroded. For instance, the proliferation of pornography is offensive to most persons, and it is also counter-productive to parental child-raising obligations.

(2) There *are* victims of so-called victimless crimes: the family, the supportive community or government, as well as the involved individual

himself. Moreover, a society which tolerates patently immoral conduct makes victims of us all.

(3) Organized crime would take over most, if not all, of "victimless" crime activities if such conduct were removed from the prohibitions of the criminal justice system. Prominent among these activities are gambling and prostitution.

(4) Relaxation of the laws to which we have referred would encourage other persons to engage in such undesirable activities—an encouragement, for instance, to young women, not otherwise inclined, to engage in prostitution.

(5) "Victimless" crime is a small percentage of law enforcement activity; its elimination would have inconsequential impact on the prosecution backlog.

(6) Shifting from criminal to civil law enforcement will only transfer the burden from the police to governmental civilian agencies, with little or no real personnel and fiscal savings for local government.

(7) The "victimless" criminal whose conduct is now unlawful is frequently a very valuable source of information regarding other more dangerous criminals. By giving him or her an occasional "pass" or other consideration, that person's cooperation can be of invaluable assistance. Were the conduct legalized, however, the incentive to cooperate would disappear.

The trend, nevertheless, is toward decriminalizing of at least certain activities which traditionally have been prohibited conduct—the use of marijuana, homosexuality, and gambling, to mention only a few. Just how far this trend will go toward removing all "victimless" crime from the criminal justice system remains to be seen.

In view of the extensive public interest in the issue of whether certain present criminal offenses should or should not be decriminalized, the reader may wish to consult the following articles: Davis, "Victimless Crimes: The Case for Continued Enforcement," *Journal of Police Science and Administration* vol. 1 (1973), pp. 11–21, and a response in the same issue (pp. 401–409) by Gitchoff, Ellenbogen, and Ellenbogen, entitled "Victimless Crimes: The Case Against Continued Enforcement." As regards the legalization of gambling, and particularly on major sports, see Hickman, "Should Gambling Be Legalized for the Major Sport Events," *Journal of Police Science and Administration* vol. 4 (1976), pp. 203–213, in which the author points out that all four major sports commissioners are unalterably opposed to such legalization.

The Sale, Possession, and Carrying of Firearms

Practically every attempt to prohibit the sale, possession, and carrying of firearms other than hunting weapons has been challenged in the courts

Offenses Affecting Public Morals

as violating the Second Amendment to the Constitution, which reads as follows:

> A well regulated Militia, being necessary to the security of a free State, the right of the people to keep and bear Arms, shall not be infringed.

It is now agreed by practically all Constitutional authorities, and the court decisions agree, that the Second Amendment does not bar the enactment of legislation dealing with the control of firearms. It is settled that the Second Amendment means simply that the federal government cannot prohibit the establishment of a state militia. Nevertheless, many gun enthusiasts continue to argue that the Second Amendment gives the private citizen an absolute right to ownership and lawful use of guns.

The extensive and increasing use of firearms, particularly handguns, in the commission of crime has generated many proposals to control the criminal use of firearms. The proposals have ranged from efforts to ban the possession of handguns by all persons except law enforcement officers and certain other designated groups, to requirements for the registration of firearms or of owners of firearms.

The absolute ban proposals have been totally rejected. The nearest approach to absolute ban are statutes which prohibit the sale, the private possession, or the interstate transportation of sawed-off shotguns and machine guns, which obviously are usable by private individuals for no other purpose than criminal activities. There is, however, one type of control effort that has been generally accepted—the registration of firearms or the registration of owners of them. The difficulty with registration laws, according to their opponents, is that the criminal element will simply not register *their* firearms. Moreover, the criminal element assumes that if caught with an unregistered firearm, the chances of any meaningful sanction are minimal. In fact, persons who are caught carrying concealed weapons in violation of the traditional state laws prohibiting such conduct (irrespective of whether or not the weapon is registered) are rarely convicted, fined, or sentenced. In one large city in 1975, over 20,000 firearms were seized by the police, practically all from the persons themselves or in automobiles they were using, and yet only about 10 percent received any meaningful penalties. Either the evidence was considered illegally seized or else the judge was persuaded that the carrying of the weapons by persons without criminal records was for self-protection. Opponents of registration use these facts to make the point that if we do not deal more firmly with violators of the law prohibiting the carrying of concealed weapons, we are not likely to impose punishment for mere failure to register a gun or failure to register oneself as a gun owner.

Despite the practical difficulties of enforcement, the proponents of gun control believe that much good would result from a ban on the sale and ownership of firearms that can be easily concealed and that are rather inexpensive (e.g., the so-called Saturday night specials). They do feel, however, that whatever is done should be done through Congressional legislation so as to prevent a person who lives in a place with local restrictions on firearm purchases, from going to a nearby city or state with lesser or possibly no restrictions at all. In any event, the problem of gun control is a difficult, controversial one which has yet to be resolved.

PUBLIC OFFICIAL CORRUPTION

The elected and appointed officials of local, state, and federal units of government wield power and authority of varying degrees. Whether the individual is the president of the United States, or a part-time village trustee, however, power is granted to him by the people with the understanding that it is to be used honestly and not for personal monetary gain beyond what has been appropriated for his official services. Because each grant of governmental power represents a corresponding abdication of personal liberty, abuses of the public trust affect all of us. In recent years there has been an increasing awareness of the problem of public official corruption at all levels of government. There also has developed a recognition of the advisability and need for the enforcement of relevant criminal laws to discourage breaches of the public trust.

Bribery

The most widely known form of public official corruption is bribery. Under state law, a person commits bribery when he promises or actually gives something of value or of some personal advantage to someone who is or is believed to be a public official with the intention of influencing the performance of an official act. A public official commits bribery by accepting or soliciting such an offer. Bribery can occur in a wide variety of circumstances in connection with law enforcement matters, zoning applications, and tax assessments, and in furthering efforts to obtain permits or government service contracts.

In some states a public official's mere failure to report a bribe offer constitutes an offense.

Example

Julian works in the county assessor's office appraising property to determine tax rates. Naomi owns a large barbeque restaurant and would like to increase her profits by decreasing her taxes. In one year, Naomi caters a large picnic for Julian's friends without charge. In return, Julian lowers Naomi's assessment and thereby

Offenses Affecting Public Morals

saves her $1,000 in taxes. Naomi and Julian are both guilty of bribery. In some jurisdictions, Julian would also be guilty of failing to report a bribe. The next year Naomi offers Julian $500 cash for another tax favor. Julian refuses. Naomi is guilty of bribery.

A provision of the federal criminal code makes it a crime to give, offer, or promise anything of value to a federal official to influence an official act in any way. A person who accepts such an offer is also guilty of federal bribery.

Extortion

Because it represents the ultimate perversion of the public trust, extortion is the most odious form of official corruption. Under a federal law called the Hobbs Act, a person who in any way or degree obstructs, delays, or affects interstate commerce by extortion "under color of official right" is subject to incarceration for up to twenty years and a $10,000 fine. "Under color of official right" means that the pressure which the victim feels is based upon the extorter's position and power as a public official.

Examples

1. Detective Smith of the vice squad collects $100 a month from bartender Roy with the understanding that Roy's customers will be harassed if he doesn't pay. Because Roy buys and serves liquor which is manufactured in another state, interstate commerce is affected and the Hobbs Act has been violated.

2. Detective Smith tells Ed, a suspected burglar, that if Ed doesn't pay $500, Smith will trump up a phony burglary charge. Although state laws have been broken, interstate commerce was not affected and the Hobbs Act has not been violated.

In recent years, the federal mail fraud statute has been utilized to combat the schemes hatched by corrupt public officials. The mail fraud statute prohibits using the mails in furtherance of any scheme to defraud. Public officials (federal as well as state) who use or cause the mails to be used in connection with schemes to defraud the citizens of their honest and faithful service as public servants violate the federal law. An official's duty is breached if he is influenced by bribery, extortion, or, as discussed below, conflict of interest.

Examples

1. Village manager Warren negotiates for the purchase of a piece of property by the village park district. Warren owns the property which is held in a secret land trust. Bids and contracts

are mailed during the course of the negotiations. Warren has used the mails in a scheme to defraud the citizens of the village of his honest and faithful service as village manager and of their right to have the business of the village conducted fairly and without regard for personal advantage.

2. State Senator Mary Plunder was chairman of the agriculture committee when she received bribes in payment for her agreement to back legislation favorable to the birdseed industry. Some of the bribe money was sent through the mail. Senator Plunder used the mails to further a scheme to defraud the citizens out of their right to have the affairs of government conducted honestly and free from bribery, corruption, and deceit. The members of the agriculture committee were defrauded out of their right to have the affairs of the committee conducted in the same fashion.

In a subsequent chapter (15) which discusses the constitutional privilege against self-incrimination, the prosecutorial value of *grants of immunity* will be discussed with respect to cases involving public official corruption.

Conflict of Interest

Public officials, be they elected or appointed, are duty bound to make decisions and to conduct themselves fairly, impartially, and without regard for personal advantage and enrichment. Accordingly, a public official cannot *self-deal;* this means, for instance, he cannot hold an undisclosed interest in a contract he negotiates or in a company with which he deals as a public servant. State statutes make it unlawful for a public official to engage in self-dealing.

Example

Mayor Jordan awards the city garbage removal contract to A-1 Garbage Service, a company in which he secretly holds a 50 percent interest. The mayor is self-dealing and his conduct is a conflict of interest.

Violations of Civil Rights

A number of statutes, both federal and state, have been enacted to protect citizens from the loss of constitutional rights at the hands of oppressive public officials. Most noteworthy of all is the federal civil rights statute (18 U.S.C. § 242) which makes it a criminal offense to utilize "color of law" to wilfully deprive a person of such rights. A companion statute (18 U.S.C. § 241) makes a conspiracy to do so punishable by up to ten years imprisonment, or up to life imprisonment if the victim dies.

Offenses Affecting Public Morals

Examples

1. Two railroad police officers discover vagrants sleeping in a boxcar. Instead of arresting the vagrants for trespassing, the police officers beat the trespassers with an axe handle. Both police officers are guilty of a crime because they acted "under color of law" to deprive the vagrants of the right to be free from summary punishment and to have their offense adjudicated by a competent tribunal.

2. Sheriff Shaw arrests two protesters for disturbing the peace. Before bringing them before a judge to answer charges, the sheriff gives the prisoners to the grand wizard of the Knights of the Strong Onion who hangs them both. Although the sheriff and the wizard are guilty of murder, they have also violated the federal civil rights law by depriving the victims of their right to life and their right to trial in accordance with the law. Because they acted in concert, the official authority or "color of law" exercised by the sheriff is attributable to the wizard.

3. A Caucasian, an Eskimo, a Negro, and an Oriental who work in the same factory get into a brawl over their respective races. The civil rights statute is inapplicable because no offender acted under color of law.

In addition to the criminal civil rights statutes there is one statute (42 U.S.C. 1983) which provides a civil remedy for civil rights violations.

State civil rights statutes may make it unlawful for a public official to discriminate on the basis of race, religion, color, or national ancestry. It also may be unlawful to deny a person access to a public accommodation for the same reasons.

Election Frauds

Fair and honest elections are central to the preservation of our democratic system of government. Accordingly, a variety of local statutes have been enacted to insure that votes are neither purchased nor coerced and that votes are cast and tallied properly. State statutes prohibit vote buying, vote selling, preventing people from voting, voting more than once, tampering with voting machines, and stuffing ballot boxes. Moreover, the federal government has invoked the civil rights statutes where vote fraud has been a substantial problem, under the theory that when an election official buys a vote or records a ghost vote he dilutes the effect of the proper votes and thereby deprives the honest voters of their constitutional right to cast a full vote. Additionally, federal statutes make it unlawful to intimidate a person with the intention of influencing his vote as well as to offer, solicit, or receive anything of value in connection with one's vote.

ANNOYING AND POTENTIALLY DANGEROUS CONDUCT

Some offensive activities are too varied or too general to be outlawed in specific terms. For that reason, a few statutes or code provisions have been rather broadly worded. Examples are laws directed at disorderly conduct and disturbing the peace.

Disorderly Conduct and Disturbing the Peace

Legislative provisions against *disorderly conduct* and *disturbing the peace* seek to prevent persons from knowingly committing acts in such an unreasonable manner as to alarm or disturb another person or persons. The gist of the offense is not so much that a person committed an offensive act, but that he knew, or should have known, that his action would tend to disturb, alarm, or provoke others. The emphasis lies in the unreasonableness of the conduct and its tendency to disturb. But what is "unreasonable" depends upon the facts of each case.

Some of the general classes of conduct traditionally considered to be disturbing or disorderly are creation or maintenance of loud and raucous noises of all sorts, threats to damage property or to cause bodily harm, careless or reckless display of fireworks, and fighting of all sorts.

Public Intoxication

A drunk weaving up and down a sidewalk is another example of annoying conduct that is usually punishable under laws declaring it an offense to be in a public place while intoxicated. Enforcement is generally reserved for the drunk whose conduct is of an annoying nature.

Although the Supreme Court has prohibited prosecutions for narcotics addiction, on the theory that such addiction is an illness, the Court has thus far refused to prohibit prosecutions of chronic alcoholics for public intoxication, holding that scientific evidence has not yet established that chronic alcoholism is an illness.

Mob Action, Unlawful Assembly, and Rioting

A group of persons acting together can commit an offense even though the conduct might not be criminal if performed by an individual. Such an offense is usually labeled *mob action, unlawful assembly,* or *rioting.* The minimum size of the group required to make the conduct unlawful is from two to twenty persons, depending upon the particular state statute involved. Some unlawful mob action statutes contain a provision that permits any individual who is harmed to recover damages against the city, county, or state in which the unlawful mob action occurred, as well as against members of the mob personally.

The activities proscribed by the statutes include the use of force or violence by a group of persons acting together and without authority

Offenses Affecting Public Morals

of law which disturbs the public peace; the assembly of a group of persons to do an unlawful act; the assembly of a group of persons, without authority of law, for the purpose of doing violence to the person or the property of anyone supposed to have been guilty of a violation of the law; and the assembly of a group of persons, without authority of law, for the purpose of violently exercising correctional or regulative powers over any person.

Examples

1. The "boys" at Joe's tavern decided one evening to do something about the college students in town who were wearing their hair long. The boys at Joe's all wore crew cuts and felt that long hair was feminine and Communist-inspired. The boys, all twenty of them, marched onto the college campus and proceeded to clip the hair, moustaches, and beards of all the students they encountered. Their conduct may be punishable as mob action. The individual crime of battery is also involved, of course.

2. The Jones family, members of a minority group, moved into an all-white neighborhood. A gang of toughs stationed themselves outside the Jones' home, vowing to rough up Mr. Jones if he came out of the house. The toughs are guilty of mob action.

3. To call attention to slum conditions in a particular area, a group of individuals banded together and marched down the street with flaming torches, threatening to burn down the town if the slum conditions were not remedied. They are guilty of rioting.

To protect the public from the results of riots, a few states recently have enacted anti-looting laws. *Looting* occurs when a person enters any building of another in which normal security of property is not present because of a hurricane, fire, "act of God," or riot and attempts or accomplishes a theft.

Example

A city was paralyzed by a severe blizzard. As a result, neighborhood stores were not able to open and the police were unable to patrol the streets. Joe and Louise observed a storm-broken window at the Big X Liquor Mart. They helped themselves to several bottles of liquor in the broken display window. In addition to committing the offense of theft, Joe and Louise are guilty of the related crime of looting.

Protest Parades and Marches

A statute requiring a parade permit as a condition to conducting a parade or march, and leaving it to the discretion of the officials to issue or refuse to issue the permit, is constitutionally void as an infringement of the First Amendment freedoms of speech and assembly. However, parade permits with limited restrictions may be constitutionally acceptable.

Some of the permissible statutory restrictions on issuing a parade permit are limitation of the number of paraders (although the limitation must relate to problems of pedestrian and vehicular traffic); reasonable notice to law enforcement officers of the organizers' names and the time and place of the parade; restrictions of the parade to nonpeak traffic periods; restriction of night-time parades in residential areas.

Restrictions on Residential Picketing

A few states have statutes which make it criminal to picket the residence of another person. Usually, however, no offense occurs if the residence is used as a place of business, if the residence is the place of employment when the person is involved in a labor dispute and is peacefully picketing, if the residence is a meeting place, or if the residence is commonly used to discuss subjects of general public interest.

Chapter 8

"White Collar" Crimes

Although crimes of violence, frequently referred to as "street" crimes, are understandably of greatest concern to the average citizen and to enforcement agencies, there are other, nonviolent types of criminal conduct which are far-reaching in their deleterious consequences and deserve citizen concern and law enforcement effort. They are generally referred to as *white collar crimes*.

Just as there are laws directed at the sneak-thief, the robber, and the rapist, there are laws which can be applied to the swindler, the con man, and other schemers seeking to cheat other persons and even the government itself. Some of the latter forms of conduct were previously discussed in chapter 7 in the section "Public Official Corruption," but there is much more that is deserving of treatment under the present heading.

Fraudulent Schemes

Individuals who devise schemes to defraud may run afoul of both state and federal statutes. Modern state theft legislation, for example, provides that a person commits theft if he or she obtains the property of another by deception. Federal laws may be used whenever the schemer utilizes the mails or makes interstate phone calls in the context of his or her fraudulent plans. Because of the greater resources and investigative facilities of the federal government, schemers may be far more vulnerable to apprehension and successful federal prosecution than those who avoid breaking federal laws. The primary emphasis in this chapter, therefore, will be upon the federal laws.

Examples
   1. Barbara is an executive for the Regal Television Company. She uses the mails in furtherance of a scheme to purchase parts from a supplier who pays her a kickback. Even though the supplier charged no more for the parts than an honest supplier would, Barbara has defrauded Regal out of her honest and faithful services as an employee.
   2. Eddie contacts Pete, Rick, and Bill, who live in another state, with a proposal to invest in a money-making shopping center which Eddie allegedly owns. Eddie mails them photographs of the complex, profit and loss statements of the stores, the bank, and the miniature golf course located at the center. After Pete, Rick, and Bill each wire $50,000 to Eddie, they learn that the pictures and statements are phony and that the only land which Eddie owns is a vacant lot alongside the center. Eddie has committed the state offense of theft by deception, and he has also violated the federal mail fraud and wire fraud statutes.
   3. An accident chaser hears of an auto crash on his radio and drives to the scene. He steers the victim, who is shaken up but not injured, to a lawyer with the advice that if the victim plays sick they can all make a lot of money. The lawyer arranges for a doctor to examine the victim and submit inflated medical bills to the insurance company. All parties share in the proceeds. Each one of them has committed theft by deception under state law, and, if the doctor bills or the insurance company check was mailed, all of them have committed mail fraud.

FALSE STATEMENTS

In a variety of situations, a false statement made to a federally insured bank or an agency of the federal government can constitute a criminal offense. The statutes which proscribe such conduct were enacted to maintain integrity in banking transactions and in federally administered programs.

Examples
   1. Leo applies for a business loan from a bank insured by the Federal Deposit Insurance Corporation (FDIC). As security for the loan, Leo pledges his furniture store as collateral. Leo values the furniture store at $500,000, although it clearly is not worth more than $75,000. Leo has violated the federal false statement law. Even if the bank did not rely on the false statement and would have issued the loan even if they had known the true value of the store, the offense has been committed.

"White Collar" Crimes

2. Larry applies for veterans' benefits to attend the **Superior Barber College**, the **Acme Truck Driving Academy**, and the **Taylor Institute of Mortuary Science**. Although he attended no classes, Larry and the administrators of each school filed forms with the Veterans Administration which sought veterans' education benefits. All have unlawfully filed false statements with the federal government.

Antitrust Activities

In order to protect and preserve the competitive nature of our economy, a number of antitrust laws have been enacted. The most famous of these laws are the Sherman Act and the Clayton Act. The Sherman Act makes illegal all contracts, combinations, and conspiracies which act in restraint of trade, and all monopolies or attempts to monopolize. The test of illegality is whether the business conduct merely regulates competition or whether it suppresses or even destroys competition. Activities such as price-fixing, division of markets, and group boycotts are therefore rendered illegal, and enforcement of the act can be accomplished by either the Antitrust Division of the Department of Justice or by private plaintiffs who have been harassed by such conduct. The Sherman Act has been supplemented by a number of statutes, including the Clayton Act, which prohibits certain types of price discrimination, exclusive dealing arrangements, and certain types of corporate mergers. Antitrust prosecutions mounted by the government can result in huge fines and imprisonment. Suits brought by private litigants can result in treble damages, which are monetary recoveries in the amount of three times the financial damages incurred.

Chapter 9
Organized Crime

THE NATURE OF ORGANIZED CRIME

Although today's organized crime is frequently termed "the Mafia," that is a misnomer, because the Mafia was an organization composed only of Sicilians, whereas today the persons who are engaged in criminal activities of an organized nature come from many national and ethnic origins. Moreover, contrary to a popular misconception, there is no single "outfit" or "syndicate" functioning as a board of directors for organized crime activities throughout the United States. Most certainly, however, there exists a considerable measure of cooperation among the various groups engaged in such profitable ventures as gambling, usurious lending ("loan-sharking" or "juice"), narcotics traffic, and, though to a considerably lesser extent, prostitution.

One fact remains undisputed, however, and that is that many criminal activities are of an organized nature, and, furthermore, the criminal element engaged in such activities have their "enforcers" or "hit" men to insure against deviations from a particular group's standards of doing business. Moreover, there is rivalry among the various groups, and that rivalry often reaches an intensity resulting in "bumping off" rival group leaders and members.

Organized crime is involved in a host of illegitimate activities. Increasingly, it is becoming entrenched in legitimate business ventures as well. Among the criminal activities engaged in by organized crime are gambling, loan-sharking, narcotics, and prostitution.

Gambling is organized crime's major source of revenue, and estimates of the annual take in this area have been as high as $50 billion. Gambling

Organized Crime

revenues come from a variety of sources, including numbers, off-track horse betting or bookmaking, and bets on sporting events. Gambling money is filtered upwards from small operators, through intermediaries and runners, into complex financial channels leading to organization kingpins. Gambling profits are used to finance other illegitimate activities and to corrupt law enforcement and other public officials.

Loan-sharking, the loaning of money at exorbitant interest rates, is organized crime's second largest source of revenue. Most often, the loan shark's prey is a debt-ridden gambler, although anyone willing to pay the usurious interest ("juice") is fair game. "Juice" payments can range upwards of 100 percent a week, but the classic "6 for 5" loan is more common. When a victim falls behind in his payments, threats and violence are the collection tools that are utilized.

Narcotics distribution brings large profits, and for years secret laboratories in France produced the heroin imported into the United States and wholesaled by organized crime. Vigorous enforcement efforts and changing crime patterns in recent years have seen a dramatic shift from the distribution of white French heroin to the widespread importation of brown Mexican heroin. Most of this brown heroin traffic is controlled by large groups and families based in rural areas of Mexico.

Not content with the profits from illegitimate activities, organized criminals are becoming increasingly engaged in legitimate businesses. This might be commendable were it not for the tendency of organized criminals to utilize criminal tactics in the operation of legitimate business ventures. Legitimate returns on an investment are viewed as inadequate, and therein rests the problem.

The extent of organized "hoodlum" penetration into legitimate businesses and its long-term effects upon the economy cannot be accurately measured. Organized crime has infiltrated the coin-operated machine industry, retail sales, transportation, and other service enterprises. Participation in such businesses may be solely to reap profit, but often it is actually an effort to provide a front or legitimate source for illegitimate income. Businesses are also used to "launder" corrupt income.

Once involved in legitimate business operations, the organized criminal element remains quite willing to promote those businesses by unlawful means. Threats and coercion are used to enlist customers and dissuade competitors. Organized crime has also made substantial inroads into labor unions. This infiltration has generated huge revenues and provides a stranglehold on legitimate businessmen.

Combating Organized Crime

The first major attack on organized crime took place during prohibition days when Elliot Ness and his Treasury Agency "untouchables" fought it out with Al Capone in Chicago and Thomas E. Dewey convicted Lucky Luciano in New York. In 1950, Senate hearings chaired by Senator Estes Kefauver heard from hundreds of witnesses and a short-lived flurry of interest in organized crime was stimulated. Not until 1957, however, when it was learned that almost one hundred organized leaders from all over the country had met in a grand strategy meeting at Apalachin, New York, did the nation realize the extent of the problem. Since then, resources have been committed and legislation drafted to meet the challenge of organized crime.

The Organized Crime and Racketeering (OCR) Section of the Department of Justice is responsible for the coordination of a nationwide effort to control and disrupt the activities of organized crime. The OCR Section receives and disseminates organized crime intelligence reports from all federal law enforcement agencies and from local enforcement agencies as well. The field work of the OCR Section is conducted by organized crime strike forces located in target cities throughout the United States.

Organized crime strike forces are staffed by special attorneys who work in close cooperation with representatives of each of the major federal law enforcement agencies. These representatives are assigned full time to the strike forces. In this manner, agents of the Federal Bureau of Investigation, Secret Service, Drug Enforcement Administration, Bureau of Alcohol, Tobacco and Firearms, and the Postal Inspection Service can and do work together with the special attorneys in coordinating the investigation and prosecution of organized crime figures and organized crime activities.

Congress has enacted legislation which is designed to facilitate the attack on organized crime. One of the main legislative tools enacted by Congress allows for the use of court-ordered wiretaps to gather information leading to criminal prosecutions. An immunity statute allows the government to immunize a witness, and thus foreclose him from invoking the Fifth Amendment as a bar to questioning by a grand jury or in court. Using immunity, a mobster can be forced to testify against his cohorts in crime or else face contempt proceedings and imprisonment. The fact that one is being compelled to testify under an immunity grant does not release him from the sanctions of the federal perjury statute. If he testifies falsely, even under a grant of immunity, he can be prosecuted.

A novel legislative tool enacted to fight organized crime is the Racketeer Influenced and Corrupt Organizations statute, labeled RICO. The RICO statute allows the federal government to move against any partnership, corporation, association, or other legal entity which is involved in or profits by a pattern of racketeering activity. Such activity includes bribery, counterfeiting, theft from interstate shipment, fraud, gambling, extortion, and loan-sharking. RICO allows the individuals involved to be fined and imprisoned and provides for the forfeiture of the defendant's interest in the business entity.

Many local law enforcement agencies, such as state bureaus of investigation and large municipal police departments, have set up special units to investigate and prepare cases on organized crime activities. A great deal of local law enforcement resources is spent fighting organized crime indirectly through vice control units. In this fashion, inroads can be made into gambling, prostitution, and narcotic-related activities.

Because the bulk of the services provided by organized crime is in response to consumer demand, one of the greatest weapons against organized crime is an informed and concerned citizenry. A social and political awareness of the evils of organized crime—its raw financial power, its effect on the quality of life, and its relationship to political corruption—could eventually lead to widespread refusal to purchase the goods and services in which organized crime is involved. To this end, state and local crime commissions make a substantial contribution towards identifying the nature of the problem and educating the community to the need for concerted action.

Chapter 10
Miscellaneous Federal Offenses

Tax Evasion

The federal government and, to a lesser extent, some state governments depend upon a voluntary system of taxation for the revenues necessary to fund government programs and services. A number of criminal statutes are utilized to insure the integrity of that system. Under federal law, it is unlawful to fail to file an income tax return, to evade taxes by failing to report certain income, or to file a return which contains false information such as the number of dependents or the amount of legitimate deductions. Because willfulness and unlawful intent are required to make such conduct unlawful, a good faith mistake may give rise to an adjustment of the tax due, but will not cause a criminal prosecution.

Examples
 1. Erma deducted as a casualty loss the cost of removing from her front yard a tree killed by Dutch elm disease. Although the deduction will be disallowed and an additional tax payment levied, no crime was committed since she acted in good faith.
 2. Alderman West received a $50,000 bribe in connection with an industrial rezoning and failed to report it on his income tax return. He can be charged with both tax evasion and the filing of a false return.

It is also a federal crime for any person to knowingly assist or aid another person in preparing a false or fraudulent return.

Example
 Joe is a *maître d'* at a fancy restaurant. He receives a nominal salary from the restaurant, but earns substantial tips from the

customers. Joe hires an accountant to assist him in preparing his income tax return. The accountant advises Joe to report only half of his gratuities, on the theory that no one will ever know the difference. Joe follows his accountant's advice and files his return. Both men are guilty of federal offenses.

There are many other types of federal taxes, and evading their payment is also a federal offense. These include taxes on alcohol, tobacco, etc., which apply primarily to manufacturers or producers rather than to citizens generally.

Immigration Law Violations

Congress has promulgated rules and regulations governing the admission, residence, and deportation of noncitizens or aliens. Fines and/or imprisonment may be imposed upon aliens who violate these provisions, as well as upon citizens of the United States who participate in immigration offenses. For example, all aliens are required to register with the United States government and provide their name, nationality, current address, fingerprints, and other information. Failure to comply with those requirements is a misdemeanor. The citizens and noncitizens alike who bypass the regular alien immigration and registration procedures in efforts to get unlawful aliens into this country are guilty of a felony punishable by a $2,000 fine and a five-year period of imprisonment. The concealment or harboring of illegal aliens is a felony as well.

Smuggling

The smuggling laws help regulate the flow of commerce to and from the United States. These statutes provide for the proper classification of and the import duties to be levied upon various items coming into the United States from foreign countries.

It is unlawful to avoid compliance with the regulations. The regulations not only cover the surreptitious personal carrying of the items but also their transportation through the mails or other facilities by means of false statements, documents, or invoices.

Example

Bea and Aaron return from a European trip. Aaron carries off the plane and into the customs inspection area a brief case in which he has concealed an undeclared valuable piece of jewelry. While in Europe Bea shipped a piece of sculpture in which she concealed a diamond ring, without making any declaration about it. Both have violated the law by attempting to evade importation duties.

COUNTERFEITING

Confidence in the obligations of the United States, such as Treasury checks, bills, notes, and securities of the United States, is protected by a number of statutes. The statutes make it a felony to forge, counterfeit, or alter any government obligation. Also unlawful and punishable as a felony is the possession of plates, stones, and engravings usable for counterfeiting. Likewise unlawful and punishable are the possession, passing, and sale of counterfeit currency or other obligations. Moreover, the possession, circulation, design, or duplication of *any likeness* of United States currency or obligations is a criminal offense, but punishable to a lesser degree as a misdemeanor.

Examples

1. Toby prints a quantity of counterfeit $20 bills and sells them to Billy and Amanda. Billy uses one to purchase cigarettes. Amanda is afraid to pass the bills herself, so she sells them to William, a neighbor, at a considerably lesser price. Toby, Billy, Amanda, and William have all violated counterfeiting laws.

2. Harry pastes small parts of different $10 bills onto a one dollar bill in an attempt to create a "raised note" which looks like a ten. Harry has committed a felony.

3. Jordan Petrunkis owns Petrunkis Brothers Van Lines. As an advertising promotion, Jordan has his printer design a handbill which looks like a $100 bill, but in the center it bears Jordan's picture and the slogan, "You can Bank on Petrunkis." Jordan and the printer are guilty of a misdemeanor and could be fined $500. As a practical matter, however, they would most likely not be prosecuted for their misguided promotion, provided that their conduct was not repeated and the plates, negatives, and handbills were surrendered to the Secret Service.

Federal statutes make it unlawful to reproduce coin currency or to possess the dies and molds intended to make them. The passage of counterfeit coins is, of course, also unlawful.

INTERFERENCE WITH THE MAILS

There is a host of federal statutes designed to protect the United States Postal Service from criminal conduct which interferes with the integrity of the mails. Statutes make it a felony to steal from the mails, be it from a mailbox, a collection box, a mailbag in transit, or from a post office itself. If the theft is from a postal employee, a ten-year prison term may result; and if a weapon is used, or if the robber is a second offender, a mandatory penalty of twenty-five years imprisonment is provided by the statute. A variety of other statutes makes it unlawful to obstruct or delay the mails, to damage any mail box, and to counterfeit postage stamps.

Examples

1. Jill works as a mail sorter and provides special handling for letters which contain currency. Jill removes some of the currency and puts it in her purse. She has embezzled from the mails, a felony.

2. Eric works as a letter carrier. While on his route he is accosted by Colin, who used a sawed-off shotgun to convince Eric to part with his mailbag. Colin could be charged with obstruction of the mails, a misdemeanor, with robbery of a letter carrier, which carries a penalty of up to ten years, or with armed robbery of a letter carrier, which carries a twenty-five year mandatory penalty.

Espionage and Sabotage

Although counterintelligence activities receive little peacetime publicity, the FBI has thousands of agents working around the clock to prevent espionage and to identify foreign intelligence operatives and American citizens who, wittingly or unwittingly, are in league with such agents. An American citizen or foreign national who gathers, receives, or transmits information pertinent to the national defense with the intent or with reason to believe that such information is to be used to the injury of the United States can be fined $10,000 and imprisoned for ten years. If such information is transmitted to a foreign government or agent, the penalty may be imprisonment for any term of years up to life or even execution.

Prosecutions of foreign agents are extremely rare. Most frequently the agents are attached to a foreign embassy, and, owing to the niceties of diplomatic relations, once identified for what he or she actually is, the agent is either fed incorrect information or else a request is made to his government for his recall. A foreign agent without a protective diplomatic cloak may, of course, be prosecuted for any acts of espionage or sabotage.

A related area which has figured prominently in the news of recent years has been the unauthorized disclosure of classified information. A federal statute protects against disclosure of information relating to intelligence gathering and intelligence communications.

A number of sabotage statutes provide extremely heavy penalties for the destruction of fortifications or national defense installations or materials and for the production of defective war material. Little used in peacetime, these statutes are divided into wartime and peacetime categories. The wartime provisions carry penalties up to thirty years imprisonment.

PIRACY AND OTHER CRIMES COMMITTED UPON THE HIGH SEAS

Although of far greater importance in the bygone buccaneering days, piracy is still a crime by federal law. In accordance with constitutional authorization (see Article 1, Section 8 in the Appendix to this text), Congress made piracy on the high seas a federal felony. It applies even though the vessel and crew involved in the piratical act are of foreign origin or registry and no United States vessel or citizens were in any way directly affected. Once a pirate vessel reaches United States waters it may be seized and the crew members prosecuted in a U.S. federal court. Crimes committed on vessels of United States registry are, of course, punishable just as though the acts were committeed on United States waters.

CRIMES AFFECTING AIRCRAFT, MOTOR VEHICLES, AND THEIR AUXILIARY FACILITIES

One of the most common aircraft offenses involves the conveying of false information concerning an alleged attempt to destroy or damage an aircraft. The act is punishable by a civil fine of up to $1,000, but if the false information is imparted maliciously or with reckless disregard for the safety of human life, the offense is a felony punishable by five years imprisonment.

Examples
 1. "Laugh-a-Minute" Cyril tells a stewardess that the camera which he carried on board flight 123 is in fact a bomb. Cyril is subject to a $1,000 civil fine.
 2. Phil is a disgruntled mechanic for Supreme Airlines. In order to punish the airline's management for what he feels to be intolerable working conditions, he makes a series of false bomb threat telephone calls which ground a number of Supreme aircraft. Phil may incur a five-year imprisonment term for each false threat.

Carrying aboard an aircraft any accessible concealed deadly weapon is an offense punishable by fine and imprisonment up to one year. The same is true of carrying aboard any explosive or incendiary device. Of course, if the weapon is used or the explosive or incendiary device is detonated, the offense is more severely punishable.

The actual skyjacking of an aircraft, described in the federal law as "aircraft piracy," or an attempt to commit such an act, is punishable by up to twenty years in prison, or, if a death results, the offender may be imprisoned for life, or executed. The same offense and penalties apply even though at the time of the act the aircraft is outside the special air-

Miscellaneous Federal Offenses

craft jurisdiction of the United States, and it is immaterial whether the aircraft is a foreign or domestic one, just so long as the offender is subsequently seized in the United States. The historical basis for jurisdiction in this latter situation is to be found in Article 1, Section 8 of the Constitution (see "Appendix") as well as in the International Convention for the Suppression of Unlawful Seizure of Aircraft.

The willful destruction or disabling of an aircraft or its parts, or of aircraft facilities such as a hangar or terminal, also constitutes a serious federal offense. The placing of a bomb or other destructive substance in or about a motor vehicle used in interstate commerce, or in or about a garage or other facility used to implement such commerce, with intent to endanger persons or to impair the usability of such a structure, is also a federal crime and severely punishable.

Travel Act Violations

A very important law, particularly for the prosecution of official corruption cases and cases involving organized crime, as well as other types of serious crime, is a statute known as the Travel Act. This statute makes it a federal felony to travel in interstate or foreign commerce, or to use a facility such as a telephone or the mails, in order to promote, manage, carry on, or facilitate any unlawful activity.

Examples

1. Apex Oil Company has its corporate headquarters in Dallas, Texas. Alderman Corn of Kansas City, Kansas, traveled to Apex' headquarters to discuss his $10,000 bribe in connection with favorable zoning for a planned Apex distribution center in Kansas City. After the meeting, Apex telephoned its Swiss bank to arrange for the transfer of the $10,000. Because Corn traveled interstate to further the unlawful activity of bribery, he violated the Travel Act. When the phone call was placed to Switzerland, the act was once again violated.

2. Spike and Nina take bets in Virginia and bring them to Mr. Big in West Virginia. The next day they return to pay off the winners. Because bookmaking is illegal in both states, Spike and Nina have violated the Travel Act both coming and going.

3. Judge Perrin of Maine takes a $25,000 bribe to put an axe murderer on probation. Perrin takes the money and drives to Las Vegas in his camper, where he gambles it all away. Although Perrin can be prosecuted in Maine for bribery, he did not violate the Travel Act because his trip took place after the crime and the interstate travel did not further or facilitate it.

The Transmission of Threatening Communications

The transmission of a threat through the use of the mails or some other avenue of interstate commerce is a federal offense. Usually such a threat would be to kidnap or injure a person, or damage his or her reputation or property. It is also a crime to transmit in such a fashion an extortionate or ransom demand. Of high national interest, of course, is the issuance of a threat to kill or injure the president or vice-president of the United States.

Crimes Committed by Military Personnel

Crimes committed by military personnel upon any military vessel, aircraft, or military installation are tried before a military tribunal. The judges are members of the military. The constitutional authorization for this stems from Article 1 of the Constitution (reproduced in the Appendix to this text). It confers upon Congress the power "to make Rules for the Government and Regulation of the land and naval forces." The Supreme Court of the United States has decided several cases which have rather strictly interpreted this authorization so that it does not cover dependents of members of the armed forces nor nonmilitary personnel employed to work on various military structures or projects in foreign countries. They can be tried only in U.S. civilian courts where they may receive the benefit of the constitutional rights of all U.S. citizens who are charged with criminal offenses. Primary among those rights is trial by a civilian jury. (Curiously enough, however, Congress has not set up a procedure whereby such persons may be tried in the federal courts; consequently, the most that ordinarily happens to them is that they are sent back home to the U.S.)

Another Supreme Court decision limits the jurisdiction of the military courts even as to military personnel themselves. If a member of the military commits a crime while off a military vessel, aircraft, or installation, but while still on U.S. territory, he is entitled to trial before a civilian court, unless the offense was "service connected." Although the meaning of that phrase is not altogether clear, it may be illustrated by a case where a member of the military, while in uniform, engages in a fight with other uniformed personnel and kills one of them in a tavern off the military base in State X. Since he was in uniform, his act is considered service related, and he would be tried in a military court.

The basis for this limitation of the military courts' jurisdiction was to accord the accused a jury trial and other rights. The limitation is inapplicable, of course, when the criminal act is committed in a foreign country which does not afford comparable constitutional protections. In

Miscellaneous Federal Offenses

such instances the military would be permitted greater jurisdiction, at least insofar as our own governmental interests are concerned. However, when the victim is a foreign country civilian or the country's property is damaged by our military personnel, that country's courts would have jurisdiction to try the case. Treaties and agreements usually govern such situations, however, and many times, especially when the incident is a relatively minor one, the matter is left to our own military authorities. Of course, in a country with which the U.S. is engaged in war or which has been occupied following the cessation of hostilities, military courts have complete jurisdiction over offenses committed.

Chapter 11

Interference with Law Enforcement and Judicial Processes

In order to insure that the workings of the criminal justice system are not frustrated or subverted, a number of statutes and court rulings have been promulgated as protective measures. They are intended to prevent overt interference with law enforcement and judicial bodies as well as to guarantee the truthfulness and integrity of information conveyed within the criminal justice system.

INTERFERENCE WITH POLICE

Most states have statutes which make it a crime to interfere with the duties of a police officer.

Example
   Officer Jones observes Lynne throw a rock at marchers in an Armed Forces Day parade. When Officer Jones identifies himself and announces that Lynne is under arrest, Lynne runs away down a side street. Officer Jones gives chase, but is stopped by three of Lynne's friends, who deliberately block Officer Jones' path, causing him to lose Lynne in the crowd. Lynne's three friends are criminally liable for their conduct.

Similarly, it is a crime in many states for a person who, upon command of a police officer, and under reasonable circumstances, refuses to aid in the apprehension of an individual or in the prevention of a crime.

Example
   Officer Smith observes Edgar looting a Bar-B-Que stand. Smith chases him. Edgar hurries to a taxi stand and begins to enter a

Interference with Law Enforcement Processes

taxi. Smith shouts his identity to the taxi driver and orders him not to drive off with Edgar. Because the driver knows Edgar's brother, he disregards Smith's order and drives off. Smith then jumps into another taxi and orders its driver to follow the taxi carrying Edgar. That driver dislikes Officer Smith and he refuses to comply. Both taxi drivers are criminally liable for failing to aid Smith in the apprehension of Edgar.

Interference with federal officers such as FBI or Treasury agents is prohibited by a federal statute which makes it a felony to forcibly assault, resist, oppose, impede, intimidate, or interfere with such officers while in the performance of their official duties.

OBSTRUCTING SERVICE OF PROCESS

The obstruction of the authorized service or execution of any civil or criminal court process or of any other court order is a violation of the law.

Example
A deputy sheriff, in uniform, goes to the high-rise apartment building where Tammi lives in order to serve a divorce summons on her. Todd, the doorman, not wishing to permit any annoyance to Tammi, refuses to permit the deputy sheriff to enter the building, on the pretext that he is not wearing the clothing required of guests in the building. Todd's conduct is criminal.

TAMPERING WITH EVIDENCE

It is a crime for a person, with the intent to prevent the apprehension of any person or to obstruct the prosecution or defense of any person, to destroy, alter, conceal, disguise, or plant evidence, or to falsify evidence, or to furnish false information.

Example
Andy and Bob, strangers to each other, meet at Charlie's tavern and engage in a fist fight. Bob falls down and accidentally hits his head on a bar stool and dies. Andy flees the tavern. Charlie, the bartender-owner, in order to protect his good customer Andy, gives the police a false physical description of him. By so doing, Charlie has committed a crime.

COMPOUNDING A CRIME OR MISPRISION OF FELONY

Society's interest in having crimes reported and prosecuted is protected by state and federal statutes which provide penalties for those who attempt to shirk their responsibility as citizens by seeking to avoid involvement in the criminal justice process. The offense of such avoidance is known either as *compounding a crime* or *misprision of felony.* They are essentially the same.

Some state statutes are phrased as follows: "A person compounds a crime when he receives or offers to another any consideration for a promise not to prosecute or aid in the prosecution of an offender."

Example

Carol steals (or embezzles) $5,000 from her employer. Carol's father offers $1,000 in restitution, upon the employer's promise not to initiate a criminal complaint. Carol's father has compounded a crime with the offer. If the employer accepts the offer, he is guilty as well.

The federal statute, under the title of "Misprision of Felony," provides that:

Whoever, having knowledge of the actual commission of a federal felony conceals and does not as soon as possible make known the same to some judge or other person in civil or military authority under the United States, shall be fined not more than $500 or imprisoned not more than three years, or both.

However, the mere failure to report a crime, without an affirmative act of concealment, does not violate the statute.

Example

Nate, the president of the Austin Community Bank, discovers that Lou, the bank's head teller, has been lining his pockets with bank funds. Because he is embarrassed by the fact that he hired Lou, Nate conceals from the bank examiners the books and records which prove the embezzlement. Heartsick over the affair, Nate confides in his friend Red and tells him the entire story. Neither Nate nor Red report the crime to the FBI. Because Nate committed an act of concealment *and* failed to report the crime, he has violated the misprision of felony statute. Because Red merely failed to report the crime but did not conceal it, he has not violated the law.

Unlawful Flight to Avoid or Hamper Prosecutions

There is a federal statute prohibiting unlawful flight to avoid prosecution (UFAP) which makes it a felony to engage in interstate or foreign flight to avoid a criminal prosecution or to avoid being a witness in a criminal trial. Unlike the other federal statutes in this section which are

Interference with Law Enforcement Processes

applicable only when the underlying proceeding is a federal one, the UFAP statute empowers the FBI to track down and apprehend fugitives from state criminal proceedings.

Example
A well-known state political leader is assassinated by a sniper. The local police investigating the murder have reason to believe that the killer has fled to another state. Even though the murder itself is not a federal crime, the FBI enters the case because of the UFAP violation and apprehends the killer.

As a practical matter, UFAP arrestees are generally not prosecuted in the federal courts for their interstate flights. Rather, they are usually returned to the state from which they fled to face only state prosecutions for the basic offense. For this reason, the UFAP statute is more a vehicle for federal apprehension than for federal prosecution. Its primary value is that it affords local law enforcement the benefit of the nationwide FBI manhunting resources.

It is a crime in many states for a person to try to prevent the apprehension of, or to obstruct the prosecution or defense of, another person by concealing himself or by leaving the state to avoid testifying, or to induce a witness who has material knowledge to conceal himself or to leave the jurisdiction.

Examples
1. Tom and Candy are high school sweethearts. Their parents are friends. One evening, in the heat of passion while parked in front of Candy's home, Tom forcibly rapes her. Although Candy's parents report the crime to the police, they have second thoughts about prosecuting Tom. Prior to Tom's trial, Candy's parents take her temporarily to another state so that she will not have to testify against Tom, thereby assuring his acquittal. The conduct of Candy's parents is a criminal offense.

2. In the foregoing case, if, after her parents pressed charges against Tom, Candy voluntarily left the state because she did not wish to testify against him, she alone would be guilty of a crime.

3. If Tom's parents had offered to pay for a trip to Europe for Candy in exchange for her failure to report Tom's crime to the police, both Candy's and Tom's parents would have been guilty of compounding a crime, or misprision of felony.

HARBORING FUGITIVES

State and federal statutes make it unlawful to harbor or conceal a person for whom an arrest warrant has been issued, although some states exempt family members from the statute's provisions. The concealment of escaped prisoners is, of course, also unlawful.

Prohibiting Communications with Jurors and Witnesses

It is a crime in most jurisdictions for a person to communicate in a manner other than that authorized by law with a person who is a juror, or reasonably believed to be a juror, with the intent to influence that person in regard to any matter which may or could be entrusted to him as a juror.

Example
Nat is a neighbor of Carl, a juror in a case in which Bette, a friend of Nat's, is on trial for a criminal offense. During the course of the trial, Nat remarks to Carl one Sunday that it is a shame Bette is in trouble and that he has learned Bette was framed. Nat's conduct would be criminal in many jurisdictions.

In some jurisdictions it is also a crime to communicate with a juror or a witness (or with a potential juror or witness) in order to intentionally produce mental anguish or emotional distress.

Examples
1. John is a juror in a case involving an alleged assault on a company executive by Bill, an employee. As John leaves his home each morning to go to court, several of Bill's fellow workers shout obscenities at John. Such conduct would be criminal in some states. If the obscenities were vile enough, of course, other criminal laws might also be violated.
2 Throughout the night before Elaine is to testify in a trial against Frank's brother, Frank telephones Elaine periodically. Each time Elaine answers the phone, Frank hangs up without saying anything. By trial time the next morning Elaine is a nervous wreck from lack of sleep. In some jurisdictions, Frank's action would violate a specific state statute.

It is a crime in most states, and within the federal system as well, for a person to communicate threats, offers of reward, or false information to any witness or potential witness with the intent to deter him or her from testifying freely, fully, and truthfully in any pending matter.

Examples
1. Andy, a member of a juvenile gang, the Tenth Street Toughs, is on trial for assaulting a police officer. Bob, a neighborhood merchant, witnessed the crime from his place of business and is sched-

Interference with Law Enforcement Processes

uled to testify. Clyde and Doug, fellow Toughs, go to Bob's store and inform him that if he testifies at Andy's trial his store windows will be broken. No matter who Clyde and Doug say will break the windows—the Toughs or some other party—the two Toughs are in violation of the criminal laws of many states.

2. Under similar factual circumstances, Clyde and Doug advise Bob, the neighborhood merchant, that they have learned that he will soon receive a package containing $1,000 on the condition that he does not testify against Andy. Even though it is clear that the money is not coming from Clyde and Doug, the communication of the offer of reward is a criminal act, in and of itself, in many states.

3. Again, under similar factual circumstances, Clyde and Doug tell Bob that he must have been mistaken in his identification of Andy, since Andy was out of the city with them at the time of the crime. Although Clyde and Doug might testify to that effect at Andy's trial, the communication of such information to a potential witness with the intent of inhibiting his testimony is against the law in many states.

PERJURY

Perjury is a false statement, made under official oath, about an issue that is before a court, legislature, grand jury, or an executive branch of government.

Examples

1. Under oath, Wendy testifies for the defense at a liquor license revocation proceeding against a tavern owner who allegedly permitted his premises to be used for selling liquor to minors. Wendy states under oath that she was in the tavern at the time of the alleged sale and that it did not occur. It is later proved that the sale occurred, as charged, and that Wendy was not in the tavern at the time. Wendy committed perjury.

2. At a recess during a criminal trial for murder by shooting, Roy walked up to the judge and told him that the defendant was his brother-in-law and had admitted to him that he murdered the deceased. The prosecution informed the judge that Roy was unrelated to the defendant and had never talked to the defendant, who was in continuous custody from the moment of the shooting. Roy did not commit perjury because his statements were not made under oath.

Perjury also occurs when a statement containing a major falsity is signed under oath or affirmation.

Example
> An application for a driver's license in state X requires a statement of the applicant's age and must be signed under affirmation. No one in the state who is over 70 years of age is granted a license. Abner, 75 years of age, signs an application under affirmation, stating that he is 69. He has committed perjury.

If someone makes contradictory statements under oath at a trial, in many jurisdictions the prosecution need not specify which of the two statements is false. On the other hand, if contradictory statements are made in the same continuous trial and the witness admits the falsity of one of his statements, he is not guilty of perjury.

Example
> In a personal injury trial, Gordon testified for the plaintiff during direct examination that the defendant drove his auto through a red light before striking the plaintiff. On cross-examination, Gordon admitted that the light was green. Gordon would be guilty of perjury unless he admitted, during cross-examination, that his first statement was false.

SUBORNATION OF PERJURY

A person commits *subornation of perjury* when he induces another to lie while under oath.

Example
> Omar punched a Secret Service agent who was interviewing him about a threatening letter he had sent to the president. Before his trial for assaulting a federal officer, Omar contacted a number of friends and convinced them to testify that they were in an adjoining room during the scuffle and saw Omar strike in self-defense. Omar has suborned perjury.

DISOBEDIENCE OF COURT ORDERS AND DISRUPTIVE COURTROOM BEHAVIOR

The dignity and procedural regularity of our courtrooms is preserved by the inherent power of the judge to insure an orderly proceeding. In some jurisdictions the power of the judge is supplemented by statutory measures.

The potent procedural tool that a judge may employ in cases of courtroom misconduct, either by authority of statute or under his inherent power, is known as *contempt of court*. It is the willful disobedience of a court ruling or regulation, or the willful performance of an act that is disrespectful to the court. Contempt can be either "direct" or "indirect."

Direct contempt occurs in the presence of the judge, in which instance he has all the facts before him and can, therefore, summarily punish the offender. For example, a person who swears at a judge in open court during a judicial proceeding may be guilty of direct contempt.

In indirect contempt, all or part of the misconduct occurs when the judge is not present. Unlike direct contempt, which can be summarily punished, a person charged with indirect contempt is entitled to a trial, at which the alleged misconduct must be proved. At this trial, he is entitled to notice, an attorney, right of cross-examination, and other due process safeguards. Indirect contempt may occur, for example, if a person falsely announces outside of court that the judge received money as a bribe.

Contempt is either *criminal* or *civil*, depending upon the nature of the penalty. If found guilty of criminal contempt, a person receives a set penalty, a fine or jail sentence, for example. A person may be jailed for direct criminal contempt for only six months. In cases of indirect criminal contempt, where the judge must determine the facts, the penalty also is restricted to a six-month term in jail. If the offender is to be penalized more than six months for indirect criminal contempt, he is entitled to a jury trial. No matter how many instances of contempt occur within a single trial, the penalty for indirect criminal contempt is limited to six months without a jury trial. In other words, at the close of a trial, a judge could not sentence a person for two contempts at the rate of six months each for a total of a one-year sentence. However, where the judge sentences summarily (not at the end of the trial) for direct contempt occurring *during a trial*, the six-month total limit is inapplicable. If it *were* applicable, the trial judge would be helpless to discipline a recalcitrant after the imposition of the first six-month penalty. If the criminal contempt charges arise out of a situation where the trial judge becomes "personally embroiled" with the accused or where the contempt charged involves a personal attack upon the judge, the law provides that the charges must be decided by another judge. In these instances, what was originally direct contempt summarily punishable by the trial judge becomes an indirect criminal contempt proceeding for trial before a different judge.

Civil contempt occurs when a person willfully disobeys a court order. The judge may sentence the offender to jail for an indefinite period until he agrees to obey the order. For example, if a judge orders a person to pay alimony to a divorced spouse and the person refuses to do so, the judge may order the offender committed to jail until he or she agrees to pay. Likewise, a witness, not suspect himself, who refuses to testify in court or before a grand jury or a legislative committee may be sent to jail until he or she complies with the court order, or until the end of the term of the court, grand jury, or legislative committee. The same is true for a suspect or an accused person who has been granted immunity from criminal prosecution. Thus protected from self-incrimination, he or she must testify or be subject to a charge of contempt.

In a number of highly publicized trials in the late 1960s and early 1970s, some so-called radical defendants and their supporters engaged in highly disruptive courtroom conduct in an effort to bring the judicial proceedings to a standstill. Such conduct is, of course, punishable by contempt proceedings. Moreover, the Supreme Court has ruled that a defendant who persists in efforts to disrupt his trial relinquishes his right to be present at the trial for as long as he indicates unwillingness to conduct himself according to appropriate standards.

Example

Wild Willy is a self-proclaimed revolutionary who is on trial for a series of bombings. He refuses to sit quietly through his trial and continues to throw pencils at the jurors and make obscene remarks to the witnesses. Wild Willy can be removed to his jail cell where he will be allowed to watch his trial continue on a closed circuit television monitor until he assures the judge that he will cease his disruptive behavior.

Chapter 12
Uncompleted Criminal Conduct and Criminal Combinations

A separate category of criminal offenses exists for conduct that falls short of a completed unlawful act. Such offenses are technically called *inchoate* offenses and fall within at least one of three groups: attempt, solicitation, and conspiracy.

ATTEMPT

A person commits the crime of *attempt* when he intends to commit a specific offense and performs an act which constitutes a substantial step toward its commission. "Mere preparation to commit a crime" does not constitute a "substantial step toward its commission." The courts hold that the difference between conduct which is a "substantial step" and that which is "mere preparation" is one of degree, and must be determined by the circumstances of each case.

Examples
   1. Joan, an employee of J. B. Smith, obtains some cyanide and puts it into a drink she serves Smith, to expedite an inheritance she was anticipating. Smith becomes suspicious and saves the drink for analysis by police laboratory technicians. Joan is guilty of attempted murder.
   2. Bob flunked his medical board exam. Disgruntled, he decided to go into the illegal abortion business. He purchased surgical equipment for that activity, but abandoned the idea before making contact with any prospective patients. Bob has not taken a "sub-

stantial step" toward completing the offense of abortion. His "mere preparation" is not criminal.

In most jurisdictions, a misunderstanding, or misapprehension, of the the circumstances which makes it impossible for the accused to commit the crime is not a defense against attempt.

Example
Tim fired a pistol at Hal, intending to kill him. But someone, without Tim's knowledge, had loaded the pistol with blanks. Even though it was impossible for Tim to kill Hal because of someone else's action, Tim's offense of attempted murder is not negated.

The federal criminal code does not have a general attempt provision. Accordingly, unless an attempt provision is included in the statute which makes the completed conduct unlawful, an unsuccessful effort to commit a federal offense is not a violation of federal law. Among the federal statutes which include a provision prohibiting attempt are those governing bank robbery, post office robbery, kidnapping, homicide, and smuggling.

Examples
1. Irving is a bungling bank robber who pulls his car alongside a drive-up teller at the Phoenix Street Savings and Loan. As he displays a meat cleaver and demands that Edith, the teller, fill a bag with all the money she has, she notices that Irving has wedged his car alongside the wall of her teller station and is unable to drive away. Edith signals the guard, who arrests Irving and turns him over to the FBI to be charged with attempted bank robbery.
2. Bette, a movie star of great beauty and wealth, is known for her fabulous million-dollar collection of jewelry. Seymour is a burglar who plans to crack Bette's wall safe and fence the jewels in a neighboring state. While Bette is attending the grand opening of her latest movie, Seymour sneaks into her house, cracks the safe, and leaves with her jewels. Seymour buys a plane ticket but is arrested before his plane takes off, and, therefore, before he crosses a state line. Because the Interstate Transportation of Stolen Property Statute contains no attempt provision, Seymour cannot be prosecuted federally. He can, of course, be prosecuted in state court for burglary.

SOLICITATION

A person who intends to have an offense committed and who commands, encourages, or requests another person to commit that offense is guilty of the crime of *solicitation*.

Example

Mack gets into an argument with the bartender at his local tavern and is ejected when he becomes too boisterous. Furious at what has occurred, he offers a passing person $10 to throw a brick into the tavern window. Mack is guilty of the offense of solicitation (for criminal damage to property).

Conspiracy

Conspiracy is the agreement between two or more persons to commit a crime. Conspiracy is a crime in and of itself, separate and distinct from the underlying substantive offense.

Conspiracy traditionally has been viewed with severity because of the feeling that secret plots involving multiple parties pose a greater threat to society than do individual offenses. Some states, however, have departed from the tradition of imposing higher penalties for conspiracies than for the substantive offenses themselves. The conspiracy need not be of the magnitude to overthrow the government or to defraud a governmental unit or the people of a community, although it is often thought of in such a context; it can involve any type of crime—robbery, burglary, etc.

The crime of conspiracy does not require formal meetings to plot a crime. The arrangement does not even require that all of the conspirators meet or talk to every member of the group. Anyone may act or speak out for all the others, so long as the purpose is in furtherance of the conspiracy. There is a sort of agency principle involved; each one is considered to be an agent for the others, and what one does or says is competent evidence against them all.

Merely talking over the possibility or the ease with which a crime may be committed does not constitute a conspiracy. There must be a planning and, according to most conspiracy laws, someone in the group must perform at least one overt act toward its accomplishment.

Examples

1. While Leo, Ronald, and Jim are playing poker one night, they discuss the vulnerability of a local supermarket to burglary and they even express a wish that they could get their hands on the Saturday night funds stored in the vault. Up to this point no crime has been committed.

2. Now, assume that in the foregoing situation the three persons decide that next Saturday night they will commit the burglary. Leo agrees to have a fourth individual, Ed, steal a car for the purpose and serve as its driver. Ronald goes to the store and prepares a sketch of its interior. Jim asks his Aunt Mary if they might

hide the loot in the basement of her house, which she refuses to do, so Jim makes other suitable arrangements for hiding the loot. Mary's maid overhears the conversation between Jim and Mary and reports it to the police.

The night of the planned burglary, the police arrest Leo, Ronald, Jim, and Ed as they get into the stolen car. All four have committed a conspiracy. At the trial the prosecutor may use the maid as a witness to the conversation between Jim and Mary, and he may prove the overt acts of the stealing of the car by Leo and the making of the sketch by Ronald. The evidence is usable to prove the guilt of all of them.

In addition to the general conspiracy laws which make it unlawful to conspire to commit *any* substantive offense, many jurisdictions, particularly the federal one, have statutes prohibiting *specific* conspiratorial conduct. For example, the federal criminal code contains, in addition to its general conspiracy statute, provisions prohibiting conspiracies to defraud the United States, to kidnap, to violate the federal homicide statutes, to violate civil rights, to commit espionage or sabotage, and to commit robbery or extortion which interferes with interstate commerce.

Conspiracy statutes have proved to be an effective means of fighting criminal activities which are otherwise difficult to control with substantive criminal statutes alone. Prime examples of these activities are organized crime gambling and loan-sharking, official corruption, and traffic in narcotics. Such activities are more readily attacked through conspiracy charges because the more important the participant, the less likely he is to get directly involved in the actual commission of the substantive offense (e.g., the collection of juice money, or the distribution of heroin).

Chapter 13
Accessories to a Crime

Although there is no legal concept in the United States for "guilt by association" as such, under certain circumstances an individual may be criminally liable for the acts of another person.

Accessory before the Fact

Broadly stated, a person who aids or assists another person in the performance of a criminal act is regarded as an *accomplice* or as an *accessory before the fact*. In most states, he is subject to the same penalty as the individual who performs the criminal act. One state deals with such conduct by means of the following statutory provision:

> When one person engages in conduct which constitutes an offense, another person is criminally liable for such conduct when, acting with the mental culpability required for the commission thereof, he solicits, requests, commands, importunes, or intentionally aids such person to engage in such conduct.

Example

Abe, Nora, and Fred agree to rob the City Bank. Abe drives Nora and Fred to the bank. Nora and Fred, armed with pistols and wearing masks, enter the bank and hold it up. Abe, unarmed, waits in the getaway car. Nora and Fred are arrested with the loot as they leave the bank. Abe is picked up later. Abe argues that he did not enter the bank or rob, was unarmed, and never was in possession of any of the loot. Abe's argument is futile. He is as liable as Nora and Fred are for the offense of robbery.

An exception is made in the law covering accessories for a person who has a change of mind and who effectively terminates his own efforts in ample time, or gives a timely warning to the police, or otherwise makes an appropriate effort to prevent the commission of the offense.

Example

Rocky and Ben, syndicate hoodlums, receive a "contract" to murder Emil. Ben changes his mind hours before the murder is to take place and telephones a warning to Emil. He also alerts the police. In spite of Ben's warnings, Rocky successfully shoots and kills Emil. By his efforts to prevent Emil's murder, Ben terminates his liability for Rocky's criminal action.

Accessory after the Fact

A person who, intending to prevent the apprehension of an offender, harbors, aids, or conceals the offender, is regarded by the law as an *accessory after the fact* and is criminally punishable. However, the penalty for accessory after the fact is usually less than that for the principal offender's crime.

Chapter 14
Mental Responsibility

A general principle of criminal law holds that a person cannot be held criminally responsible for an act unless the act was accompanied by an "evil-meaning" mind. In other words, a prohibited act is ordinarily not punishable unless performed with what is variously described as *criminal intent, felonious intent, malice aforethought, fraudulent intent, willfulness, guilty knowledge,* and so on. In general, however, this restrictive principle is confined to serious offenses. Certain other acts—the relatively minor ones—may be punishable even when the offender's mind is not "evil meaning."

Examples
   1. Linda, a customer leaving a restaurant, takes a coat off a coat rack, puts it on, and walks off with it. It belongs to someone else, but Linda mistook it for her own and did not realize her mistake until the owner of the coat caught up with her several blocks away. Linda is not guilty of larceny or of any other criminal offense.
   2. Max is stopped by a traffic officer for crossing an intersection without stopping. Max said he did not see the stop sign. His failure to see it is no defense, and he is guilty of a traffic violation even though he was not "evil meaning."

Generally speaking, therefore, when the prohibited act is a relatively minor one, and when the social need to discourage the act would be severely jeopardized by the difficulty of proving the intent, the courts permit guilt to be established merely on the basis of the conduct itself.

The Defense of Infancy

In earlier days the very young were not exempt from punishment as criminals. A ten-year-old boy, for instance, once was convicted and executed for killing his companion; a child of eight who had burned down a barn was executed. Under modern concepts, however, a person under a certain age (thirteen years old in some states) is considered incapable of harboring an "evil-meaning" mind and is therefore immune from criminal prosecution. Children under that age who commit prohibited acts are, of course, subject to juvenile court proceedings, and they may be placed in non-penal institutions for their own welfare (with the expectation of rehabilitating them) and for the protection of others.

The Defenses of Compulsion and Necessity

A person who is compelled by someone else to commit a criminal act may invoke the defense of *compulsion,* but not if it involves the taking of, or an attempt to take, the life of an innocent person.

Example
> A bank employee points a loaded revolver at another employee and threatens to kill him unless he makes a false ledger entry in order to conceal an act of embezzlement committed by the threatening party. Acting under such compulsion does not constitute a crime.

Necessity is a similar defense. If a person desperately needs to take or use someone else's personal property or to intrude upon real property, his need constitutes a valid defense against criminal prosecution. If a hunter is caught in the mountains in a blizzard without food, he is not guilty of burglary or larceny if he breaks into a cabin and eats what he needs to keep alive. But the defense of necessity is a life-or-death proposition. Consequently, a modern day Robin Hood could not take a wealthy person's money or goods and defend his actions by saying that he and others needed the property more than the victim did.

The Defense of Intoxication

A person who is so intoxicated that he does not know what he is doing is not criminally liable for an offense for which "specific intent" is required. If the town drunk picks up someone else's property and makes off with it, he may successfully defend himself against a charge of larceny if the court or jury decides that his intoxication was of such a degree that he could not have intended to permanently deprive the owner of his

Mental Responsibility

property. On the other hand, the defense of intoxication cannot be invoked if the offense involves only "general intent," or "recklessness." A motorist who kills someone while driving recklessly because of his intoxication cannot defend his negligent action by saying that he did not know what he was doing.

THE DEFENSE OF ENTRAPMENT

Out of consideration for the frailties of human nature (and the cynical notion that "every man has his price"), the courts have established the principle that if the police "entice or induce" a person to commit a crime, that person should not be punished for what he did. The feeling prevails that were it not for police persuasion and temptation, the individual might have remained an honest, law-abiding citizen. Accordingly, the courts have provided the defense of *entrapment,* which means, in effect, that he is granted immunity for what he did as a result of police encouragement. On the other hand, if the police merely afford a person an *opportunity* to commit a crime, the person has no such defense.

Examples

1. Police Detective Healy suspects that Paul obtains income by some illegal means, although Paul has never been arrested or convicted of any crime. One day Healy, posing as an ex-con, has a conversation in a bar with Paul. He tells Paul that Mrs. Healy is in need of medical attention which he cannot afford without getting some big money quick and easy, but he needs Paul's help on a fifty-fifty basis. Healy tells Paul that he can make an easy score at the home of Banker Adam, who is taking his wife to the opera that night. Healy tells Paul how to gain easy access to the home. Then Healy arranges for a group of police officers to close in just as Paul breaks into Banker Adam's home. Paul cannot be convicted of burglary. Police officer Healy "enticed and induced" him to commit the act. The idea did not originate with Paul. The defense of entrapment is valid.

2. Druggist Rex is suspected of selling narcotics unlawfully. The police arrange for a known addict, Alex, to try to make a "buy" from Rex. Alex is given marked money, goes to Rex, and asks if he can buy a "fix" of heroin. Rex says he can let him have one for $20. Rex hands the heroin to Alex, and Alex gives him the marked money. After Alex gets out of the store and the substance is verified to be heroin, officers enter the store, arrest Rex, and find the marked money in the cash register. This is not entrapment. Rex was only given an opportunity to make the sale; he was not enticed or induced to do so.

The Defense of Insanity

According to a long established rule, a person is not criminally responsible for an act committed while he was insane. The best known early test of insanity was that laid down in the famous M'Naghten case in 1843. In that case, the English House of Lords ruled that, although every person is presumed to be sane, no one could be held criminally responsible for an act if, at the time of its commission, and because of a "diseased mind," he did not know "right from wrong."

For many years the M'Naghten "right-wrong" test was the one that prevailed throughout the United States. Then it was supplemented by the "irresistible impulse" test: even if a person knew right from wrong, he could not be held criminally responsible if, because of a "diseased mind," he was unable to avoid doing wrong.

The most widely used test of insanity today is, in effect, a combination of the two aforementioned ones. It is known as the "A.L.I." test, one that was formulated and proposed by the American Law Institute. It reads as follows:

> 1. A person is not responsible for criminal conduct if at the time of such conduct as a result of mental disease or defect he lacks substantial capacity either to appreciate the criminality of his conduct or conform his conduct to the requirements of law.
> 2. The terms "mental disease or defect" do not include an abnormality manifested only by repeated criminal or otherwise anti-social conduct.

A person who is found by any legal test for insanity to have been insane at the time of perpetration is always acquitted of the offense charged against him. If mental examinations conducted after his acquittal establish that he should be placed in a mental institution for care and treatment, however, he may be so committed in a civil proceeding.

Mental Incompetence

Regardless of an accused person's state of mind at the time of the act he is alleged to have committed, he cannot be brought to trial if his present mental condition is such that he is "unable to understand the nature and purpose of the proceedings against him, or to assist in his defense." In such situations, he would be committed to a mental institution and could be tried thereafter only if his mental condition were to improve sufficiently to satisfy the two requirements just quoted. In death penalty cases, there can be no execution if, prior to the time of the scheduled execution, the sentenced person develops a mental condition that does not permit him "to understand the nature and purpose" of the death sentence.

Part III

CRIMINAL INVESTIGATIONS AND THE POWERS OF LAW ENFORCEMENT OFFICERS

Chapter 15
General Investigative Procedures

An Overview

At the outset of our discussion of criminal investigations it is advisable to consider briefly the constitutional privilege against self-incrimination because its impact is felt on the investigative level as well as in the courtroom. It will be discussed in detail in chapter 21.

Suffice it to state for present purposes that no person can be compelled to incriminate himself, but the privilege applies only to testimonial evidence and not to physical evidence. *Testimonial evidence* is that which is communicative in nature, either in the form of spoken or written words, or else by some conduct which carries with it a meaning, such as a nod of the head or a demonstration of how a crime itself was committed. *Physical evidence,* insofar as the self-incrimination privilege is concerned, is evidence which is not communicative but merely subject to observation by and evaluation of a person other than the one under suspicion or accusation. Compulsory fingerprinting is a good example.

Police Investigative Techniques

The interview process is the mainstay of criminal investigations. It may result from the need to initially identify and locate the suspect or from an effort to gather sufficient proof to charge an already identified person. Information regarding the physical description of a person or vehicle, speech patterns, and prior contacts among certain individuals may all be of importance. Then, too, there is the obvious need to secure as much information as possible as to how, when, and where the event occurred and the possible motives. In this investigative process the primary persons to be interviewed are the victim, if possible, and the eyewitnesses, if any, but the process may extend far beyond that ambit—to anyone who may furnish a possible lead or clue. Informers, usually denizens of the underworld who are paid or offered deals with respect to their own lesser crimes in return for the information they supply, are extremely important in the investigative process.

Because of the constitutional privilege against self-incrimination, the interview of the suspect himself presents special problems. These problems will be discussed in chapter 20.

Although many crimes are solved by the interview process, and by the hard work and common sense of the police investigators, scientific crime detection laboratory personnel and facilities are often helpful. However, contrary to a popular misconception generated by fictionalization in books, movies, and television, very few crimes lend themselves to solution by scientific methods alone. In fact, in most instances the greatest value of science is in supplementing and verifying information already gathered through traditional police efforts. (The many scientific methods that may be brought to bear in criminal cases are described in *Scientific Police Investigation* by Inbau, Moenssens, and Vitullo [Chilton, 1972].)

INVESTIGATIVE EFFORTS OF THE PROSECUTOR AND THE GRAND JURY

In routine cases the prosecutor generally does not become involved until an arrest is made and the defendant makes his initial court appearance. In complex cases such as bank embezzlements, fraud schemes, organized crime, and official corruption, however, the prosecutor may play an integral part in the investigation from its very inception. This "investigative lawyer" concept is beneficial in such cases because the prosecutor is able to anticipate probable defenses, gaps in evidence, and other problems as the investigation proceeds. Working hand in hand with the police detective or special agent, the investigative lawyer will plan strategy, suggest avenues of further inquiry, and interview witnesses. More important, however, is the prosecutor's access to the grand jury itself as an investigative body.

The grand jury, which is discussed further in chapter 22, usually consists of twenty-three citizens, selected at random. Most of a grand jury's function is of a rather routine nature, namely, a consideration of evidence presented by the prosecutor to determine whether there are reasonable grounds for the return of an *indictment*. However, the grand jury is also available to the prosecutor as a powerful investigative device. This is largely because of the grand jury's power to subpoena persons to appear before the jury as witnesses and relate what they know about the matter under investigation, or to produce documents or other physical evidence that may be relevant to the investigation. A failure to appear, in the absence of a valid claim to the self-incrimination privilege, is punishable as contempt of court by the judge who acts as overseer of the grand jury.

GRANTS OF IMMUNITY

Even though a person properly asserts his self-incrimination privilege, there still remains a means for the prosecutor to obtain from him the desired information. A request may be made of the court to grant that person immunity from prosecution based on the testimony or evidence he presents under compulsion. In some states the immunity statutes are sufficiently broad to completely bar prosecution for any offense about which he has testified or presented any evidence.

If, after a grant of immunity, a person still refuses to cooperate, he may be imprisoned for the length of the term of the grand jury, which may be as long as eighteen months. Figuratively speaking, however, the incarcerated person holds the key to his own cell. Upon a change of mind, the appearance and presentation of information to the grand jury terminates the incarceration. There are two factors, though, which may inhibit the subpoenaed person's willingness to cooperate under a grant of immunity and present his evidence—vengeance from the persons who may be adversely affected by his testimony, as may well occur in an investigation of organized crime, or a possible perjury prosecution if the subpoenaed person lies to the grand jury.

The prosecutor's utilization of the immunity practice to ferret out evidence usable at criminal trials has not escaped criticism. The basis for the criticism is the undeniable fact that the immunized criminal goes free, while the confederates in crime whose criminality he discloses, and for whom he furnishes the proof of guilt in court, go to the penitentiary. The usual prosecutorial response given to this criticism is, first, that immunity is not granted with abandon but only in serious cases where the information of an insider is absolutely essential for a successful prosecution. Secondly, without the benefit of the immunized person's information and evidence, *no one* in the crime under investigation would have his guilt revealed and proved beyond a reasonable doubt.

United States Supreme Court Justice Byron R. White, in commenting upon the practice of granting immunity, pinpointed its value when he stated in an opinion of the Court that immunity statutes have long been employed "for the investigation of offenses, chiefly whose proof and punishment were otherwise impracticable, such as political bribery, extortion, gambling, consumer frauds, liquor violations, commercial larceny and various forms of racketeering." The justice's observations were based upon the differences in the availability of evidence needed to prove various crimes. For example, after a bank robbery, a willing teller provides a description, a cooperative guard produces the film from the surveillance cameras, and agents dust for fingerprints. Those arguing for the use of immunity contrast that situation, where an abundance of evidence is readily available, with a secret zoning bribe deal between a group of well-heeled land speculators and a corrupt mayor, an act of extortion between a crooked tax assessor and a frightened tax payer, or a clandestine mail fraud scheme. In the latter situations, only an insider can provide crucial details of the offense. When, as is often the case, the insiders seek to withhold their testimony based upon the Fifth Amendment privilege, proponents of immunity suggest that its grant is the only way to compel that testimony and uncover the scheme.

Deciding when to immunize and whom to immunize is a carefully considered process which brings into play a number of general guidelines:

(a) Immunity is a last resort, used only when necessary to the investigation or prosecution, and only when the evidence cannot be obtained under other circumstances. (With rare exceptions, immunity is demanded by the witness' attorney as a condition of his cooperation.)

(b) A person should not be immunized if he is someone who abused the public trust and will remain in a position to continue to do so.

(c) The most evidence should be obtained for the smallest loss of a guilty defendant.

(d) As few persons as possible should be immunized in order to get to as many offenders as possible.

(e) Whenever possible, there should be a prosecution and conviction prior to immunization.

(f) Corroboration of the testimony or evidence offered by the witness should precede any grant of immunity.

On the federal level, the decision to immunize involves an exhaustive review procedure which considers the foregoing guidelines at every stage —by the prosecutor handling the case, his deputy chief and division chief, the first assistant United States attorney, the United States attorney, and on up to and including the Department of Justice in Washington. Only when the immunity request is approved in Washington is the request formally made before the district court judge, who then enters the order. State immunization procedures vary from jurisdiction to jurisdiction, but the chief judge of the local criminal court usually enters the immunity order pursuant to the provisions of a state statute.

Critics often suggest that the judiciary should play an even more prominent role in determining when and to whom immunity should be granted. This would help protect against its use to harass and intimidate and also its use, along with the contempt of court sanctions, to prosecute and incarcerate a person against whom a substantive criminal violation cannot be proved. The reliability of immunized testimony in court has also incurred a great deal of attention from its critics.

Proponents of immunity point out that the presentation of immunized testimony in an actual criminal trial is subject to rigorous inspection and reflection. The jury or judge in a bench trial observes the demeanor of the witness throughout his direct testimony and during cross-examination. The testimony is similarly attacked and questioned during the defendant's closing argument. A jury is specifically instructed how to weigh the immunized testimony. Judicial review of the evidence is present at both the trial and appellate levels. Critics counter, however, that it is nearly impossible to overcome a jury's realization that the *government* believes the witness and that, in any event, it is the government which decides whether the immunized witness has testified truthfully or should be prosecuted for perjury.

Ironically, from the standpoint of a defendant about to stand trial, the grant of immunity to one of his confederates in crime may at times accord him an advantage that he would not otherwise have. Because "deal making" has always been a part of the criminal justice system when insider testimony was needed, a defendant often faced the difficult task of countering testimony obtained through informal promises and unwritten expectations. With a grant of immunity, however, all cards are on the table, and the jurors can read the terms of the immunity grant themselves. The defense may argue that the witness is testifying to pay for his immunity, whereas the government can point out that the witness' only fear is the commission of perjury. Based upon all the facts and evidence of the case as well as the demeanor and interest of the immunized witness, the trier of fact will reach a decision. In this fashion, immunity constitutes "part of our constitutional fabric," and it plays an important role in the administration of justice.

Chapter 16

Specific Police Powers and Their Limitations

An *arrest* may be defined generally as taking a person into custody for the purpose of charging him with having committed some kind of prohibited conduct. An arrest does not include questioning a witness to a crime. It does not cover stopping a motorist to check his driver's license or vehicle ownership registration, or to give him a traffic ticket. Only when custody occurs does a stopping become an arrest. Arrest, therefore, occurs only when a police officer shows his intention to take a person to a police station or before a magistrate or another judicial officer. The two forms of arrest are arrest without a warrant and arrest with a warrant.

Arrests without a Warrant

A police officer may make an arrest without a court order (warrant) when he has "probable cause" to believe a suspect has committed a crime. Some state statutes phrase the probable cause test in terms of an officer having "reasonable grounds," or "reasonable cause," to believe that the person in question has committed an offense, but such terms are just other ways of phrasing the probable cause test.

The probable cause requirement stems from the provision in the Fourth Amendment to the United States Constitution and from comparable state constitutional provisions protecting persons from "unreasonable seizures" and requiring that "no warrants shall issue, but upon probable cause." The two provisions have been read to mean that an arrest without a warrant must also be upon probable cause, because, otherwise, it would be "unreasonable."

"Probable cause" does not mean actual knowledge: the officer need not

Specific Police Powers and Their Limitations

have personally observed the commission of a crime. He need only have knowledge of facts and circumstances that would lead a reasonable man to conclude that the suspect in all probability has committed a crime.

Evidence Required for Probable Cause

The amount of proof necessary to satisfy the probable cause test is less than that required to prove in court that the suspect committed the crime. At the trial, the prosecution must present evidence to prove the accused person's guilt beyond a reasonable doubt. To make an arrest, however, a police officer needs only to show probable cause—that is, enough facts to cause him to believe, upon reasonable grounds, that the suspect has committed an offense. The following are illustrations of the fulfillment of the probable cause requirement:

Examples
   1. While cruising in his patrol car, Officer Marla heard a voice from an alley, yelling, "Help! Thief!" Seconds later she observed Jerry running down an alley away from the source of the shouts for help. Marla chased Jerry and apprehended him. Marla had probable cause to arrest Jerry, even though subsequent events established that Jerry was not the thief.
   2. Cruising in a patrol car at three a.m. in a neighborhood that had recently experienced a number of burglaries, Officer Leonard observed Marty walking down an alley carrying a portable TV set, a small leather case, and several other objects. When Marty saw the police car, he dropped the items he was carrying and started to run away. Leonard had probable cause to arrest him.

Mere suspicion or a hunch, however, does not justify an arrest.

Example
   Julius, known by the police to be a dope peddler, was seen by Officer Howard walking hastily to get into a cab. The officer arrested and searched him for narcotics. Howard's action was not based upon probable cause, and the arrest and search were illegal.

Hearsay Evidence and Informers' Tips

Under most circumstances, *hearsay evidence*, which may be described loosely as secondhand evidence, cannot be used at the trial of an accused person. Most often, it is information received by the police from an informer, and as such it may be used to establish probable cause for an arrest if it can be corroborated in some way. Confirmation of hearsay evidence is possible in either of two ways:

(a) If a police officer observes certain suspicious activities or has knowledge of pertinent facts or circumstances which substantiate the tip given by an informer, probable cause exists for an arrest.

Example

Sarah told Officer Potts that Marvin was selling policy tickets on a street corner. Officer Potts, in an unmarked parked car, later saw Marvin conduct suspicious transactions with about twenty people in the course of half an hour. Each person gave Marvin something in return for something else. Although Officer Potts could not tell exactly what was exchanged, his observations, coupled with the informer's tip, gave him probable cause to arrest Marvin.

(b) If a police officer has contact with an informer who has previously given him consistently reliable tips, he may rely, in substantial measure, upon that informer's information to make an arrest.

Example

Leroy told Officer Roberts that he saw Hank selling narcotics. Leroy described Hank and said where he would be that night for the purpose of making his sales. Upon several prior occasions, whenever Leroy gave Officer Roberts such information, Roberts always found narcotics on the person "fingered" by Leroy. Under the circumstances, Roberts would have probable cause to arrest Hank.

Of interest in connection with hearsay evidence situations is the fact that, when an informer has furnished such information, his identity does not have to be disclosed at the defendant's trial *unless* the informer participated in the transaction, the informer was a witness to the particular crime for which the arrest was made, or the informer was present at the time of arrest.

Consequences of an Invalid Arrest

There are several consequences of an invalid arrest by a police officer:

(1) Any evidence that is obtained as a result of an invalid arrest will be suppressed and excluded at the trial. The theory behind this "exclusionary rule" is that it will discourage illegal police actions.

(2) Any invalid arrest can also result in a successful false arrest action against the arresting officer; a successful federal civil rights action against the arresting officer in the federal court; and (a remedy to be subsequently discussed) departmental disciplinary action.

An invalid arrest by itself, however, will not result in the acquittal of an accused person whose guilt can be proved beyond a reasonable doubt by other, independent evidence—that is, by evidence untainted by the invalid arrest.

Arrests with a Warrant

The legal requirements for an arrest made with a court warrant are the same as those for an arrest without a warrant. Both must be based

Specific Police Powers and Their Limitations

upon probable cause. A warrant for an arrest may be obtained by presenting to a judge or magistrate a *complaint* (charge), made under oath, which contains statements that establish a probable cause to believe that the person named in the warrant committed the crime described. The same kind of evidence that may establish probable cause for an arrest without a warrant (e.g., hearsay bolstered by other factors, as previously illustrated) may also justify the issuance of a warrant by a judge or magistrate.

Examples

1. Carla is a hotel keeper. Joe tells her that Sadie performs acts of prostitution in her hotel room. Joe says that he too had engaged Sadie's services. On several occasions, Carla sees six men enter and leave Sadie's room at intervals of about a half hour. Such information, submitted by Carla under oath, is enough to show probable cause and would justify an arrest warrant.

2. Bill, a brother-in-law of Officer Mason, tells Mason that several persons have told him that Rose engages in prostitution in her hotel room. Without more information, Officer Mason's affidavit of what his brother-in-law told him is not enough to show probable cause and would not justify an arrest warrant.

3. Charles stated that Maureen told him that Guy was a receiver of stolen property. Charles then stated in detail, without corroboration, the alleged illegal transactions of Guy as told to him by Maureen. Any complaint presented under these circumstances would be based solely on unsubstantiated hearsay and would not show probable cause.

In cases in which corroboration of an informant's tip is unavailable, the only recourse is to have the informant himself sign the complaint. That is seldom done, however, because the complaint and the warrant are public records, without the protection of anonymity. Most informants are not willing to risk disclosing their identities. Some jurisdictions permit an informant-complainant to use an alias in signing a complaint for an arresting warrant. But if he becomes a witness at the trial, he is required to disclose his real name. The arrest warrant must be signed by a judge or magistrate. Most state statutes also require that the judge or magistrate first examine the complainant about the matters set forth in the complaint.

The Warrant Requirement

Even though time and circumstances may afford the police an opportunity to obtain an arrest warrant, an arrest may nevertheless be made without one whenever there exists probable cause to do so. In other words, although there are situations in which a warrant arrest may be considered advisable, there is no compelling legal necessity for a warrant when the requirement of probable cause can be otherwise established. Furthermore, any officer who has reasonable grounds for believing that a warrant has been issued for a person can make a valid arrest of that person.

Example
> Police Officers Al and Bob went to the home of Franklin for the purpose of arresting him. They had very reliable information about Franklin's activities for several days. Officer Al thought that Officer Bob had signed a complaint and secured an arrest warrant before arriving at Franklin's home. Bob thought the same thing. Neither officer had in fact procured the warrant. The arrest of Franklin is nevertheless proper because both Al and Bob had probable cause to arrest him without a warrant.

The Valid Warrant

An invalid arrest warrant voids an arrest. But not every irregularity in a warrant will invalidate it: the irregularity must adversely affect the substantial rights of the suspect.

Examples
> 1. The name of the person to be arrested was spelled correctly as "John Q. Smith" in six out of the seven places it appeared in the complaint and warrant. In one place it was incorrectly spelled as "John Q. Smythe." The misspelling is an inconsequential error and the warrant is valid.
>
> 2. The state arrest warrant statute requires that all complaints be "sworn to." Complainant Carl told Police Officer Jones about a crime committed by Sam. Jones prepared a complaint for Carl's signature. In the excitement, Jones neglected to make sure that the complaint was sworn to before executing the warrant of arrest. The judge who signed the warrant also failed to notice that the complaint was not under oath. After Sam was in custody, Jones presented the complaint to the judge and it was sworn to by Carl at that time. Such an irregularity affects Sam's substantial right to be arrested only on the basis of a warrant issued upon *sworn* complaint. Consequently, the arrest is invalid.

Consequences of an Invalid Warrant

Whenever the counsel for an arrested person seeks to attack the validity of a warrant, he must file in court, before trial, what is known as a motion to quash the warrant of arrest. If he is successful—in other words, if the motion is granted—the arrest will be declared illegal and any evidence obtained as a result of the arrest will be suppressed and cannot be used at the trial. In many instances, if the motion to quash is granted, there

Specific Police Powers and Their Limitations 111

will be no trial and the accused person will go free because, without the suppressed evidence, the prosecution would be unable to prove guilt beyond a reasonable doubt.

Example

Pat was arrested for robbery-murder with a warrant based upon an unsworn complaint. When the officers searched Pat, they found a loaded pistol in his pocket. In this case, the pistol cannot be used as evidence against Pat at the robbery-murder trial; nor can it be used as evidence at a trial for the crime of carrying a concealed weapon.

When a warrant is declared void because of a substantial defect, the arrest itself might still be valid, and the seized evidence admissible at a trial, if the circumstances under which the arrest was made would have justified an arrest even without a warrant.

Example

A warrant is obtained for the arrest of Tony on the charge of raping a child. Officer Parson, looking for Tony near Tony's home, sees him pick up another child in his car and speed off. Officer Parson chases and ultimately arrests Tony. In his car, and within clear view of Officer Parson, there is a child's garment that is later identified as belonging to the raped child. On Tony's trousers there is a stain that is later determined to be blood of the same type as that of the raped victim.

Even though the arrest warrant may contain a defect and be declared invalid, the garment and the blood would be admissible as evidence at the trial because, under the circumstances, Officer Parson could have made a valid arrest even without an arrest warrant.

A person who in good faith is successful in obtaining a warrant is relieved of personal liability if the warrant or the affidavit upon which it is issued is ultimately declared invalid.

Arrests by Federal Officers

There is no single congressional statute regarding the general powers of arrest by federal officers. The matter is dealt with by separate statutes pertaining to particular groups of officers. For instance, there is a separate provision for FBI agents which authorizes an arrest without warrant for "any offense against the United States committed in their presence, or for any felony cognizable under the laws of the United States if they have reasonable grounds to believe that the person to be arrested has committed or is committing such felony." Another statute confers a similar power upon marshals and their deputies. Still another prescribes similar powers of arrest for agents of the Drug Enforcement Administration. The various powers of arrest by members of the Secret Service are also separately defined, as is true of other governmental units such as the Postal Inspection Service and the Bureau of Prisons.

Legal Geographic Boundaries for State and Local Police Arrests

A non-federal officer may make an arrest only within the boundaries of the governmental unit he serves. Therefore a state police officer may arrest persons throughout the state, whereas a city officer's powers are confined to the city itself, although by special statute some states permit arrests within adjacent cities. Nevertheless, while outside his own jurisdiction, an officer may effect a lawful arrest in his capacity as an ordinary citizen, provided it is within the legal limitations set for that jurisdiction's citizen arrest powers. Moreover, a police officer who observes a person commit a crime in his jurisdiction may chase the offender into another jurisdiction and lawfully arrest him there. This is commonly referred to as the doctrine of "hot pursuit."

Example

X and Y are adjoining municipalities. Pam is a police officer in X. While on patrol she sees Woody snatch a purse from a woman on a street in City X. Woody jumps into a car and drives away. Pat chases him on her motorcycle. Woody makes it to City Y, where Officer Pam curbs Woody's car and arrests him. The arrest is valid even though Pam is not a police officer in City Y.

In many jurisdictions a warrant of arrest may be executed by any police officer of the state in which it was issued, but a police officer in one state may not execute an arrest warrant in another state. To apprehend an out-of-state suspect or fugitive, legal proceedings must be begun for his extradition from the other state. A federal arrest warrant, however, may be executed by a federal officer in any state.

Citizen Arrests

For certain crimes and under certain conditions, a private citizen may make an arrest. The scope of his arrest power and the limitations upon it are usually specified in state statutes or in municipal or county ordinances. As a general rule, a private citizen may arrest for a serious offense, such as a felony, when it is committed in his presence. He may also arrest a person who has committed a felony elsewhere, other than in his presence. But he may not, in most states, arrest for minor offenses, particularly city or county ordinance violations, even when committed in his presence.

Illinois has one of the most liberal citizen-arrest authorizations. Its Criminal Code provides that a private citizen "may arrest another when he has reasonable grounds to believe that an offense other than an ordinance violation is being committed."

A private citizen, in making an authorized arrest, may use the same force as a police officer. But he usually may not use force which is likely to cause death or great bodily harm, even in the case of a felony, unless that degree of force is necessary to protect him or another person from death or great bodily harm at the hands of the person he is seeking to arrest. In a number of states, any male over 18 years of age is bound by law to assist a police officer in making an arrest if he is commanded to do so.

Permissible Force in Making Arrests

A police officer may use such force as he reasonably believes to be necessary to make a lawful arrest and to protect himself and other persons from bodily harm while doing so. When the offense for which the arrest is attempted is a dangerous one, the officer is generally privileged to use even deadly force, while for minor offenses he may not resort to either deadly force or great bodily harm, except in defense of himself or others.

Example
Officer Joan sees Jeff, a juvenile, steal several quarters from a newsstand and ride away on his motorbike. Joan is on foot. Joan fires her revolver at the fleeing boy. Officer Joan used excessive and illegal force in seeking to apprehend Jeff.

Post-Arrest Obligations

The laws of practically all jurisdictions require that when an arrest is made without a warrant the arrested person must be taken before the nearest judge or magistrate "without unnecessary delay." When the arrest is made with a warrant, the arrested person must be taken before the judge who issued the warrant or, in his absence, before the nearest judge or magistrate in the same county.

"Unnecessary delay," as used in the various statutory provisions, is generally interpreted to mean a delay for any reason other than the unavailability of a judge or magistrate, or circumstances such as distance or lack of ready transportation. Some state courts give the phrase a more liberal interpretation by saying that it means only an "unreasonable" delay, and consequently the police are permitted to retain custody over an arrested person for a reasonable length of time, reasonableness being determined by all the surrounding circumstances of the particular case. (One such circumstance, to be discussed separately in the next section, is the need in many cases to have an arrestee viewed by victims or other witnesses to ascertain whether or not he is identified as the offender.)

Examples

1. Burt is arrested by the police in City Y at ten a.m. as he leaves the scene of a burglary. The police put him in a jail cell and keep him there until ten a.m. the next morning, even though a judge was in a courthouse six blocks away. Such a delay is "unnecessary" and "unreasonable."

2. Five people see two men commit a robbery at two p.m. A witness to the crime, Wilma, was shot in the foot as the result of an accidental discharge of a robber's gun. The police soon apprehend suspect Frank, who fits the description of one of the robbers, but they cannot locate Frank's brother, Bob, who fits the description of the other robber and who has a criminal record for robbery. The police delay taking Frank before a magistrate so that they can conduct a line-up for identification purposes the next morning when Wilma is expected to be released from the hospital. By that time, they also expect to have Bob in custody. A delay of that duration and for such purposes is "necessary" and "reasonable."

Although arrest statutes usually fail to prescribe the procedure to be followed in a citizen arrest, the reasonable presumption is that the citizen's obligations are fulfilled when he turns the arrestee over to a police officer, except for court testimony that may later be required.

Legal Alternatives to Arrest

Most jurisdictions have alternatives other than arrest for taking a suspect into custody to stand trial for a crime. The alternatives are a *notice to appear* and a *summons*. They are most commonly used in traffic offenses. For example, the parking ticket instructing the owner of an automobile to appear in court on a specific date to answer charges is a notice to appear. The ticket given by an officer to a motorist for a moving violation is a summons requiring the motorist to appear in court on a specific date to answer the charge lodged against him. If a person ignores a summons or a notice to appear, a warrant may be issued for his arrest.

In recent years, the notice to appear and the summons have been used by some jurisdictions with increased frequency in non-traffic crimes. These procedures are especially effective for use in cases of minor crimes and in cases in which the suspect is a responsible member of the community and there is little or no expectation that he will flee from the jurisdiction before his trial date.

Chapter 17
Eye-Witness Identification Procedures

As will be discussed in chapter 19, evidence of a physical nature may be obtained from an arrestee without his consent or, under certain conditions, even over his objection. The same is true with respect to viewing the arrestee by the victims or witnesses to a crime; the arrestee cannot prevent the viewing by invoking the self-incrimination privilege. However, there is another constitutional right that is a factor at this stage of the police investigative process. The Sixth Amendment provides that in "all criminal prosecutions, the accused shall enjoy the right ... to have the assistance of counsel for his defense." Does the Sixth Amendment right to counsel then mean that when the police arrange for a viewing of the arrestee he is entitled to have a lawyer present?

In answer to this question, the Supreme Court has held that, in view of the wording of the amendment, there is no constitutional right to counsel at a viewing unless it is conducted *after an indictment or other formal charge* has been filed against the arrestee. Even then it is a right which the arrestee may waive. (It is obvious, of course, that there is no problem with respect to a suspect who is not under arrest and who willingly submits to the viewing.)

The reason given by the Supreme Court for according an arrestee the right to counsel at a viewing after indictment or other formal charge is that the viewing is then considered a critical stage in the judicial process, and counsel's presence will serve to insure fairness in the viewing procedure. If it is not fair, counsel will be able to disclose that fact at the trial. Because of the limited circumstances covered by the Sixth Amendment, the same reasoning has not been applied to viewings prior to the start of the judicial process. Nevertheless, no viewing, regardless of when conducted, may be of a "suggestive nature." Therefore, presenting a single suspected person to a victim or other witness, which is known as a *show-up,* is very likely to be considered suggestive. The better procedure by far is to have the suspect viewed among a group of other persons (four, five, or so) with somewhat comparable physical characteristics, and then ascertain whether he can be identified as the offender. This is known as a *line-up.*

There may be emergency situations or other factors, of course, which may render a line-up impractical, but wherever feasible this procedure should be employed. An example of an excusable circumstance is where a victim has been seriously injured and might not survive long enough to permit arrangements for a line-up.

Where no suspect has been apprehended or no one is even known to the police to be a suspect, a victim or witness may be requested to look at the photographs, or mug shots, of prior offenders on file in the police department. Here again, for obvious reasons, the showing of a single picture should be avoided in favor of a presentation of several photographs with instructions to the viewer to pick out the picture, if any, that looks like that of the offender.

If it is determined that any unfairness was present in the viewing procedure, the identifying evidence obtained from the viewing may be rejected, either at the time of the viewing or when presented in the courtroom by a witness whose courtroom identification may have stemmed from what occurred at the police station.

Chapter 18
Stop-and-Frisk

Although the police practice of stopping and frisking people under circumstances reasonably indicative of criminality is a long-standing one, the constitutional authorization for and the legal limitations upon the practice were shrouded with uncertainty until the 1968 United States Supreme Court decision in the case of *Terry v. Ohio*. The decision did not dispel all of the uncertainty, but it did sanction the stop-and-frisk practice in general, and in it the Court attempted to lay down some understandable rules for police to follow.

LEGAL GUIDELINES AND LIMITATIONS

In *Terry v. Ohio*, the Court held that when a police officer

(1) "observes unusual conduct which leads him reasonably to conclude in light of his experience that criminality may be afoot and that the persons with whom he is dealing may be armed and presently dangerous," and when

(2) "in the course of investigating this behavior he identifies himself as a policeman and makes reasonable inquiries," and when

(3) "nothing in the initial stages of the encounter serves to dispel his reasonable fear for his own or others' safety,"

then the officer "is entitled for the protection of himself and others in the area to conduct a carefully limited search of the outer clothing of such persons in an attempt to discover weapons which might be used to assault him."

Essentially what the Supreme Court ruled was that a *stop-and-frisk* could be conducted upon *reasonable suspicion,* which is a less restrictive standard than that of reasonable grounds or probable cause which is required to justify an arrest. The underlying reason for the distinction is the difference in consequences between a stop-and-frisk and an arrest; the former is a relatively minor intrusion upon an individual's freedom of movement and privacy, whereas the latter involves a taking into custody, the usual consequences of which are a trip to a police station and an appearance in court. Coupled with this, of course, is the practical need for the stop-and-frisk power to help prevent crime and to afford the police officer a right to protect himself from physical harm. Note should be made, however, that the Court's language in the *Terry* case strictly limits the circumstances that justify the stop and the scope of the frisk. Unless all of the prerequisites spelled out by the Court are met, an investigating officer's conduct may lack legal validity, and, among other possible consequences, a seized weapon could be suppressed as evidence.

Examples

1. Tom, Dick, and Harry were seen by Officer Jones standing and talking on a street corner. All three men took turns walking to a jewelry store half-way down the block. One man would look into the store and report back to the other two. One man kept his right hand in his overcoat pocket most of the time. Officer Jones approached the men, identified himself, and asked their names and the reason for being in the area. They said nothing (or else they gave an implausible explanation). Jones frisked them and recovered a revolver from the overcoat pocket of one of them. Jones' stop-and-frisk of the three suspects was proper, and the evidence seized is usable in court.

2. For several hours, Officer Smith watched Sam standing in front of a restaurant. During that time, Sam spoke with eight known addicts. He entered the restaurant and spoke with three more addicts. Officer Smith entered the restaurant, identified himself, told Sam to come outside and said, "You know what I am after." Sam mumbled an inaudible response and Smith reached into Sam's pocket and pulled out several glassine envelopes of heroin. Smith's action was improper because he acted not for his own protection and because he reached into Sam's pocket without first "patting him down."

3. Millie was a beauty contestant from Turkey in the Miss World Contest held in Des Moines, Iowa. Officer Sherlock posed as a judge in the beauty contest in order to gather information about narcotics that were being smuggled into Des Moines from the Middle East. In order to get a date with Millie, Sherlock led her to believe he would vote for her. They parked in Sherlock's car.

He noticed a strange bulge in Millie's clothing. Thinking it was a knife, he proceeded to "pat her down." Wishing not to offend the contest judge, Millie let Sherlock continue until she discovered that in the process he had recovered the knife and heroin as well. Sherlock's conduct was improper. He was required to identify himself as a police officer.

4. There were several strong-arm robberies by juveniles in the 19th Police District. On Saturday night, Captain Tracy saturated the district with officers and set up a dragnet. During the evening 100 youths were stopped and frisked. Such police action was improper because there were no reasonable grounds to believe that any particular youth was involved in criminal activity.

Although the right of a police officer to conduct a stop-and-frisk is not based upon legislative authorization, a number of states have nevertheless enacted stop-and-frisk statutes to reinforce this essential police practice.

Permissible Force

An officer may use reasonable, minimal force in executing a stop-and-frisk search. He may never use force that is likely to cause death or serious bodily harm. Resort to the latter is permissible only when necessary for the officer to protect himself or others from dangerous action that may be taken by the person stopped.

Example

While Officers Bob and Bill were making a stop-and-frisk search of two juvenile robbery suspects in front of a pool hall, the two youths started to run away. Bob and Bill chased the youths, caught and tackled them. Such police conduct was proper, but it would have been improper for the officers to fire their revolvers at the fleeing suspects.

The legal limitations upon the questioning of suspects who are stopped and frisked will be discussed in chapter 20.

Chapter 19
Search and Seizure

In addition to the authority to stop-and-frisk and to make arrests, the police are authorized to conduct a full search for, and to seize, weapons and evidence of guilt on any person who has been lawfully arrested. Various limitations have been placed upon the general power to search for and to seize evidence, however, and it must be done in the vicinity of the arrest, as in a car or a home. In an effort to insure police compliance, apart from the inherent threat of civil suits or even criminal prosecutions against errant or abusive police, a court rule was created whereby evidence illegally seized could not be used against the accused at his trial. It became known as the *exclusionary rule*. At first it was applied only in federal cases. Then a number of state appellate courts adopted it. Ultimately, in the 1961 case of *Mapp v. Ohio,* the Supreme Court of the United States held in a 5 to 4 decision that the exclusionary rule was required by the Constitution. This meant, of course, that the rule had to be adopted by all of the states. The pertinent constitutional provision is the Fourth Amendment's prohibition against "unreasonable" searches and seizures, and the permission of searches and seizures only when based upon "probable cause" (meaning, in effect, "reasonable grounds").

A considerable amount of criticism of the exclusionary rule has evolved, on two principal grounds: (1) one consequence of the rule is the nullification of positive evidence of guilt of the person who is its direct beneficiary, e.g., the carrier of a dangerous weapon, the possessor of stolen property, the possessor of heroin or other narcotics; (2) the rule has proved ineffective in controlling police conduct, and alternative measures can be utilized toward that end, without society having to suffer the penalty of freeing the guilty for the purpose of teaching the police a lesson.

One of the most outspoken and respected exponents for the abolition of the exclusionary rule has been the Chief Justice of the Supreme Court, Warren E. Burger. As of mid-1977, however, the exclusionary rule still prevails. *Mapp v. Ohio* has not been overruled, and, moreover, even if the Supreme Court should overrule it, the various state supreme courts could decide to retain it on the theory that it is implicitly mandated by their own state constitutions. Or the state legislatures or even Congress would be privileged to retain it through legislative enactments.

Regardless of the ultimate future of the exclusionary rule, there will still remain the need to know the nature of the scope and restrictions upon police searches and seizures. This information is presented under the various titles which follow. The discussion and the examples which appear are based upon the assumption of the continued existence of the exclusionary rule.

Search without a Warrant

Search Incident to Arrest

As previously stated, once a lawful arrest has been effected, a *full* search may be made of the arrestee *for evidence of crime as well as for weapons*. Further searching, however, is subject to certain limitations.

In addition to searching the person of the arrestee, there obviously may be a search of the area of the arrest if it is in a public place. When, however, the arrest is in one's home or other private place, there can only be a search of the immediate surrounding area; it is from that area, of course, that the arrestee might obtain a weapon or gain possession and destroy an object that could be used as evidence against him at trial. No search can be made beyond the immediate area without a search warrant, the requirements for which will be discussed below under "Search Warrants." Consequently, if a person is arrested in one room of his apartment the police may not search the other rooms, with the exception that the police may look into other rooms as a protective measure to prevent harm to themselves from other persons.

Generally speaking, a search connected, or *incident,* to arrest must be made at the time of the arrest, and a search of the immediately surrounding area must be made in the arrestee's presence. Obviously, therefore, a person who is arrested on the street may not be taken to his home or office for a search there as one incident to an arrest. However, once a person is taken to a police station, he, as well as his luggage or car, may be subjected to an *inventory search*. This is to afford the arrestee protection from the loss or theft of his personal property and at the same time protect the police from a subsequent false accusation of stealing the arrestee's property. If, in the course of such a lawfully permissible search, they discover contraband or other evidence of crime, it is properly seizable.

A police officer who makes an arrest with an arrest warrant may make the same kind of search that may be made incident to a probable cause arrest without a warrant. In most states, the arresting officer does not have to be in possession of the warrant at the time of the arrest. It is sufficient if he knows that the warrant has been issued.

In instances where the driver of a vehicle is arrested for an "evidentiary" offense such as a burglary, a search may be made of the vehicle for the loot or for weapons. However, if the arrest is for some other type of offense for which the car is only used as a transportation device for the arrestee, a search is permissible merely for weapons within reach of the driver. Obviously, no search can be made pursuant to a stop simply for a traffic violation, for a traffic stop is not even viewed as an arrest.

Some jurisdictions provide, by statute, that if a motor vehicle is used in the commission of a contraband offense, such as one involving narcotics, the vehicle may be seized and permanently confiscated by the government or state. Under this authorization, once a driver is arrested for an offense of this type, the car and the contraband within it may be seized.

Search Independent of Arrest

Consent Search

Irrespective of the issue of probable cause, a search is a legal one if made with consent, either on the part of the person to be affected by it or by someone authorized to act in his stead. For instance, a relative who lives with a suspect may consent to the search of jointly inhabited premises because both of them have an equal right to the use and possession of the premises.

Example

Hal is a murder suspect. The police believe that the gun he used in the killing is in his home, from which they know he is absent. They go to the home. Hal's wife permits them to enter and to search for the gun, which they find. The search is valid and the gun may be used as evidence against Hal.

The rule permitting a consent search by a joint tenant in order to bind a non-consenting joint tenant applies even though the co-tenants are not husband and wife or otherwise related. In the absence of a familial relationship, the existence of an equal right to usage and posses-

Search and Seizure

sion may be inferred when the consenting person has a property right or another connection with the premises, or with the defendant, that signifies that he is entitled to bring guests onto the premises. In other words, it must be adequately shown that the consenting party has a right equal to that of the non-consenting defendant to use and possess the premises being searched.

Example
>Ralph's girl friend, who occasionally spent the night at his apartment, consents to the search of Ralph's apartment while he is at a tavern getting some beer. Ralph's girl friend's consent is invalid. She did not have equal rights in the apartment.

Under most circumstances, a hotel keeper may not validly consent to the search of a guest's or tenant's room. Nor can a landlord give valid consent to search rented premises.

Plain View Seizure and Seizure of Abandoned Property

Objects or materials which are not subject to lawful possession (contraband such as narcotics, for example) may be seized if they are within "plain view" of a police officer in a place where he is lawfully entitled to be. Obviously, a police officer is entitled to be in a public place, or in any otherwise private place to which the public is invited. Equally obvious is the situation where a police officer is in a private place to execute an arrest warrant or a search warrant; once there he may seize contraband which is in his plain view even though there is no relationship between it and the offense for which the warrant is being served.

Anything which is abandoned is clearly seizable, even though the abandonment occurs during a police chase.

Examples
>1. Officer O'Malley, equipped with a warrant to search Alfredo's summer home for gambling paraphernalia, saw in plain view a sawed-off shotgun in the home. Since its possession is unlawful, the gun could be seized.
>
>2. Officer Burns observed Paula walking down the street. Paula threw away a package. Burns retrieved the package, which appeared to contain narcotics. The contents were field-tested and were found to be heroin. Paula was then arrested. The package was admissible as evidence at Paula's trial for the sale of heroin because the package was not taken by search and seizure, but was within the plain view of Officer Burns.

Emergency Search

There are occasions when the police are confronted with situations calling for their immediate attention and which involve the searching of a person or place with less than probable cause to believe that the person has committed a crime or that the place invaded contains evidence of a crime.

Example
A man is found unconscious in an alley. To ascertain his identity the police search into his pockets. They find several envelopes of heroin. The seizure is lawful and the evidence may be usable in the prosecution of the person as a possessor of the narcotic, or, with additional evidence, perhaps as a seller.

This type of emergency search is characterized by some courts as a "good Samaritan" search.

Vehicle Search

Mention has already been made of the inventory search of vehicles, and the search of them where the driver is arrested for an evidentiary crime. There are other circumstances permissive of a search without a warrant, the principal justification being the ready movability of vehicles. This probable cause search is permitted without a warrant because of what the courts call "exigent circumstances."

Example
A police officer has probable cause to believe that a large quantity of stolen shoes were stored in a trailer parked in a private lot. A reliable informant had told him that the vehicle was soon to be removed to another location. The search of the trailer and the seizure of the shoes are legal.

Border Search

It has long been established that searches at our nation's borders are permissible without any showing of probable cause. The mere fact that a person crosses the border is justification for a customs search. Statutes enacted by Congress grant the authorization, and there is the element of implied consent on the part of all travelers.

Not only are searches at the border authorized, but also the stopping and brief questioning of occupants of vehicles at fixed check points in the vicinity of the border. Beyond such areas, however, the usual constitutional limitations apply; in other words, the probable cause element must be satisfied.

"Shocking" Search

A search for evidence upon a person, even though there may be probable cause to believe it is upon him or her, must be conducted in such a manner as not to "shock the conscience" of the courts. Otherwise the

Search and Seizure

evidence may be suppressed either on the basis of the rule against illegal searches and seizures or as a violation of constitutional due process.

Examples

1. The police are about to arrest, upon probable cause, a suspected narcotics peddler. He puts into his mouth and swallows something that obviously contains narcotics. He is taken to a hospital where, over his objection, a member of the medical staff uses a stomach pump on him and recovers the material. This was considered to shock the conscience of the court (the Supreme Court) and the evidence was suppressed.

2. A man is arrested for drunk driving in a hospital to which he had been taken for treatment of injuries received in an accident. At the direction of the police, a doctor, over the patient's objection, extracted a specimen of blood, which, when later tested, established the fact of intoxication. The evidence was considered usable at his trial. The Supreme Court did not view the conduct here as shocking.

Search Warrants

Like an arrest with a warrant, a search may be authorized by a judge or magistrate by issuing a warrant authorizing the search of an automobile, home, office, or any other place. A search warrant may be executed without effecting an arrest. The search warrant is not conditional on any arrest. Indeed, there are times when the owner of a car or premises to be searched may be in custody already, or he may be many miles away. On some occasions, however, arrests are made at the time of, or following, a search that is conducted with a warrant.

Objects Subject to Seizure

At one time, in most states, the objects that could be seized via a search warrant were very limited—generally, they were limited to the instruments of a crime (e.g., a gun), or the fruits of the crime (the stolen property). Today, however, most, if not all, search warrant statutes permit the seizure of additional items, including any instruments, articles, or things which may constitute evidence of an offense (for example, a blood- or semen-stained undergarment worn by a rapist); a human fetus (for example, in an abortion investigation); and a human corpse (for example, in a murder investigation).

Form of Complaint for a Search Warrant

A complaint, or request, for a search warrant must be signed under oath or affirmation by either a police officer or a private citizen. This person is called the *affiant* or *complainant*. The complaint must state *facts* to show probable cause that the item to be seized will be found on the person or place described in the complaint. However, the complaint may be based in part on corroborated secondary information, known as *hearsay*, if there is "a substantial basis for crediting the hearsay."

Example

Officer Brown was told by Sid Green that a gambling operation was being run at Smith's barber shop. Green, who had given Brown reliable tips before, showed him a betting slip he said he obtained from Smith's barber shop. Brown surveyed the barber shop and saw a number of known gamblers come and go. Brown's complaint for a search warrant, based in part upon the corroborated information given to him by Green, was adequate for the issuance of a search warrant.

The facts to show probable cause may be obtained by an affiant who is an undercover, plainclothes police officer.

Example

Officer Green, in plain clothes, visited Joe's Cigar Store and asked where he could place a bet. He was invited to the rear of the cigar store where a wire room was operating. Green, although in disguise, was not a trespasser. Since he made no "affirmative misrepresentation" and had been invited to a place "open to the public," his complaint for a warrant was valid.

The complaint for a search warrant must particularly describe the place or persons to be searched and the things to be seized. The complaint and the warrant based upon it must leave the police officer who will execute it with no doubt regarding the place or person to search and specifically what to seize.

The premises where the search is to occur must be described in such detail that it excludes any other premises. The address, apartment number, apartment location, and any other descriptive data should be detailed. Usually a slight error in the address, however, will not invalidate an otherwise correct complaint.

Example

A complaint described a premises as apartment 2B in a three-story red brick building with the address of 2300 South State Street. The description was correct but the address should have been 2310 instead of 2300. But there was only one building in the 2300 block of South State Street, so the complaint was considered valid.

The complaint must describe in detail the objects to be seized. General and broad descriptions are inadequate, especially in obscenity cases.

Search and Seizure

Example

A complaint stated that at Edna's book store the owner kept "dirty, prurient, obscene and offensive books" underneath the counter. This description is inadequate. The complaint should state the titles of the books and contain other descriptive data such as author and type of book. If at all possible, a copy of the book should be attached to the complaint. (It should also be recalled from the earlier discussion on obscenity that special, speedy court procedures to determine the obscenity of books seized are also required.)

When a search warrant is for the search of a premises, the complaint does not have to identify the owner or the person in charge. Nor does it have to name the person in possession of the things to be seized, or any particular offender.

Form of the Search Warrant

Most of the descriptive data of the complaint (place to be searched and objects to be seized) must be repeated in the warrant. But a search warrant usually will not be quashed, nor the evidence suppressed, because of technical irregularities that do not affect the substantial rights of the accused.

Example

A warrant listed "Charles F. Smith" in three out of four places where the name was mentioned. In the fourth place, his name was inadvertently stated to be "Charlie Smith." The warrant is, nevertheless, valid.

Any major defect, however, will render a warrant void and result in the suppression of the evidence seized.

Issuance and Execution

A reasonable delay between the date the items to be seized are first observed and the date of the issuance (signing by the judge or magistrate) of the search warrant does not render the warrant void. However, the warrant itself must be executed (served and the search made) within a reasonable time after its issuance, usually within three or four days. It may be executed either at night or during the day.

The length of time during which the search is conducted does not affect the validity of the search warrant. Nor is the validity of a warrant affected by an invalid search that is made simultaneously with the search based on the warrant.

Example

Police officers obtained a valid search warrant to search apartment 25 of the Jet Hotel. They proceeded to the hotel and searched apartment 25. But while in the hotel they also searched apartment 26, for which they had no warrant. The unlawful search of 26 does not affect the validity of the search of 25.

Only necessary and reasonable force may be used to gain entry into any building or other place to execute a search warrant. While executing a search warrant, a police officer may reasonably detain and search any person in the place at that time, for the purpose of protecting himself from attack or preventing the disposal of the objects described in the warrant.

Warrants for Administrative Agency Search

Health inspectors and representatives of other administrative agencies must secure search warrants whenever the occupant of a premises refuses to permit inspectors or entries. Such warrants, however, may be obtained with affidavits based upon less than the probable cause required for police searches in criminal cases. Moreover, where licensed businesses are involved, warrantless searches may be made of the unlocked portions of the premises which are in public view.

Court Orders for Procurement of Physical Evidence from Suspected Persons upon Less Than Probable Cause

There are certain criminal case situations in which it would be extremely helpful to have an examination made of a person's body or clothing for possible evidence of a crime, but probable cause for an arrest is lacking. For instance, a young woman is found raped and murdered in the dining room of her apartment. On the table there are an empty bottle of wine and two wine glasses. Some of her fingerprints are found on one glass and on portions of the bottle. Some other person's fingerprints are found on the second glass and also on parts of the bottle. There was no forced entry into the apartment, so there exists a reasonable assumption that the other person was a friend or acquaintance. Among her known friends, however, none is under suspicion. Nevertheless, it would be helpful to have their fingerprints for comparison purposes, but not all have fingerprints on file with any governmental agency. Is there any way for obtaining them, since there is no basis for an arrest and the attendant right to fingerprint the arrestee? The answer is "yes," for the Supreme Court has clearly indicated that court orders may be obtained in such instances for the taking of prints either at a police station or elsewhere. The individual would not be subjected to the indignity of an arrest, only the taking of his fingerprints under conditions of considerable privacy.

Another example of the use of court orders for such limited purposes are cases where a person's fingernail scrapings or hair specimens might be helpful in an investigation. To take care of instances such as these, at least two state supreme courts have formulated rules of court whereby such court orders are obtainable. A frequently used alternative, however, is to have a grand jury subpoena issued for the purpose of securing the desired objects or materials.

Procedures and Requirements for Having Evidence Rejected

In order for a court to consider whether seized evidence should be rejected because of illegal seizure, there must be filed, usually in advance of trial, what is known as a *motion to suppress*. This is a written request by defense counsel which urges the court to declare the evidence unusable and states the reasons in support of that position. The motion to suppress can also cover evidence "derivatively obtained," i.e., from leads produced by the illegally seized evidence.

In practically all states and in the federal system, the person on whose behalf the motion to suppress is filed must be one whose own rights have been violated. Either the evidence must be owned by him, or taken from his person or from a vehicle or premises in which he has a proprietary interest. As known within the legal profession, he must have "standing."

Example
   The police make an illegal entry into Jones' home. There they find new transistor radios stolen from a company where Jones' friend Smith works in the shipping department. They bear shipping tags, signed by Smith, designating delivery to temporary premises rented by Jones under a fictitious name. Although the discovered evidence could not be used against Jones, it could be used against Smith because Smith has no standing to object; the police violated only Jones' rights, not Smith's.

However, one state supreme court, that of California, does not require that standing be established, reasoning that since the purpose of the exclusionary rule is to discourage illegal police practices, anyone adversely affected thereby has a right to have the illegally seized evidence suppressed.

In a number of states and in the federal system, the prosecutor may appeal a pre-trial suppression order. This appeal does not constitute a violation of the defendant's protection against double jeopardy because jeopardy does not apply until the defendant is put on trial. (For an explanation of double jeopardy, see "Motion to Quash the Indictment" under "Pre-Trial Motions" in chapter 22.)

Chapter 20
Interrogations and Confessions

THE TEST OF VOLUNTARINESS

Torture or any other form of physical abuse, or the threat of such treatment, might make an innocent person confess to a crime. For that reason, the courts have refused for many years to accept as evidence of guilt any confession obtained by force or threat of force. The courts exercised that power by invoking the constitutional guarantee that no person shall be deprived of his life, liberty, or property without due process of law.

A similar view has prevailed regarding confessions obtained after a promise had been made to a suspect or to an accused person that, if he confessed, the court would impose no punishment at all, or only a light sentence. The underlying theory behind that rule was that a person caught in a web of strong circumstantial evidence might readily confess if he were offered immunity or leniency, rather than continue to protest his innocence and risk a severe penalty, which in a murder case could mean death.

The general rule developed, and still prevails, that only a "voluntary" confession can be used in court as evidence of guilt.

Examples

1. The police suspected that Joe had committed a murder. They handcuffed him to a chair and started hitting him over the head with a large book or some other such object. They told him that the beating would continue until he confessed. Joe confessed. Joe's confession cannot be used as court evidence. The same result would prevail if it were the victim's relatives, rather than the po-

lice, who indulged in such conduct. The physical and mental effect would be the same and the risk of a false confession would be just as great.

2. Fran is told that, unless she confesses to the robbery-murder for which she is a suspect, she will be pushed out of a fifth floor window, turned over to a lynch mob, or subjected to a physical beating by the police. Fran confesses. Fran's confession is not valid.

3. One evening, Pete got into a fight with Ed outside a tavern. Several hours later, Pete was seen leaving the rooming house where Ed lived. Shortly thereafter, a neighbor found Ed dead in his room. He had been stabbed to death. When Pete was questioned by the police, he readily admitted the fight, but denied killing Ed. As for his being at Ed's rooming house, he stated that he went there to look for a former girl friend whose name he had forgotten and whom he was unable to locate. He also said that while in the rooming house hall, he encountered Ed, but that they only swore at each other and that no physical encounter occurred. Pete's shirt had blood on it of the same blood type as Ed's, but Pete said it got there at the time of the tavern brawl. Pete was seen with a knife in his possession while in the tavern, but he had no knife in his possession when taken into police custody.

The police pointed out to Pete the implausibility of his story of innocence. They told him that a conviction for murder was a sure thing. They also told him that since Ed was a skid row bum and his death a good riddance, if Pete confessed they would recommend that only a charge of manslaughter be placed against him. They informed him that it might result in a one-year sentence and he would thereby avoid the risk of life imprisonment or death if found guilty of murder.

A confession obtained after such a promise of leniency would not be usable as evidence. It lacks the requirements of voluntariness, and, more particularly, trustworthiness.

Until recently, if any of the suspects in these examples had told the police interrogator where he had hidden the murder weapon or the victim's jewelry or other valuables, and if these items had been found at that location, both they and that portion of the confession thus substantiated could be used as evidence. The courts considered the element of trustworthiness as overriding that of voluntariness because the voluntariness test had been developed only as a protection for the innocent. The theory was that a person who disclosed such details must have been telling the truth, even though the truth had been forced out of him. But the present judicial viewpoint is to outlaw such evidence in order to discourage the police from resorting to brutal interrogation practices.

POLICE DETENTION

In a democratic society, the police cannot have and are not given unlimited privileges regarding the length of time they may detain arrested persons, either for interrogation or for any other purpose. One requirement imposed upon the police is that the arrestee must be taken before a judicial magistrate or judge "without unnecessary delay." State courts have admitted as evidence confessions obtained during a period of unnecessary delay provided they were voluntary. The federal courts, however, for a number of years have rejected confessions obtained by federal officers during a period of unnecessary delay, and unnecessary delay was interpreted to mean anything other than promptly or immediately. This exclusion was applied without regard to the voluntariness or truthworthiness of the confession. The underlying court purpose was to force the police to comply with the requirement of an early presentation of an arrestee to the court. Recently, however, because many criminal offenders whose guilt was indisputable were going free because their confessions were not obtained "promptly," Congress legislated this exclusionary rule out of existence. Congress had authority to do so since the United States Supreme Court had not said that the rule was constitutionally required. When it originally established the rule, the Court had only invoked its "supervisory power" and said no *federal* court could use confessions obtained during a period of unnecessary delay. It had also held that the state courts were not obligated to follow this rule, since the use of such confessions, if voluntarily given, did not offend due process.

As matters now stand, therefore, in both federal and state courts, a confession obtained during a period of delay in getting an arrestee before a magistrate will not necessarily be rejected. However, the delay may be considered as a factor in the over-all determination of whether or not the confession was a voluntary one.

WARNINGS OF CONSTITUTIONAL RIGHTS

The Supreme Court of the United States, in the 1966 case of *Miranda v. Arizona*, held, by a 5 to 4 decision, that the police must give the following warnings before they can interrogate a criminal suspect who is "in custody" or who "has been deprived of his freedom in any significant way":

(a) You have a right to remain silent and you need not answer any questions.

(b) If you do answer qustions, your answers can be used as evidence against you.

(c) You have a right to consult with a lawyer before or during our questioning of you.

(d) If you cannot afford to hire a lawyer, one will be provided for you without cost.

The Court decided that these warnings were required in order that all persons who were to be interrogated by the police while restrained of their freedom would have made known to them that they had a right to remain silent—in other words, to invoke their constitutional privilege against self-incrimination. The reason the Court held that the restrained person was entitled to a lawyer before police questioning was to add assurance that the privilege would be known and understood by the person subject to questioning.

Under the *Miranda* decision, the only time the police can interrogate a suspect who is "in custody" or "otherwise deprived of his freedom in any significant way" is *after* he has been given the warnings and *after* he has clearly evidenced his willingness to talk without a lawyer being present.

The *Miranda* rules have met with disapproval from many quarters on the grounds that they are not constitutionally required and that they have severely handicapped the police in their efforts to solve serious crimes. The Congress of the United States, subscribing to this disapproval, passed a statute in June, 1968, aimed at nullifying the *Miranda* rules and substituting the original test of whether or not a confession was given voluntarily. Although the statute was necessarily directed only toward interrogations by federal officers and trials in federal courts (Congress having no such authority over state cases), if declared constitutional, it will ultimately have a considerable impact on interrogations by state officers and on trials in state courts, too. However, until the Supreme Court acts in some future case, state and local police officers and the courts of the various states must continue to comply with the *Miranda* requirements. Even federal officers must comply with the *Miranda* rules.

Since the *Miranda* decision was based upon constitutional grounds, most legal authorities are of the opinion that the congressional effort to nullify it will be considered unconstitutional. It is important to note, however, that the composition of the Court has changed from what it was at the time of the *Miranda* decision, and that in a series of cases decided since 1971 the present Court has indulged in what has been described by Justice William J. Brennan, Jr., who was with the majority in *Miranda*, as "erosions" of that case's holding. He has also predicted in one of his dissenting opinions that *Miranda* will ultimately be overruled. Moreover, two of the Justices who were with the minority in the *Miranda* case have continued to express their disapproval of it. Even if *Miranda* should be overruled by the Supreme Court, however, the state courts or the state legislatures may decide to retain it for application within their own jurisdictions.

Two aspects of *Miranda* should be clearly understood: (1) only the police are required to give the warnings, and (2) the warnings are required only when the police are to interrogate someone who is under restraint by them, or as the Court put it, "in custody" or "otherwise deprived of his freedom of action in any significant way."

It must also be understood that someone may decline to have a lawyer, or may change his mind to that effect after once having expressed a desire for one. However, when someone actually has a lawyer who has advised him not to discuss the matter under investigation and who has also instructed the police not to indulge in any interrogation, any abandonment by that person of his lawyer's advice or any waiver of his right to continue to have a lawyer would have to be shown very clearly and definitely. Otherwise an ensuing confession, according to the Supreme Court, would violate the Sixth Amendment right to counsel. (Right to counsel was not the question in the *Miranda* case; the *Miranda* rules relate only to the right to remain silent.)

GENERAL GUIDELINE FOR INTERROGATORS

As for what interrogation tactics and techniques the police may use *after* they have told an arrested person about his rights and privileges as prescribed in the *Miranda* warnings, and *after* the arrestee has waived his right to remain silent and his right to counsel, the only general rule is that the police must scrupulously avoid doing or saying anything that might make an innocent person confess to a crime. They may thus fulfill the basic requirement of voluntariness.

Chapter 21

The Privilege Against Self-Incrimination

Although there has been some discussion of the privilege against self-incrimination in various preceding chapters, the subject is deserving of a more extensive treatment.

In addition to the right a person has to refuse to talk to law enforcement officers about his possible guilt in a criminal offense, his self-incrimination privilege also protects him from compulsory testimony before such governmental agencies as coroner's inquests, legislative hearings, and, of course, at trials or other types of judicial proceedings such as hearings before grand juries.

History and Policy of the Privilege

The self-incrimination privilege, in contrast to the involuntary confession rule, was not created primarily for the protection of the innocent. It arose out of an early practice in England in which persons suspected of heresy were brought into the church courts and ordered to answer to the charges made against them. A sufficient feeling of opposition to the practice gradually developed so that the church courts ultimately stopped it. Shortly thereafter, the law courts felt impelled to discard the practice of compelling testimony. In other words, no person accused of *any* offense was to be compelled to incriminate himself.

In addition to the historical basis for the privilege against self-incrimination, there was another consideration for its acceptance and incorporation into our federal and state constitutions. There was a feeling that the police should be required to search for other and more reliable evidence than merely what a court or some other governmental unit could extract from the accused. The self-incrimination privilege, therefore, is largely founded upon a policy consideration—the sheer distaste for the idea that a person ought to be required to incriminate himself orally.

Limitations upon the Privilege

In view of the historical origin and the policy reasons in support of the self-incrimination privilege, clear distinctions must be drawn as to just what kind of protection is offered by the privilege. In the first place, one must distinguish between *testimonial* evidence and *physical* evidence; only the former is protected. As stated at the beginning of Part III, evidence is testimonial if it is communicative, whether spoken, written, or a physical act which conveys a meaning such as the nod of a head. Evidence is physical in nature and unprotected by the privilege if it is not communicative and is merely subject to observation by and evaluation of a party other than the defendant. As previously stated in chapter 19, "Search and Seizure," however, even physical evidence which may be gathered against a subject's will may not be utilized against him unless it is obtained by "reasonable force" and under "reasonable circumstances."

The following are kinds of physical evidence that may be obtained without the consent of an arrestee, by exercising reasonable force under reasonable circumstances, or pursuant to a grand jury subpoena: mug photographs; fingerprints; fingernail scrapings; samples of hair; specimens of blood, urine, or breath; objects concealed in bodily cavities, even in the anus or vagina.

An arrestee may also be required to permit the removal of clothing to be searched for concealed items such as narcotics or jewelry; permit an inspection of his body for tattoo marks, scratches, etc.; try on articles of clothing (e.g., a hat left at scene of crime); appear in a police line-up for identification purposes; speak for purposes of voice identification by witnesses to an offense; and provide specimens of his handwriting (e.g., in an extortion or kidnapping case).

Even when the evidence comes from the mouth, or through the voice, of the arrested person (or through some other act on his part), no violation of the self-incrimination privilege is involved, provided that it is to be used only for its physical characteristics and not for its value as "testimony." For instance, if an arrestee is ordered to utter the words "stick 'em up," so that a robbery victim can compare his voice with that of the robber, or so that a laboratory voiceprint analysis may be conducted, the evidence thus obtainable is considered to be of a physical nature only. The same is true of a specimen of handwriting that an arrestee may be ordered to furnish; it is solely for the purpose of a comparison between its physical characteristics and those of the document in question (e.g., a ransom note, or a forged check). On the other hand, of course, an arrestee

The Privilege Against Self-Incrimination

cannot be compelled to furnish a specimen of his handwriting in the form of a statement of his whereabouts at the time of the crime.

Assuming that the evidence sought is "testimonial," in order for its production in court to be banned by the Fifth Amendment, it must be compelled from the defendant himself. This is because the privilege is personal in nature.

Examples

1. Gronek is a sex deviate who assaults young children. After each attack, Gronek describes the incident in a diary which he places in a locked box and entrusts to his sister Mary for safekeeping. Gronek is arrested and brought to trial, and the diary, which is still in Mary's possession, is subpoenaed. Gronek cannot ban the production of the diary with a Fifth Amendment claim because *he* is not compelled to produce it. Mary cannot invoke the Fifth Amendment privilege of her brother because the privilege is personal to him.

2. Bobby is an executive of a prominent retail sales corporation which has been defrauding the state government out of sales tax which is collected from its customers. Bobby is subpoenaed by the grand jury and is ordered to produce business records and testify about the company's operations. Even though the corporation is a subject of the investigation, it has no Fifth Amendment right, and its officers cannot invoke the privilege on behalf of the corporation. However, if Bobby is also a target of the investigation or is asked questions which may incriminate him, he can invoke *his* Fifth Amendment privilege to avoid testifying.

When one appears before a grand jury or in court as a subpoenaed witness, the Fifth Amendment cannot be used as a blanket shield to avoid testimony; it can only be used to protect against self-incrimination. One who does not have a reasonable good-faith fear that the compelled testimony would criminally incriminate him cannot invoke the privilege.

Example

June sees Steve snatch Patti's purse from her. Because June knows Steve and does not want him to lose his job, June is reluctant to cooperate with the police. At trial, June invokes the Fifth Amendment and refuses to identify Steve. June can be forced to answer truthfully or face contempt charges and imprisonment. Because she was uninvolved in the theft and cannot incriminate herself with her testimony, she cannot invoke the Fifth Amendment.

Part IV
PROCEEDINGS BETWEEN ARREST AND APPEAL

After law enforcement authorities are notified of the commission of a crime, it becomes their duty to attempt to arrest the violator. If he is not arrested during the commission of the crime or at the scene immediately after its commission, the police must begin their investigation, and only when the investigation establishes probable cause that a certain person or persons committed the crime may the police make an arrest, either with or without a warrant.

Following an arrest, the court process begins. Although the legal procedures prescribed for criminal cases are not uniform among the states, the differences in basic concepts and principles are slight. Similarly, there are few basic differences between the procedure used in the state courts and that within the federal system.

Chapter 22
Pre-Trial Rights and Procedures

RIGHT TO COUNSEL

Once an arrestee is formally charged with an offense—in other words, when the judicial process has begun—he is entitled to legal representation. This right is guaranteed by the Sixth Amendment, and, as interpreted by the Supreme Court, it is absolute whenever the penalty for the charged offense may be incarceration for *any* length of time.

The right to counsel following a formal charge is to be distinguished from the *Miranda* warning with respect to counsel. At the police custody pre-charge stage, the right to counsel at an interrogation, as declared by the Supreme Court in the *Miranda* case, was for the purpose of insuring that the suspect would be made aware of his privilege against self-incrimination. In other words, the right to counsel at that point is a secondary, supplemental right. After a formal charge, however, the right to counsel is a primary one, for the Sixth Amendment specifically states that "in all criminal prosecutions the accused shall enjoy the right to have the assistance of counsel for his defense."

Once an accused has an attorney, unless he waives his right to continued legal representation, the police and prosecutor are not privileged to question the accused about the case without permission of his attorney.

PRELIMINARY HEARING

As previously stated, an arrested person must be taken without unnecessary delay before the nearest judge or magistrate. An exception to this rule occurs in instances of arrests for traffic violations or for other very minor offenses, which, as discussed below under "Bail," may be disposed of at the police station level. Another exception is where the police soon ascertain that the arrestee is innocent; in many jurisdictions he may be promptly released without having to appear before a judge.

What happens after presentation to the judge or magistrate depends upon whether the arrested person is accused of a felony or a misdemeanor. If the charge is a misdemeanor, the judge or magistrate may proceed with the trial, unless the accused demands a trial by jury or unless a *continuance* (an adjournment of the proceedings until a future specified date) is requested or ordered for some reason. If the offense is a felony, the judge or magistrate before whom the accused is first brought conducts a *preliminary hearing*.

A preliminary hearing is a relatively informal proceeding to determine whether there are reasonable grounds for believing that the accused committed the offense; that is, under the circumstances, is the charge upon which he was arrested sufficiently supported by evidence to require the accused to stand trial? If, after the hearing, the judge or magistrate decides that the accusation is without probable cause, the accused is discharged from custody. Such a discharge does not bar a subsequent grand jury indictment; and in jurisdictions without a grand jury system, the discharge will not prevent a trial itself based upon a prosecutor's re-filing of his charge, known as an "information."

If the judge or magistrate at the preliminary hearing decides that the accusation is a reasonable one, the accused is "bound over" to the grand jury or for trial, and he is held in jail until the charge against him is disposed of, or, if the offense is bailable, the accused may be released after a bail bond is posted, which is intended to insure his presence at the subsequent proceeding.

Habeas Corpus Writ

In the event an arrested person is not formally charged with an offense and is not taken before a judge or magistrate "without unnecessary delay," he, or someone on his behalf, may petition a judge for a writ of habeas corpus and thereby attempt a release, or at least compel the police to file a specific charge against him, in which event he may be released on bail.

The Role of Coroner or Medical Examiner

Peculiar to homicide cases and soon after a killing or unexplained death occurs, an ancient proceeding known as a coroner's inquest may be conducted. In most states which have preserved the coroner's system, the position of coroner is an elective one, and there is no requirement that the coroner be a person with medical training.

Pre-Trial Rights and Procedures

The coroner's jury is composed, in some states, of six laymen selected by the coroner or by one of his deputies. The verdict of the coroner's jury is not binding on the prosecuting attorney, grand jury, or court. In effect, the inquest results in merely an advisory finding which can be either accepted or completely ignored. Even though a coroner's jury may return a verdict of accidental death, a grand jury, either on its own initiative or on evidence presented by the prosecutor, can find that death resulted from someone's criminal act, and then charge that person with the offense. Likewise, a charge may be filed by the prosecutor despite a finding of a coroner's jury favorable to the suspect.

The trend in many jurisdictions is to eliminate the coroner's office and to replace the coroner with an appointed medical examiner, who should be a doctor of medicine with special training as a forensic pathologist; in other words, the doctor must be one who has pursued post-graduate medical studies in determining such facts as the cause and time of death. His findings become a matter of public record. They may serve the dual purpose of providing the prosecution with valuable evidence to establish someone's guilt or as the basis for exonerating innocent persons who are suspected or accused of homicides.

Grand Jury

A discussion has already been presented (in chapter 15) of the value of a grand jury as an investigative aid. Presently we seek only to describe its function as an auxiliary to the judicial process.

In many states, a grand jury, usually composed of twenty-three citizens, sixteen of whom constitute a quorum, must consider the evidence produced by the prosecution before there can be a prosecution of anyone for a felony. If the evidence is convincing, the grand jury may return an indictment, which is sometimes referred to as a "true bill." On the other hand, if the grand jury is not convinced, it may refuse to return an indictment, and its findings to that effect may be termed a "no bill."

Although grand jury indictments are not required by the United States Constitution as a basis for state criminal prosecutions, indictments are constitutionally required for federal criminal prosecutions. The reason for the federal requirement—and for the adoption of the grand jury system in many state constitutions—is the belief that there should be some means for citizens to guard against arbitrary or politically motivated conduct on the part of a prosecuting attorney. Today that concern has diminished, however, and many states have abolished the grand jury altogether, as has England, where the concept originated.

According to the 1970 Illinois Constitution, the state legislature is empowered to abolish the grand jury or to modify its powers and functions. Legislation enacted under this constitutional provision permits the prosecutor to proceed by information if a defendant is first afforded a preliminary hearing. If there is no prior preliminary hearing, the prosecutor may proceed by information only where the defendant formally waives his right to proceed by indictment. In Illinois, the grand jury is still used for some felony cases, particularly those requiring the use of the grand jury as an investigative body or in sensitive cases where the prosecutor's own independent charge by information might be viewed as of questionable motivation. The net result of this dual indictment/information charging system has been to speed up the processing of ordinary felony cases.

The consideration of a felony charge by a grand jury is in no sense a criminal trial. Only the prosecution's evidence is presented, and even then, just enough to satisfy the grand jurors that there should be a prosecution. There is no requirement of "proof of guilt beyond a reasonable doubt," as is necessary for a conviction before a jury or a judge hearing a case without a jury.

Traditionally, grand jury hearings have been secret; only the prosecutor or an assistant was permitted to be present, along with a stenographer to record the proceedings. Recently, some states have passed statutes allowing the attorney for a "target" of an investigation to be present if his client has consented to testify, so that the client and attorney may confer during the questioning process. But the attorney is not permitted to present any witnesses or present any evidence on behalf of his client, nor can he remain to hear the testimony of other witnesses. During the deliberations of grand juries, all persons are banned from the room, including prosecutors and stenographic reporters.

In some states, *after* indictment, the attorney for a defendant is entitled to inspect the record of the grand jury proceedings. In others, the inspection right is a limited one, being confined to inspection of the testimony of witnesses who are to testify in court. Within the federal system there is no general inspection privilege; only after a witness has testified at trial is the defense entitled to inspect that witness' grand jury testimony.

Unlike felony cases, lesser offenses (misdemeanors) traditionally did not and still do not require grand jury consideration; they are subject to prosecution upon a complaint or an information filed in court by the prosecuting attorney. Moreover, as already alluded to, informations in felony cases are permissible in state courts where authorized by state statutes. Such informations are usually based upon the sworn complaint of the victim of a crime or some other person who has first-hand knowledge about the crime.

Bail

The average citizen only encounters the bail process in connection with a traffic violation arrest at the time he is taken to a police station. In many jurisdictions provision is made for release upon the payment in the police station of a bail bond amount previously set by a court for that particular kind of offense. At that time, the arrestee will not be appearing before a judge; the matter is handled on the police level. The same procedure is often followed in certain other minor cases.

Except for the types of cases handled at the police station level, a judge will determine whether and under what conditions an accused person will be released on bail. This may occur at the preliminary hearing, or, in some jurisdictions, in a separate proceeding at a later stage.

In capital offense cases, where "the proof is evident and the presumption great," bail may be denied altogether. In practically all other types of cases, there is a constitutional right to bail, although, as a practical matter, the amount set is sometimes beyond that procurable by the accused.

The criteria a judge uses in setting bail provide that the amount be

(1) sufficient to assure compliance with the conditions set forth in the bail bond;
(2) not oppressive;
(3) commensurate with the nature of the offense charged;
(4) considerate of the past criminal acts and conduct of the defendant; and
(5) considerate of the financial ability of the accused.

There are two rather diverse trends in regard to setting of bail. First, for less serious offenses committed by first offenders, a so-called recognizance bond is increasingly being utilized. Under this procedure, the defendant is released on his own signed promise to appear in court at the designated time, without being required to put up a cash bond. The penalty for violating the terms of the recognizance bond is the same as a violation of a cash bond—the incarceration of the defendant until the trial is completed. Second, where a defendant is charged with committing another offense while free on bond pending the disposition of a first charge, many jurisdictions are now either refusing bond for the other charge or else revoking bond on the earlier one.

Where a bond other than a recognizance bond has been set, the procedures vary from state to state as to how the bond may be satisfied. The various types of satisfactions are as follows:

(1) Cash bond—The entire bond is satisfied by cash.
(2) Percentage deposit—A percentage of the amount of the bond must be posted, usually 10 percent; if the conditions of the bond are violated, the balance must be paid to the court, but upon compliance the defendant receives a refund of almost all of the percentage deposit, with the remainder withheld as court costs.
(3) Professional bail bond—For a premium (usually 10 percent of the

amount of the bond) a professional bailbondsman will post the bond. Even upon full compliance the defendant receives none of the premium back.

(4) Real estate or securities—Title to realty, stocks, or bonds, usually valued in an amount double that of the bond set, is posted as security.

Prosecutorial Discretion

The prosecutor is the single most powerful officer in the criminal justice system. This power is the product of two factors: (a) the influence he exercises upon the actions of other agencies within the system, and (b) his freedom from judicial review—except in the most extraordinary circumstances—of the decisions he makes as to whether or not to prosecute. His power to decide whether or not to prosecute is called *prosecutorial discretion*.

Many variables play roles in the exercise of prosecutorial discretion. The applicability and importance of each varies greatly from jurisdiction to jurisdiction. Factors that may be considered include the severity of the crime; the amount of money involved; the prior record of the accused; the quality of the prosecution's evidence and the probability of success with the accusation; the age of the case; the cooperation of the accused in making other cases; alternatives to prosecution such as restitution, administrative action, or prosecution in another jurisdiction; and the advisability of so-called diversionary programs in place of criminal prosecutions. The last named factor deserves special consideration.

Pre-Trial Diversionary Programs

Pre-trial diversionary programs are a way of dealing with certain criminal offenders without going through a trial and conviction, and they have become increasingly popular in recent years. There are two major reasons for their increasing popularity. First, our overburdened criminal justice system requires that priority be given to certain types of crime, usually those involving violence or repeat offenders. Therefore, and even if for no other reason, new methods must be explored for dealing with the less serious crimes, and particularly with those committed by first offenders. Second, since it has become very apparent that our penal institutions do not rehabilitate their inmates, it seems wise to find some alternative to penal incarceration for the young, nonviolent first offender. Pre-trial diversion may offer a desirable alternative, even to the probation system.

There are two types of pre-trial diversion. The first type occurs at the police station level. It is often called *station adjustment*. The charges against the offender are dropped on condition that he perform some

Pre-Trial Rights and Procedures

agreed task or tasks. No court trial occurs and the offender acquires no criminal record.

Example

After drinking a few beers, Phil, a teen-ager, throws a rock through a window of the lobby of the local hospital. This is his first trouble with the law. The hospital authorities agree with the police not to press charges, provided that Phil pay for the cost of the new window and volunteers to work at the hospital each Saturday afternoon for the next three months.

The second type of pre-trial diversion is more structured. Charges are actually filed against the offender; however, the case is continued until the defendant performs certain agreed-upon actions. After he successfully performs them, charges are dropped by the prosecution. In some jurisdictions, this type of pre-trial diversion is termed *supervision*.

Example

Harry, a young man with apparent emotional troubles, in a jealous rage attacks and beats Fred, who was talking with Harry's wife at a party. Harry and his wife have had marital problems ever since their marriage a year earlier. Harry had never before been in trouble with the law. The court, the prosecution, and Harry's attorney agree to continue the case for one year. During this period Harry is to pursue regular psychiatric care. In addition, Harry and his wife are to see a marriage counselor. At the end of the year, if Harry faithfully adheres to the agreed program, the criminal charges against him are dismissed.

Some pre-trial diversion programs are administered by the court; others are administered by the probation department or the prosecutor's office. The advantage to the defendant in any pre-trial diversionary program, as opposed to a probationary program, is that he receives no conviction and does not obtain a criminal record.

In addition to the employment of diversionary programs in ordinary criminal case situations, the concept has been invoked in drunk-driving cases. If the accused has an alcohol problem and agrees, after having the benefit of consultation with his attorney, to submit to a sound, meaningful therapeutic treatment, the drunk-driving charge will be held in abeyance for a period of about a year, at the end of which time the charge will be dismissed, provided there has been full cooperation on the part of the accused.

Arraignment and Plea

Following an indictment or the filing of an information, the next step is the appearance of the accused before a judge who has the power to try felony cases. The charge is read to the defendant, or the essence of its contents is made known to him; in other words, he is advised of the accusations against him. This is known as the *arraignment*. If he pleads guilty, the judge can sentence him immediately. If he pleads not guilty, a date is then set for the trial. In some states, and in the federal system, the defendant may enter a plea of *nolo contendere,* a plea which has the same effect as a plea of guilty, except that the admission thereby made by the accused cannot be used as evidence in any other action against him (e.g., in a civil suit by the crime victim). Whether such a plea will be accepted is usually within the court's discretion.

Pre-Trial Motions

After the formal charge has been made against the accused, he may, in advance of trial, make a request to the court (file a motion) for certain court orders that can assist him in his defense or in the implementation of his constitutional rights. Descriptions of some of the most frequently used motions follow.

Motion to Quash the Indictment

With a *motion to quash the indictment* the defendant may question the legal sufficiency of the indictment. If the court decides that the indictment adequately charges a criminal offense, and that it was obtained in accordance with the prescribed legal procedures, the motion will be overruled; otherwise, the indictment will be considered invalid and "quashed." Even after an indictment has been rejected and set aside, the prosecutor may proceed to obtain another and proper indictment. The prosecution is entitled to appeal from a court order quashing an indictment, since at this stage of the proceedings the defendant has not been placed in jeopardy (i.e., his actual guilt or innocence has not yet been under consideration); consequently, a subsequent indictment and trial would not constitute a violation of his constitutional protection against *double jeopardy.* The protection against double jeopardy means that an individual is not required to stand trial more than once for the same offense, whether he was previously acquitted or not. (A motion to quash an information might also be filed, but it is rarely done.)

Motion for a Change of Venue

A defendant may attempt to avoid trial before a particular judge or in the city, county, or district where the crime occurred by seeking a *change of venue.* In instances in which it appears to be necessary in order for the defendant to receive a fair trial, the motion for a change of venue is granted.

Pre-Trial Rights and Procedures

Motion to Suppress Evidence

A defendant has the privilege of filing with the court, normally in advance of trial, a *motion to suppress evidence* if he contends that evidence has been obtained from him in an unconstitutional manner. The evidence in question may be a tangible item such as a gun, narcotics, or stolen property or an intangible item such as a confession. If the court is satisfied that the evidence has been illegally obtained, it orders the evidence suppressed, which means that it cannot be used at the trial. If the court decides that the evidence was lawfully obtained, it is usable against the defendant at the trial.

PLEA BARGAINING

Primarily because of the rising crime rate and population growth, the criminal justice system in most urban areas of this country has encountered great difficulty in processing criminal cases in the traditional manner. In order to alleviate the situation, the practice of *plea bargaining* has developed as an alternative to formal criminal trials with the judge or jury setting the penalty following a verdict of guilty. In fact, a reliable estimate has been made that 90 percent of our criminal cases are disposed of by the plea bargaining process.

There are essentially two types of plea bargaining. In the first, the defendant bargains that he will plead guilty (or enter a plea of nolo contendere) in return for a specific sentence within the statutory range provided for the crime with which he is charged. In the second type, referred to as a *negotiated plea,* the prosecution agrees to reduce the charge to a less serious one with a correspondingly lower specific sentence.

In some jurisdictions the judge will participate to a certain extent in the plea bargaining discussion; in others he will merely accept or reject what has been agreed upon by the prosecution and defense. In still other jurisdictions, usually rural, and in the federal system, judicial involvement in plea bargaining is not officially permitted. Even so, however, it is permissible for the prosecutor, after discussions with the defense, to *recommend* to the judge a particular sentence, but it is in no way binding upon him. A plea where the judge does not participate in the plea bargaining and where there is no certainty that he will follow the prosecutor's recommendation is often referred to as a *blind plea.*

There is no longer any question as to the constitutionality of the plea bargaining process. In a 1971 decision the Supreme Court of the United States held that plea bargaining is "an essential component of the administration of justice," and, "when properly administered, it is to be encouraged."

Despite its constitutionality and the fact that it has become an integral part of the criminal justice system, there has been considerable criticism of plea bargaining within the legal profession and also from the news media. In 1973, for instance, the convenors of the National Conference on Criminal Justice recommended the abolition of plea bargaining "as soon as possible, but in no event later than 1978." Those who attended the conferences—including judges, prosecutors, defense counsel, and penologists—overwhelmingly rejected this recommendation. They did so not because of satisfaction with the practice but due to the fact that there is no suitable alternative.

Victims of crime, the police, and members of the public at large are skeptical, and sometimes cynical, of having justice consummated behind closed doors. Then, too, even though there is acceptance of plea bargaining within the legal profession, there is a recognition within the profession that plea bargaining should be so structured and so conducted that the best interests of society as well as fairness to the defendant are adequately protected. With this goal in mind, in the American Bar Association Standards Relating to Pleas of Guilty, a number of recommendations have been made with respect to plea bargaining procedures. The recommendations are essentially as follows:

1. Where it appears that the interest of the public in the effective administration of criminal justice would thereby be served, the prosecutor may enter into discussions toward reaching an agreement with the defendant through his attorney, unless he has waived his right to one. The prosecutor may agree to (a) make, or not oppose, favorable recommendations as to sentence; (b) seek, or not oppose, dismissal of the charge against the defendant upon his pleading guilty (or nolo contendere) to another offense reasonably related to the instant one; or (c) seek, or not oppose, a dismissal of the pending charges.

2. Defense counsel should only conclude an agreement after obtaining his client's consent following his being made aware by the attorney of other available alternatives.

3. The trial judge should not participate in the plea discussions, although he will, of course, have the option to accept or reject the agreement reached by the parties.

Although the ABA Standards contain the recommendation that the judge should not participate in the plea bargaining process, in some states the judge is authorized to participate when requested to do so by both the prosecution and the defense.

Since plea bargaining will not be eliminated soon under present conditions, the trend in many jurisdictions is to refine its procedures and seek to eliminate potential abuses.

Chapter 23
The Trial

THE LAW OF EVIDENCE—WHAT CAN AND WHAT CANNOT BE USED AT TRIAL

In order to insure that trials are conducted in a rational and impartial manner, a considerable number of rules have developed regarding what evidence may or may not be used, and the manner in which admissible evidence should be presented.

Admissibility and Weight of Evidence

Admissibility of Evidence

The question of whether certain evidence is admissible is simply this: should the real or testimonial evidence (a gun, or the identification testimony of a witness, for example) be the subject of consideration by the trier of the fact, which may be either the jury or, where there is no jury, the judge himself? The judge makes this determination of admissibility even when he is also the trier of fact in a non-jury case.

Ordinarily, in a jury trial, the issue arises in the following manner: as the real evidence is presented, or as a witness is asked a question by the prosecution or by defense counsel, the opposing attorney will say to the judge, "I object." Ordinarily he must do so immediately, for a delay may be looked upon as a *waiver* (a relinquishing of his right to object), and the evidence is in the case even though a timely objection might have caused the judge to reject it.

In rare instances a judge may hold evidence inadmissible even though no objection is voiced by counsel. He will do this in a criminal case whenever he believes that its use would violate some substantial right of the accused.

In addition to the general requirement of a timely objection, the objecting attorney is expected to give the reasons for his objection so as to pinpoint the issue to the judge. Here, again, a waiver may be imposed upon the objecting lawyer who fails to give the reason for his objection, because if there is any legal justification whatsoever for letting the evidence in, a reviewing court usually will not fault a judge who could have kept it out for the very reason the objecting lawyer had in mind but which he failed to articulate.

If the judge decides that the tendered evidence is admissible, he will overrule the objection; if he determines that it is inadmissible, he will sustain the objection.

Under some circumstances involving the sustaining of an objection, the lawyer whose evidence is thus being kept out is required to make an *offer of proof,* which means he must tell the judge what he was attempting to get into evidence and perhaps the reason why. In the absence of an offer of proof, an erroneous ruling by the trial judge may be looked upon as inconsequential by a reviewing court. In other words, it is not likely to be considered reversible error, because without an offer of proof the reviewing court will not know how harmful the error might have been.

Rules of Evidence

There are three cardinal rules governing the admissibility of evidence. The first rule is that the evidence must be *competent,* that is, it must come from a reliable source. Where an extensive amount of proof must be offered to establish competence, the process is called *laying a foundation.*

Example

Donald is on trial for molesting a six-year-old girl. She is the only witness against him. The judge must determine if her testimony would be competent—in other words, reliable. In this case the judge would question the girl privately in order to see if she could remember properly, could relate adequately what she had remembered, and if she knew that it was wrong not to tell the truth. If the judge is satisfied that she meets these tests, he would rule that she is competent to testify. (This same procedure would also be used if mental defectives or insane persons were to be used as witnesses.)

The second rule of evidence is that it must be *relevant,* that is, the evidence must be pertinent or applicable to a determination of a fact

The Trial

question in issue at the trial. In other words, does the evidence relate to the issues in the particular case?

Example

Dickenson is on trial for a theft committed in Detroit. The prosecution seeks to prove that prior to coming to Detroit, Dickenson had lived in Cincinnati, Cleveland, and Indianapolis. This would be irrelevant to the issue of whether or not Dickenson had committed a theft in Detroit.

The third rule is that the evidence must be *material* to the issue. This rule is similar and in some instances identical in application to the rule of relevance. Materiality means that the evidence is not too remote from the issue in the case. It must have some probative value. In other words, would the admission of the evidence probably influence or affect significantly the decision upon the issue involved?

Example

Warren is on trial for murder by shooting with a shotgun. The prosecutor presents a witness to testify that Warren was an excellent skeet shooter. Such evidence would be relevant and material if there was an issue in the case as to whether Warren knew how to use a shotgun, or whether he was an accurate shooter, but it would not be either relevant or material in a case where the victim was shot at very close range.

These three cardinal rules are supplemented, of course, by many other rules of evidence which are discussed in detail below. For example, the evidence may be ruled inadmissible because it is unduly prejudicial, is against public policy, is privileged, or was obtained by a violation of constitutional rights.

Evidence which normally would be inadmissible because of its prejudicial or inflammatory nature might nonetheless be admissible if it is competent, relevant, and material to the issues in the case. For instance, a color photograph of a murder victim might ordinarily be inadmissible because of the inflammatory (prejudicial) effect it might have on the jury, but it could be ruled admissible if color in the photograph was needed to adequately show the nature of the wound in a case where its nature may be helpful in determining whether it was or was not self-inflicted.

Weight of Evidence

Weight of the evidence means the degree of believability or persuasiveness, from 0 to 100 percent, that the trier of fact may attribute to it once it has been ruled admissible. This evaluation is made by the jury in a jury case, and by the judge in a trial without a jury. (The latter is referred to as a *bench trial.*)

Example

Lionel is on trial for a murder to which he had confessed to the police. Before the confession can be offered into evidence the judge conducts a preliminary hearing, out of the presence of the jury, to determine whether proper legal procedures were followed in obtaining the confession. If he decides they were not, he will rule the confession is inadmissible, after which no further mention may be made of it to the jury. If the judge holds that the confession is admissible, the jury returns to the courtroom and they hear evidence as to how the confession was obtained so that they can decide what significance, if any, they will attach to it; in other words, they will decide what weight it should receive. For instance, if they believe Lionel's testimony that he made the false confession only to protect his wife, or that it was forced out of him, the jury may disregard the confession, even though the judge had decided earlier that it could be admitted as evidence.

The Exclusionary Rule

The exclusionary rule says that illegally seized evidence cannot be used against the defendant. The rule is discussed in detail in chapter 19.

The Hearsay Rule

The hearsay rule is probably the most misunderstood concept in the law. It is basically a rule that embraces a preference for first-hand evidence. The rule requires that when a witness in court tells of facts, circumstances, and events, he should speak only about those of which he has *personal knowledge.* Stated in its simplest terms it means that the court and jury should hear what he knows, not what someone told him.

Phrased in legalistic terms, the hearsay rule may be described as one which prohibits the use in evidence of an assertion of an alleged fact unless the person to whom the assertion is attributed is available for cross-examination by the party adversely affected by it.

The reason for the traditional insistence upon the right of cross-examination is to guard against untruthful or unreliable evidence. In other words, a person who takes the witness stand and testifies to certain alleged facts based upon his own personal observations or experiences may be cross-examined about such matters as his physical or psychological capacity to have made an accurate observation of the occurrence or event in question. For instance, was he really able to see one person hit another from the place where he said he was standing at the time? Was his eyesight good enough? Was he or was he not wearing his contact lenses at the

The Trial

time? Was he so shaken up psychologically by preceding events that he was unable to maintain his composure to observe accurately the main occurrence he purports to have observed? Is his relation to the defendant, or to the crime victim, such that he may have a motive to lie as he relates his testimony? Or might he, by virtue of some other factor, be subject to an unconscious incentive to distort the truth? Or could he have been bribed to say what he said on direct examination?

Inquiries into any one or more such possibilities may result in the court or jury disregarding part or all of what the witness said on direct examination when he was being questioned by a friendly attorney.

However, few if any of the foregoing opportunities are available to the adverse party if all the witness testifies to is what someone told him. He can be cross-examined, of course, as to whether he is telling the truth about what someone told him, but beyond that there is nothing more to be disclosed; he cannot be asked anything about the occurrence or the event itself, for the simple reason that he was not there to obtain first-hand information. Consequently, the courts as a general rule insist upon first-hand information.

Examples

1. Sheryl tells the police that Dennis told her that Burns killed Thomas. At Burns's trial Sheryl will not be permitted to testify as to what Dennis told her; she herself does not *know* from her own independent knowledge that Burns killed Thomas, nor can she be cross-examined about the killing since the limit of her information is what Dennis *told* her.

2. Brown is on trial for shooting Smith. Wilcox takes the witness stand and says, "I saw Brown shoot Smith." Brown's attorney on cross-examination can question Wilcox fully in order to see if he is telling the truth, if he observed the situation correctly, if he has any reason to lie. Wilcox's testimony would not be hearsay because Wilcox is now speaking of his own knowledge.

3. Officer Williams arrests Hales for the theft of an automobile he is driving. Hales admits that the car was stolen by his friend Ganz and that he was with Ganz at the time of the theft. Ganz is arrested and both he and Hales are charged with theft. No attempt was made to interrogate Ganz, or to obtain any evidence of his guilt beyond what Hales had said and acknowledged in a written, signed confession.

Upon arraignment. Hales and Ganz both plead not guilty. Without Hales' testimony in court as a witness, the prosecution of Ganz would fail, unless there was other adequate proof of guilt. The hearsay rule would prohibit the use of Hales' confession against Ganz.

One very important point about the hearsay rule must be remembered. It is only applicable to those cases in which we are concerned with whether or not what the declarant said was *truthful* or *accurate.* In some cases it is of no consequence whether the statement of the declarant was truthful or not; the only fact of interest is whether or not he said it. In these cases the hearsay rule does not apply.

Example

Arnold, a chemist, tells his friend Phillips that he has felt a big lump in his throat and that he is sure it is cancerous because his father died of throat cancer. That night Arnold is found dead of potassium cyanide poisoning. His wife, also a chemist, is suspected and accused of killing him, because the investigation reveals she was having an affair with another man, and she had been heard to say she would like to get rid of Arnold.

At the trial of Arnold's wife, Phillips may testify about what Arnold had said. Whether Arnold did or did not have a cancerous lump in his neck is immaterial; however, his concern over cancer may have caused him to commit suicide, a factor obviously deserving of consideration in a case where someone is being tried for his murder.

Because certain hearsay declarations are made under conditions which provide substantial guarantees of reliability, exceptions to the hearsay rule have been carved out. The out-of-court admissions of a defendant (or, under certain other conditions, someone other than the defendant) which implicate him in a crime may be testified to by a third party witness because the defendant is not likely to make such statements unless true. The assertions contained in business records and documents are hearsay insofar as they reflect past occurrences and transactions; because such documents, however, are regularly relied upon they are admissible in evidence if they were prepared and maintained in the regular and ordinary course of business. Public records and other public documents are admissible under a similar rationale. More often seen on television than in the courtroom is the "dying declaration." This exception to the hearsay rule provides that a mortally wounded victim's identification of his assailant made just prior to death will be admissible testimony after his death because of the generally prevailing belief that it is unlikely a person will die with a lie on his lips.

The Best Evidence Rule

Of greater importance before the advent of the photocopier, the best evidence rule provides that before introducing a copy of a document into evidence, the lack of the original must be explained. The original is considered far more dependable.

The Trial

Privileges

Privileged communications are the result of a delicate balance between the judicial system's right to an effective search for truth and the public policy of encouraging certain types of communication or protecting certain privacies. The most well-known privilege is the Fifth Amendment privilege against self-incrimination, previously discussed in detail in chapter 21. Another widely publicized privilege is the attorney-client privilege. This privilege precludes the communications of a client to his attorney from being used against him in a trial, and the privilege can only be waived by the client himself. The privilege does not protect against discussions which plan a crime or which are themselves criminal in nature.

Examples

1. Williams is at a cocktail party and gets into conversation with a stranger. Williams asks the stranger what he does for a living and receives the reply "I am an attorney." Williams says, "Do you know what? I've been cheating on my taxes for the past ten years." Assuming that Williams is not attempting to retain his new acquaintance to represent him, Williams would not be protected by the attorney-client privilege.

2. Jackson goes to an attorney and says, "I want to retain you. Please research all of the cases in which men have been acquitted of killing their wives, and then develop me a foolproof legal plan to kill mine." This communication would not be privileged because Jackson consulted the attorney in order to plan a crime.

Another generally accepted privilege is the doctor-patient privilege. This privilege prohibits the disclosure of confidential communications made by a patient to a treating physician in connection with that treatment. The rule is designed to encourage full disclosures by a patient in order to promote the health of the patient even at the expense of concealing the truth in court.

The public policy of encouraging frank and honest communication between spouses has led to the marital privilege. In order to be privileged, such communications must be private and must have been made while the parties were married. Obviously, the privilege is inapplicable where one spouse is charged with a crime against the other.

In some jurisdictions there is an accountant-client privilege, a social worker-client privilege, a news reporter-source privilege, or a pastor-confessor privilege. These, however, are not recognized in the federal system except for the pastor-confessor privilege.

The Opinion Rule

As a general proposition, a witness is required to testify to observable fact rather than opinion. An exception to this rule is the testimony of an expert witness. A witness who by virtue of special training or skill has expert knowledge in a science, art, business, or occupation that is beyond the capacity of the ordinary layman may render opinions based upon facts in evidence or in response to hypothetical questions relevant to the case issue.

Example

A partially burned dead body is removed from a fire scene. A forensic pathologist performs an autopsy and conducts various chemical tests. He finds no evidence of carbon monoxide in the victim's respiratory system, nor in the blood stream, but he does find a fracture of the hyoid bone ("Adam's apple") in the neck. To a layman these two facts may not mean much. To the forensic pathologist, however, they mean that the victim was dead because of causes other than smoke and fire. They signify suffocation by means of strangulation. He may so testify at a trial of a person charged with the criminal homicide.

Right to a Speedy (Early) Trial

In all states, and in the federal system, the accused is entitled to "a speedy trial." The right to an early trial is guaranteed by the various constitutions, and the constitutional provisions are generally supplemented by legislative enactments particularizing and specifically limiting the pre-trial detention period. In Illinois, for instance, when a person is jailed on a criminal charge, he must be tried within 120 days, unless a delay has been requested by him or an additional length of time up to 60 days has been allowed by the court to the prosecution for the purpose of obtaining further evidence. If the accused is out on bail, he can demand a trial within 120 days, although in this instance, too, the court can allow the prosecution an additional 60 days. Unless an accused person is prosecuted within the specified period of time, he must be released; thereafter he is immune from prosecution for that offense.

Congress has enacted a Federal Speedy Trial Act which will become fully effective in 1979. At that time, all federal criminal trials will commence within 60 days of arrest. In many jurisdictions, such speedy trial legislation has placed civil cases on "the back burner" and has merely transferred delay from one type of case to another. In addition, specified speedy trial provisions have proved to be a major contributing factor in the increasing use of plea bargaining.

Time Limitations for the Initiation of Prosecutions

Somewhat related to the issue of the right to a speedy trial is the concept that after the lapse of a certain period of time following the commission of a crime no one can be prosecuted for it. The reason for this is the great difficulty or perhaps impossibility of someone adequately defending himself years later, by reason of unavailability of witnesses, etc. The period of time, set by statute, varies with the type of crime; it may be three years for most felonies, and one year for most misdemeanors. For criminal homicides, arson, or for treason there usually is no limit, the view being that the seriousness of those crimes outweighs the consideration of the difficulty of defending oneself against such charges. The legislation prescribing the various time limits is known as a *statute of limitation*.

Right to Trial by Jury

An accused person is constitutionally entitled to trial by jury, but he may waive his right to a jury trial and be tried by a judge alone. If the case is tried without a jury, the judge hears the evidence and decides himself whether the defendant is guilty or not guilty. This is known as a *bench trial*. If the trial is by jury, that body determines the facts and the judge serves more or less as an umpire or referee; it is his function to determine what testimony or evidence is legally admissible, that is, to decide what should be heard and considered by the jury. The ultimate verdict is made by the jury alone.

As trial time approaches, one of the first and most important decisions defense counsel must make is whether to ask for a jury trial or a bench trial. The defendant in most jurisdictions has the absolute right to waive a jury trial if he (through his lawyer) decides to do so; upon such a waiver there will be a bench trial because the prosecution may not demand a jury trial. In the federal system, however, the government has a statutory right to a jury trial and can demand a jury trial even though the defendant elects to waive trial by jury.

The Respective Functions of Judge and Jury

In a jury trial the judge rules upon the legal issues; the jury alone is the trier of fact and it will decide all factual questions and determine whether the defendant is guilty or innocent. Sometimes, however, a trial issue involves both legal and factual questions, and both the judge and jury may have to consider the same issue as part of their respective duties. For example, a judge must determine whether a confession is legally admissible as evidence; in other words, whether it was voluntarily made or was coerced. Once that confession is determined admissible by the judge, the jury will then have the responsibility of deciding what weight or probative value to give to it. In so doing, the jury will examine to what extent there were elements of coercion involved in its making.

A clear case of a decision to be made exclusively by the judge in a confession case is whether or not the *Miranda* warnings had been timely issued by the police interrogator in circumstances which required their issuance.

In most jurisdictions if there is a conviction, the judge rather than the jury will determine what the sentence will be.

Composition of the Jury

Twelve-person juries are used for felonies in most jurisdictions, and six persons usually compose a jury for misdemeanors. In most jurisdictions the jury verdict must be unanimous for all offenses, although statutes permitting less than unanimous verdicts are constitutionally permissible.

The array of jurors, namely, the persons subpoenaed for prospective jury service, must be selected on the basis of a fair representation of the citizens in the community where the trial is occurring. In other words, the prospective jurors cannot be an unfair sampling of the residents of the community so as to exclude potential jurors by reasons of race or sex.

Questioning of Prospective Jurors

In selecting a jury, both the prosecutor and defense attorney have the same number of what are known as *peremptory challenges*. A peremptory challenge is used to exclude a prospective juror without requiring a showing that the excluded juror would be unfair; an intuitive feeling on the part of either prosecutor or defense attorney will suffice. In most jurisdictions, there are more peremptory challenges provided by statute for felonies than for misdemeanors, and more for capital cases than for noncapital felonies. Also, if there are multiple defendants, the prosecutor receives the same number of peremptory challenges for each one of the defendants. In contrast to the limitation upon peremptory challenges, both the prosecution and defense have an unlimited number of *challenges for cause*. A challenge for cause will be allowed in instances where either attorney can convince the judge that a prospective juror, by his answers to the questions, has indicated that there is a reasonable likelihood he may not be able to give the examining attorney's side a fair trial.

The questioning of prospective jurors is called the *voir dire* examination. There are two basic approaches to such questioning. In many jurisdictions the judge will ask the prospective jurors some general questions and then permit the attorneys for both sides to ask their own specific questions. In other jurisdictions, such as the federal system, the judge will ask all the questions, although counsel are permitted to submit suggested questions to him. The trend is toward the latter approach. It is faster and re-

The Trial

moves the hazard of the *voir dire* examination being used by attorneys for purposes other than selection of a fair and impartial jury.

The questioning of the jurors is designed solely to exclude prejudicial or potentially unfair jurors. Its purpose is not for the attorneys to "brainwash" the jurors to decide in a particular manner or to "charm" the jurors so as to precondition them in favor of a particular attorney, or in favor of either the prosecution or the defense. For that reason, questions cannot be repetitive, cannot contain arguments of facts to be proved, and cannot deal with questions of law. In spite of these restrictions, however, in most jurisdictions where the attorneys are permitted to participate in the questioning, abuse of that privilege is not uncommon.

Jurors are usually selected in panels of four. Under this procedure, four jurors would be selected and sworn in at a time, rather than have the attorneys agree upon one juror at a time.

Before asking a single question, many trial practitioners, depending upon the juror's background, will attempt to "cubbyhole" that juror as to how she or he is likely to decide the case. Thus, through the years there has developed a folklore as to which prospective jurors are likely to be "defense-minded" or "prosecution-minded" jurors. Depending upon the offense being tried, the folklore is that the age, sex, race, ethnic background, family status, religion, occupation, economic status, and the education of the juror will determine whether that juror will be inclined toward the prosecution or defense. For example, this folklore would dictate that, in an armed robbery case, an elderly, wealthy Swedish Lutheran, married, male, college graduate accountant, would be an ideal prosecution juror, whereas, a young, poor Italian Catholic, single, female, high school graduate waitress, would be perfect for the defense. Modern trial attorneys do not place as much importance on this folklore as do some of the old-time practitioners.

There has developed a trend toward relying upon the advice of non-lawyer experts in this *voir dire* selection of jurors. A psychologist, psychiatrist, or sociologist, for example, may assist in the preparation of questions aimed at ferreting out hidden biases and predispositions on the part of a prospective juror. This expert may also sit at the counsel table to help evaluate the answers and demeanor of the prospective juror. To date, these experts have been used by the defense and only in a few celebrated cases involving a wealthy defendant, or an otherwise well-funded defense. Non-lawyer experts rarely if ever have been employed for this purpose by prosecutors.

Opening Statements

After the jury is selected, both the prosecuting attorney and the defense lawyer are entitled to make *opening statements* in which each outlines what he intends to prove. The purpose is to acquaint the jurors with each side of the case so that it will be easier for them to follow the evidence as it is presented.

The Prosecutor's Evidence

After the opening statements, the prosecuting attorney presents the prosecution's testimony and evidence. Since the defendant is cloaked with a "presumption of innocence," which remains with him throughout the trial, the prosecution must overcome this presumption and must assume the burden of proving its case "beyond a reasonable doubt."

If, at the close of the prosecution's case, the judge is of the opinion that reasonable jurors could not conclude that the charge against the defendant has been proved, he will "direct a verdict" of acquittal. That ends the matter and the defendant goes free—forever immune from further prosecution for the crime, just the same as if a jury had heard all the evidence and found him not guilty.

The prosecutor's evidence may take a number of forms. It may be presented in the form of live testimony by witnesses; it may consist of physical evidence such as money, a gun, or a document; or it may take the form of agreements between the opposing attorneys (known as *stipulations*) as to certain bits of fact or testimony. Evidence may be *direct*, such as an observed fact, or it may be *circumstantial*, which requires that a conclusion be drawn from an observable fact.

The Defendant's Evidence

If the court does not direct the jury to find the defendant not guilty, the defendant may present evidence in refutation. He himself may or may not testify, and if he chooses not to appear as a witness, the prosecuting attorney is not permitted to comment on that fact to the jury. The basis for not obligating the defendant to speak in his own behalf is the constitutional privilege which protects a person from self-incrimination.

Just as with the prosecution, the defendant's evidence may be direct or circumstantial. It may be testimonial, physical, or by way of stipulation. On the other hand, because the prosecution bears the burden of proof, the defendant need not present any evidence at all and can argue that the prosecution did not meet its burden beyond a reasonable doubt. If the defendant elects to present evidence, he may introduce it in denial of the act (through alibi testimony, for example); or he may present an affirmative defense such as insanity, self-defense, etc.; or he may argue for an acquittal based solely upon evidence of good character (in other words, as a good person he could not have committed such an offense).

The prosecution is given an opportunity to rebut the defendant's evi-

The Trial

dence, if any, and the presentation of testimony usually ends at that point. Then, once more, defense counsel tries to persuade the judge to direct a verdict in favor of the defendant. If the court decides to let the case go to the jury, the prosecuting attorney and the defense counsel make their *closing arguments*.

Closing Arguments

In their closing arguments, the prosecution and the defense review and analyze the evidence and attempt to persuade the jury (or a judge hearing the case without a jury) to favor their respective positions. The arguments themselves, of course, do not constitute evidence.

The prosecution speaks first, followed by the defense. The prosecution may then speak last in a *rebuttal* argument because it bears the never-shifting burden of proof.

The Court's Instructions to the Jury

Following the closing arguments, the judge, in most jurisdictions, advises the jury members of the applicable legal principles which they should, to the best of their ability, apply to the facts of the case as they know them. The judge also presents the jury with written copies of his instructions and with certain written forms for the possible verdicts. The jury then retires to the jury room to deliberate the case.

Jury Deliberation and Verdict

During the course of the jury selection, prospective jurors are not permitted to discuss the case with anyone—not even amongst themselves. Nor during a trial are jurors to discuss the case at all. Only after hearing all the evidence, arguments, and the instructions of law by the judge, may the jurors, as a group, discuss the case. This is called *jury deliberation*. After the deliberation, the jury will return a verdict for or against the defendant.

The foreman, usually selected by the jurors themselves to serve as their leader and spokesman, announces the verdict of the jury. Insofar as jury participation is concerned the case is then ended.

If the verdict is not guilty, the defendant is free forever from any further prosecution for the crime for which he was tried. The prosecutor may not seek a new trial, because of the constitutional prohibition against double jeopardy.

If the verdict is guilty, in most types of cases and in most jurisdictions, it becomes the function of the trial judge to fix the sentence within the legislatively prescribed limitations.

In the event the jurors are unable to agree on a verdict—and agreement must be unanimous in most states—the jury (commonly referred to as a "hung jury") is discharged, and a new trial date is set for a retrial of the case before another jury. Such a retrial is not a violation of the constitutional protection against double jeopardy because there has not yet been a determination of guilt or innocence.

If the jury does reach a verdict, the losing side may ask the court that the jury be "polled." The judge or his clerk will then ask each juror separately to state what was his or her individual verdict.

THE MOTION FOR A NEW TRIAL

After a verdict of guilty, the defendant is still provided with certain opportunities to obtain his freedom. He may file a *motion for a new trial* in which he alleges that certain errors were committed in the course of his trial. If the trial judge agrees, the conviction is set aside and the defendant may be tried again by a new jury and usually before a different judge. If the motion for a new trial is overruled or denied, the judge proceeds to sentence the defendant.

THE ETHICS OF CRIMINAL LAW PRACTITIONERS

The ethical question most often asked by the layman is "How can a lawyer defend a person he knows is guilty?"

One response sometimes offered is that it is not the function of defense counsel to make a judgment as to whether a person is guilty, because guilt can only be determined by adjudication in court. Ordinarily this response is not a satisfying one. Perhaps the best answer is that by compelling the government, federal or state, to come up with the required proof of guilt beyond a reasonable doubt *in all cases*—and defense counsel is needed to insure this is done—the government will not be lackadaisical with its prosecutions and, in consequence, there will be far less likelihood of convicting the innocent. In any event, every accused person is entitled to a vigorous defense.

The right of the defense to make the prosecution prove its case includes efforts to exclude evidence of questionable admissibility and to cross-examine the prosecution's witnesses to disclose flaws in what they say, even though defense counsel may be satisfied as to the validity of the testimony. He may not, however, by the process of cross-examination seek to "destroy" a witness he knows is telling the truth.

According to the American Bar Association Standards, it is unprofessional conduct for a lawyer to knowingly offer false evidence, whether by documents, tangible evidence, or the testimony of witnesses. The latter includes the situation where the defendant himself wants to take the wit-

The Trial

ness stand after having told his lawyer he is willing to take his chances on lying. It also includes a situation where defendant says that a relative or friend is willing to testify to a false alibi.

A dilemma confronts defense counsel when in the midst of the trial his client expresses a desire to testify falsely. To withdraw as his attorney would create a very awkward problem because, in effect, he would be revealing what his client had related, and thereby perhaps violate the attorney-client privilege. One practical solution adopted by defense counsel is to let the witness take the stand and testify without asking him any questions about the case; in other words, avoid participation in the perjury.

Also provided in the Standards are prohibitions against knowingly offering inadmissible evidence, asking legally objectionable questions, and making impermissible comments in the presence of the judge or jury.

A prosecutor is also bound by comparable ethical restrictions. Furthermore, there is an additional restraint upon him. It is the right of defense counsel to secure a mistrial or a reversal upon appeal because of erroneous conduct on the part of the prosecutor. A comparable right is unavailable to the prosecutor with respect to defense counsel misconduct. Although a mistrial might occur, there is no prosecution right to appeal.

Chapter 24
Sentences

Sentencing is the final stage in the judicial aspect of the criminal justice system. For many years it was neglected by criminologists and lawyers alike, but now it is one of the most controversial and widely discussed issues in criminal law.

Goals of Sentencing

Many reasons, often seemingly conflicting in philosophy, are traditionally offered for imposing sentence in a criminal case. The primary rationales are as follows:

(1) The deterrence of the defendant from committing additional crime in the future.

(2) The incapacitation of the defendant, so that he cannot commit future crime. This second concept differs from the first in that, under the former, sentence is imposed in the belief that *after* experiencing his term of confinement the defendant will refrain from further criminality. Under the second concept, however, the sentence itself, by its very nature, prevents the defendant from committing future offenses. The death penalty certainly would, and the incapacity during prison confinement is apparent.

(3) The deterrence of *others*, by the example set in any one case, from committing similar crimes. For instance, by sentencing an income tax evader to prison, it is hoped that others will prepare their income tax returns honestly.

(4) The infliction of punishment on the defendant in return for the suffering he has caused others. In other words, since the defendant has

Sentences

inflicted pain or suffering on his victim, and grief upon his friends and relatives, there is a deserved measure of punishment to the defendant himself.

(5) The possible rehabilitation of the defendant in order that he may successfully return to society as a law-abiding and productive citizen—through vocational training or psychiatric counseling during imprisonment.

(6) The compensation to the victim of the crime by the defendant whenever circumstances permit. For example, the defendant may be required to make restitution of the property stolen or to pay for the medical bills of the victim of a battery in lieu of serving time or accompanying a shortening of sentence.

(7) The expression of society's outrage at criminal conduct. This, of course, is the traditional rationale for making the statutory penalty for homicide greater than that for any other crime.

TYPES OF SENTENCES

In order to implement what are believed to be appropriate sentencing goals, the legislatures in every jurisdiction have different sentencing concepts. It is important, therefore, to examine the laws of a particular jurisdiction to determine whether a particular statutory sentencing option is available. Following, however, are the principal types of sentences in use today, and they are often used in combination:

(1) Fine—This is a monetary penalty that is frequently the only penalty in cases of minor offenses. In major offenses, a fine may also be imposed along with some form of incarceration or probation.

(2) Supervision—This is really not a sentence in the true sense of the word, because it does not contemplate a conviction. Under this procedure, the trial is continued (postponed) by agreement of the parties until the accused has completed some agreed task; e.g., undertaking a drug rehabilitation program. Thereafter, on successful fulfillment of the agreement, the criminal charges are withdrawn.

Supervision actually is a form of pre-trial diversion employed within the court system. Other types of pre-trial diversion, previously discussed, occur at the police station level before any charges are placed.

(3) Jail and penitentiary confinement—A jail is a place of confinement in which a sentence, usually of less than a year, is served in a penal institution located within the local community. It is used in misdemeanor sentencing or in conjunction with probation in felony sentencing. A penitentiary, on the other hand, is either a federal or state institution reserved for felons where the sentence is usually a year or longer.

There are two types of penitentiary sentences currently in vogue: *determinate* and *indeterminate*. In a jurisdiction that uses determinate sentences, a defendant is sentenced to a fixed term of years, e.g., five years. In those jurisdictions using indeterminate sentencing, he is sentenced to a range of years in prison, e.g., five to fifteen years. As to the actual time of the release of an inmate, that is discussed in chapter 25.

PROBATION

In certain types of cases, a judge is empowered by statute to grant *probation* to a convicted person, which means that instead of sending the defendant to the penitentiary the court permits him to remain at liberty, on certain conditions prescribed by law and by the judge. His background first must be investigated by a probation officer for the purpose of determining if he is the kind of person who may have "learned his lesson" by the mere fact of being caught and convicted, or if he could be rehabilitated better outside of prison than behind prison walls. In other words, would any useful purpose be served for him or for society by sending him to prison?

For a specified number of years, usually a year in misdemeanor cases and up to five years in felony cases, a probationer must remain on good behavior, keep in contact with his probation officer, and fulfill any of the special conditions of probation set forth by the trial court. These conditions often include making restitution to the victim for loss of property or for medical expenses related to the crime, support of family, attendance at drug or alcohol rehabilitation programs, psychiatric care, social work or vocational therapy, gainful employment, etc. A judge may also order that the defendant, as part of his probation, spend a short period of time in jail. If a defendant violates any of the conditions of probation, he will be brought back before the sentencing judge and resentenced, usually to jail or prison. For the less serious offenses a structured program such as the foregoing one may not be required. The probationer, usually referred to as a "non-reporting probationer," is simply ordered to stay out of trouble for a given period of years. He does not report to a probation officer and usually there are no special conditions imposed by the trial court. Of course, if he commits another violation during his period of non-reporting probation, he is subject to the same penalty as other probation violators.

WORK-RELEASE

Under a so-called work-release program, a person who is sentenced to jail may be released for limited periods of time in order to work, attend school, or take care of his family. The work-release program is also used in conjunction with probation, and specifically in conjunction with a restitution program for the victim.

Work release as part of a sentence by the trial court is not to be confused with work furlough or college release programs used by the correction departments in many jurisdictions. Under the latter schemes, a defendant sentenced to prison by the trial court is permitted, after he has demonstrated the appropriate degree of trustworthiness to the prison authorities, to work or attend school outside the penitentiary. This program is normally employed during the latter stages of a defendant's prison stay.

Chapter 25
Parole, Pardons, and Commutations

PAROLE

A prison inmate, regardless of whether his sentence is a determinate or indeterminate one, may be the recipient of "good time" for exemplary behavior. For example, a person who has been sentenced to 5 years might be eligible for conditioned early release (parole) after 3½ years if he behaves well in prison. Similarly, one sentenced from 5 to 15 years may receive parole eligibility after 3½ years of good behavior. In most jurisdictions, even those where the sentence is for life imprisonment, the inmate is *eligible* for parole (which, of course, means only that he may receive it) after a given number of years, usually in the range of 10 to 20 years, regardless of the length of sentence. Also, a person sentenced to as much as 100 years imprisonment could be eligible for parole (early release conditioned on continued good behavior after release) upon the completion of a shorter term, such as 12 years.

The period of parole is usually the difference between the date of release and the expiration of the period of sentence. Just as with probationers, parolees must, during their period of parole, abide by the rules prescribed by law, or by the parole board. They require what may be generally described as "good behavior." A breach of the rules can result in their return to prison for the remaining period of the court sentence.

PARDONS AND COMMUTATIONS

The governor of a state has the legal authority to grand a *pardon* for any crime committed within the state against state law. A pardon, which may be granted either before or after sentence has been served, has the effect of removing the stigma of criminality. In some states, it restores the defendant's civil rights to vote or hold public office. The president of the United States also has the legal authority to grant pardons, but only for federal offenses.

An executive action similar to the pardon is the *commutation* of sentence. It has the effect of reducing or shortening the sentence rather than eliminating it, as in the case of a pardon. A governor may change the death penalty to life imprisonment, for instance, or reduce a twenty-five-year sentence to ten years. Some states have a pardon board that conducts hearings and advises the governor on whether to grant or to deny pardon or commutation.

Chapter 26
Current Trends in Sentencing and Penology

Rejection of the Concept of Rehabilitation for Prisoners

Until recently, the penitentiary was regarded as an environment for the rehabilitation of an offender. Unfortunately, it has been found that few penitentiary inmates have been rehabilitated. Most experts in the criminal justice system now have more modest expectations of our prisons. Most agree that imprisonment obviously incapacitates a dangerous felon—in other words, while incarcerated he will be unable to commit crimes against persons in the free society—but they do not view the penitentiary experience as a means of rehabilitation.

The Determinate Sentence

The trend in state legislatures is toward defining determinate (specific) sentences, known as "flat" time, and away from sentences for an indeterminate time between a minimum and a maximum number of years.

Standardized Sentences

Not only is the current trend toward the abolition of discretion on the part of prison authorities by switching to a "flat" time sentencing scheme, but the parole system has also come under attack. Currently being advocated is the abolition of parole and its replacement by a standardized automatic release date for inmates based upon the determinate sentences less statutory "good time." The trend also is toward narrowing the sentencing range by the trial judge, resulting in further standardization of sentencing. In addition, many jurisdictions now allow a defendant to appeal his sentence.

Mandatory Sentences

Many persons in the criminal justice community are currently advocating mandatory prison sentences. The "hard liners" argue that this will stop judges who are "soft on crime" from giving "slap on the wrist" sentences to serious offenders. The "liberals" argue that one cause of prison unrest is disparity of sentencing, and that if all inmates received the same sentence for the same offense, prison unrest and inmate bitterness would subside. It is arguable that both of the foregoing viewpoints are faulty. First, abolishing judicial discretion in sentencing merely shifts that discretion to the prosecutor who can undercharge, overcharge, or reduce charges to make the punishment fit the aggravating or mitigating factors in the individual offense. Secondly, to sentence all offenders the same is to sentence none of them fairly. Persons familiar with court practices know that the backgrounds of the offenders and the aggravating/mitigating facts of the crime vary greatly from offense to offense.

Unresolved Problems

Violence, homosexual rape, and drug abuse in prisons are some of the major unresolved problems on the contemporary penitentiary scene. Among some of the suggested answers are conjugal visitations in prison, and segregation of "experienced" older inmates from young first-offenders.

Chapter 27
Post-Conviction Legal Remedies

APPEAL

After sentence has been pronounced, the defendant may appeal his conviction to a reviewing court, which examines all or part of the written record of what happened at the trial and considers the written and oral arguments of both the defense attorney and the prosecutor. It then renders a written decision, which either reverses or affirms the trial court's conviction and states the reasons for the decision. If the trial court's decision is "reversed and remanded," it means that the defendant's conviction is nullified, although he may be tried over again by another jury. A "reversed" decision ordinarily means that in addition to an improper trial there appears to be insufficient evidence upon which to try the defendant again, and consequently the prosecuting attorney may not make a second attempt to win a conviction.

A decision by the state's highest court affirming a conviction is, in nearly all instances, the final disposition of the case, and there is nothing else the convicted person can do but submit to the judgment of the trial court. But if the appeal involved a *federal* constitutional question or issue the defendant is entitled to seek a review of the state appellate court decision by the Supreme Court of the United States. Such requests, known as petitions for a *writ of certiorari*, are rarely granted.

As earlier stated, the prosecution has no right to appeal from a verdict of not guilty. Regardless of the impropriety of such a verdict, a prosecution appeal is disallowed. A long-standing decision of the Supreme Court held that such appeals are implicitly prohibited by the double jeopardy clause of the Fifth Amendment. In many jurisdictions, however, the prosecution may appeal from pre-trial court orders suppressing the charges against the defendant and also evidence declared by the trial court to be inadmissible because of the nature by which it was obtained.

COLLATERAL ATTACK

Besides direct appeal, nearly all states in recent years have provided post-conviction remedies by means of which a defendant may attack his conviction. Such "collateral" remedies most often are known as proceedings in habeas corpus or post-conviction petitions.

Even after a conviction is upheld against a collateral attack in the state courts, if a federal constitutional question has at any time been presented, the convicted person has yet another remedy available to him —the *federal* writ of habeas corpus. In considering the petition for the writ, a federal judge has the power to return the case to the state court for a new trial or to release the defendant, depending upon the kind of error committed, and the evidence still available to the state. Any such ruling, however, may be appealed to a higher federal court.

Part V

THE CITIZEN'S DUTY AND HIS PROTECTION FROM POLICE ABUSES

Chapter 28

The Citizen as a Court Witness and as a Juror

WITNESS

It is quite common and natural for a person who, for the first time, is called as a witness in a criminal case to be apprehensive about testifying. The solemnity of the courtroom and the prevalence of certain myths that portray the ordeal of cross-examination contribute to this feeling of fear and anxiety. To lessen the apprehension, and to encourage effective testimony, we are presenting a number of basic rules of conduct for a citizen-witness in a criminal case.

(1) *Tell the truth.* Never exaggerate or knowingly hide anything. A witness who is telling the truth as well as he can does not have to fear cross-examination by the opposing lawyer.

(2) *Understand the question before answering.* A witness should never answer a question unless he is absolutely satisfied that he understands it. This advice is particularly pertinent regarding cross-examination.

If you do not understand a question, ask the lawyer to repeat it. He will probably ask the court reporter to read the question to you from his shorthand notes. If, after hearing it again, you still do not understand it, say so. If counsel persists in requiring an answer, you can always turn to the judge for protection. He will make sure you are asked an understandable question.

(3) *Don't venture a guess in answering a question.* If you do not know the answer to a question, say so. Never guess. Inferences are for the court or jury to make.

(4) *Think before answering.* Give each question as much thought as is required for a responsible answer.

When opposing counsel asks you a question that is objected to by the attorney who called you as a witness, do not answer the question until the judge makes a ruling upon the objection. If any objection is raised during your answer, stop talking and wait for a ruling from the judge.

In announcing his ruling the judge may say "objection sustained," which means that the objection was a valid one and the question should not be answered by the witness. If the judge says "objection overruled," it means that the objection was without merit and that the question must be answered.

(5) *Answer questions precisely and objectively.* In your answer, come directly to the point of the question. State the facts as you know them. Do not offer an opinion (e.g., the speed of a car) unless one is asked of you.

Do not volunteer information. Remember that you are a witness, not the prosecutor or defense counsel. Leave the presentation of evidence up to them. Your job is solely to testify to the facts, not to secure a conviction or an acquittal.

(6) *Speak so that you can be heard.* In a jury case you must speak loudly enough for the jury to hear you. One reason many lawyers stand at the far end of the jury box when they ask their questions is that if they can hear your answers so can the jurors.

A witness should not put his hands to his mouth while he talks, nor should he ever chew gum.

Do not nod or shake your head in answer to a question. Some jurors, and even the judge, may not observe the head shake. Moreover, the court reporter who is recording your testimony in shorthand or on a stenotype machine will not be able to record your answer, and it will cause an interruption and a request for an audible answer.

(7) *Be forthright with your answers.* When opposing counsel asks you a question, do not look to the lawyer who called you as a witness before giving your answer. Such a gesture may create the impression that you are reluctant to tell the truth and want some help to suppress it. If the question is understandable to you, be forthright with your answer. If, for any reason, the question is an improper one, counsel or the judge will exercise the responsibility of sparing you the answer.

(8) *Testify in as positive a manner as circumstances permit.* Answer understandable questions without hedging. If you know you will be asked certain questions about the speed of a vehicle or the time of an occurrence, have the specific answers clearly in mind and state them in a positive manner, even though you may say "about fifty miles an hour" or "about ten o'clock."

(9) *Maintain a correct posture.* A witness should sit up straight in the witness chair. He should avoid slouching, squirming, or turning around

unnecessarily. Any such activity may become a distraction that will lessen the effectiveness of the testimony.

(10) *Be courteous.* When addressing the judge, refer to him as "Your Honor." When opposing counsel asks you a question like "Are you sure?" respond with "Yes sir, I am" or "No, sir"—each is an effective courteous response.

(11) *Be serious.* A courtroom is no place for wisecracks. Your testimony affects both the liberty (and possibly the life) of an individual and the protection of society. A person who acts in a flippant manner may be regarded as a "smart aleck" by the jury and his testimony may be given little credence.

(12) *Don't argue with counsel.* Never argue or fence with opposing counsel. You will rarely win because he is far better prepared to handle an encounter than you are. Even if you should win an argument, the jury may rate you a "wise guy" and may make an appropriate discount of your testimony.

(13) *Do not lose your temper.* No matter how hard you are pressed, try not to lose your temper while under cross-examination. To do so will lessen your effectiveness as a witness. Some cross-examiners will make a deliberate effort to rattle you for the purpose of accomplishing that objective. If you succumb, you will be playing right into the hands of opposing counsel.

(14) *Dress neatly.* First impressions are often received from the manner in which a person dresses. A jury's evaluation of a witness's testimony may be based on their first impression of him.

You should appear neatly dressed, but no witness should ever be flashy or overdressed. For example, a loud sport jacket, or a cocktail dress or mini skirt or exotic hairdo, would not be appropriate. A business suit, white shirt, and tie for a male, and a modestly designed dress or suit for a female, are more suitable for the occasion.

In addition to the negative over-all impression that inappropriate attire can create, it can also distract and lessen the effectiveness of a witness's testimony.

(15) *Be prepared.* Prior to appearing in court, the testimony of a witness should be discussed between the witness and the lawyer who has called him to testify. This is a perfectly ethical practice, and it is indispensable for effective testimony.

If you are asked on the witness stand whether you talked to anyone about the case, respond unhesitatingly with "Yes." When asked with whom, say "With Attorney ———." Also admit, if asked, that you talked to other persons about the case, in the event that you did have other discussions.

(16) *Avoid contacts with jurors.* Do not talk to, or in any way contact,

any member of the jury sitting in the case in which you are appearing as a witness. Regardless of how innocuous or unrelated the matter you discussed may be to the case itself, such conduct may cause a mistrial or a reversal of the case on appeal, and you yourself may sustain considerable embarrassment.

Juror

Serving as a juror in both the trial courts and on grand juries constitutes a solemn obligation of citizenship as well as a most meaningful contribution to our system of jurisprudence. Judgments made by juries of one's peers are a fundamental tenet of our system of justice, and participation in that process is a rewarding experience as well.

Prospective jurors are generally selected by lot from among the citizens within the court's geographic area of jurisdiction. In some jurisdictions, preliminary questionnaires are mailed to prospective jurors in an effort to gather information which may warrant disqualification from jury duty. Preliminary disqualification may result from non-citizenship, inability to read and write English, mental infirmity, or felony conviction. Some persons whose occupations provide certain types of service to the public are exempted from jury service. Included in this category are doctors, dentists, policemen, firemen, and officers of the executive or legislative branches of government. Persons for whom jury service may cause an undue and unavoidable hardship, or cause extreme inconvenience, may also be excused from service. Appropriate circumstances include mothers of infants and sole proprietors of businesses.

Once a jury pool has been assembled, some of its members may be selected very quickly for grand jury service. The nature of one's service will vary greatly depending upon the type of grand jury being impaneled. Regular grand juries are usually impaneled for a period of one month. Special grand juries are usually impaneled for eighteen months and may be extended for an additional period of time, if necessary. Special grand juries generally only meet once or twice a week and, accordingly, such service is not the burden it might seem at first glance. Grand juries hear and review evidence, question witnesses, and vote indictments. When the need arises, they may issue written reports on subjects such as organized crime and misconduct or malfeasance by public officials. Grand juries are generally composed of twenty-three members and are chaired by a foreman whom they elect. The grand jury returns indictments by majority vote.

The vast majority of jury pool members for service in trial courts are divided into panels and sent to the various courtrooms where they participate in the process of jury selection described in chapter 23. Some prospective jurors may sit on a number of juries during their month of jury service. In rare cases of great notoriety, a jury may be "sequestered" or insulated from uncontrolled contact during the course of the trial in order to avoid the taint of prejudicial publicity. In the typical case, however, jurors leave the courtroom in late afternoon and go home after an admonition from the judge that they not discuss the case with anyone nor arrive at conclusions before their solemn deliberations begin.

Chapter 29

The Citizen's Legal Actions Against the Police and Other Law Enforcement Officers

As discussed earlier, police misconduct in wrongfully seizing evidence may result in the acquittal of the suspect. In addition, the citizen is afforded other protections under the law against improper or corrupt police conduct. The police officer himself may be subject to criminal prosecution for improper official actions, and the citizen who is harmed by police misconduct may file a civil suit and recover monetary damages.

State Criminal Liability of Police

The elements of many criminal offenses are such that an erring police officer might well fall within their scope. Some of the criminal offenses for which a police officer can be prosecuted for acts committed while serving in his official capacity are described below.

Although the instances of prosecution of police officers under state criminal statutes are infrequent, there is no question about their applicability to errant police conduct. In most states, the commission of any of these offenses, whether prosecuted or not, constitutes grounds for discharge of the officer from the force.

Intimidation

A police officer who threatens to detain and question a relative of an accused person in order to induce the accused to cooperate is guilty of intimidation.

Extortion

A police officer who threatens a person with arrest or with physical brutality in order to procure money from that person is guilty of extortion.

The Citizen's Legal Actions Against the Police

Example
A police officer threatens a prostitute with arrest or physical violence unless she pays him a certain amount of money each week. The officer has committed the offense of extortion.

Coercing a Confession

Some states have laws which make it a crime to obtain a confession by means of physical force or by threat of physical force.

Example
A police officer, in attempting to obtain a confession, tells the accused that unless he cooperates some other police officers who are not as sympathetic as he might physically abuse him. The crime of coercion has been committed.

Assault and Battery

A police officer who threatens to abuse an accused person may be guilty of the crime of assault. If his threat is carried out, the offense of battery occurs.

Electronic Surveillance

The subject of "wiretapping" and "bugging" of conversations received attention in chapter 5, with a discussion of what is and what is not permissible. Whether a citizen has a cause of action for any such intrusions upon his privacy will depend almost entirely upon whether the relevant state or federal laws have been violated. We need only add at this point that the ordinary citizen has very little to fear with respect to electronic overhearing or recording of his conversations *by law enforcement officers*. Apart from the prohibitory laws and moral considerations, such operations are costly and time consuming, and there are simpler and less expensive ways for dishonest law enforcement personnel to obtain evidence against an ordinary citizen for purposes of shakedown or embarrassment. Private detectives, employed by businesses or suspecting spouses, are far more likely to run the legal risks and ignore the moral considerations of such nefarious practices.

The Watergate exposures and penal consequences constitute another dissuasive factor for repetition of any unlawful electronic interception of conversations in the future.

Unauthorized Deadly Weapons

Although most police officers are permitted to carry concealed pistols, knives, and other weapons that an ordinary citizen is not permitted to carry, there are certain weapons that even a police officer, in most jurisdictions, is not permitted to carry. Usually listed among these prohibited weapons are gun silencers, sandclubs, brass knuckles, switchblade knives, and sawed-off shotguns.

Aiding Escape

It is a crime to help any prisoner escape from custody. A police officer who does not try to apprehend an escaping prisoner is guilty of this offense.

Perjury and Subornation of Perjury

A police officer-witness who knowingly testifies falsely in a criminal trial commits perjury. If an officer induces a witness to testify falsely, the officer is guilty of the crime of subornation of perjury. The false statement must be made under oath and it must be material to the issue before the court in order for a crime to be committed. The police officer must also know that the false statement is not true.

Harassing Witnesses or Jurors

It is a crime to harass or coerce a juror or witness regarding his participation in a criminal trial. A police officer who attempts to coerce a witness not to testify is guilty of this offense. A policeman who attempts to influence a juror, other than while testifying as a witness, also falls within this provision.

Bribery

It is a crime to offer or to accept a bribe. A bribe is something of value offered or accepted with the intention of influencing official performance. For example, a police officer who accepts a "gratuity" from a motorist in order to give the motorist a "pass" is guilty of bribery. Similarly, a police officer who offers a bribe to another public official is guilty of the offense. It is also a crime for a police officer to solicit a bribe from a citizen.

Failure to Report a Bribe

The statutes of many jurisdictions require a public official to report an attempted bribe to the prosecutor or to the chief of police. Failure to do so constitutes an offense. A police officer who fails to report an attempted bribe to his appropriate supervisor is guilty of this offense.

Tampering with Public Records

It is an offense to destroy, tamper with, or remove a public record. Therefore, a police officer who wrongfully alters a station's booking record or removes an arrest record violates this provision.

Official Misconduct

By state statute, it is a crime for a public official to exert his official authority to the detriment of another person in an unlawful manner. For example, a policeman who uses his office in order to collect money for a private collection firm is guilty of official misconduct.

Violating Rights of Accused

Many states have recently adopted legislation providing criminal penalties for police officers who violate specified statutory rights afforded a person accused of a crime. For example, a police officer who refuses to permit an accused person to call his attorney may fall within this provision.

STATE CIVIL LIABILITY OF POLICE

Three types of civil tort cases for damage awards are frequently filed against police officers in connection with the performance of their duties. These are actions for false arrest and false imprisonment, malicious prosecution, and negligence.

False Arrest and Imprisonment

Since arrest and custody usually occur simultaneously, actions for false arrest often contain an additional count for false imprisonment, which is the unlawful restraint of an individual's personal liberty or freedom.

In addition to being a part of false arrest, false imprisonment may exist independently of false arrest. It might occur in a situation in which there is probable cause to make an arrest but later investigation indicates that the arrested person did not commit the crime and should be released. The police officer who persists in detaining the arrested person under such circumstances may be liable for false imprisonment, but only in those states that permit an officer to release an arrestee without a court order to that effect.

Malicious Prosecution

Malicious prosecution occurs whenever a police officer (or any other citizen) knowingly signs a complaint or causes a complaint to be signed against a person who he knows did not commit a crime. Malice is an essential element of malicious prosecution. The prosecution of a person with any motive other than that of bringing a guilty party to justice is a malicious prosecution, but this civil error is not established merely by the fact that the party bringing the suit was acquitted of a criminal charge.

Action for Negligence

A police officer who injures someone through ordinary negligence during the course of his official duties could be sued successfully in a civil proceeding. For example, a police officer who attempts to apprehend a suspect and fires his weapon negligently, thereby injuring an innocent bystander, is subject to civil liability. Negligent conduct in the use of a police vehicle also subjects an officer to civil liability.

Indemnification of Police Officers

A police officer is primarily liable for any judgment obtained against him, which means that he must pay out of his own pocket any money awarded to the person who successfully sues him. Most police officers do not have substantial finances, and ordinarily a large money judgment against one of them would be difficult to satisfy. To protect their officers, some jurisdictions have enacted indemnification statutes or ordinances which provide that the state, city, or county, as the case may be, will reimburse a police officer for any money damages awarded against him arising out of negligent conduct performed in the course of his official duties. Therefore, although a police officer may be without assets, the citizen, ultimately, will be compensated by the government employing the officer.

FEDERAL CRIMINAL LIABILITY OF POLICE

The Federal Civil Rights Act provides for criminal prosecution of police officers who deprive citizens of any federal right under the United States Constitution or the federal law. This prosecution may occur in addition to the remedy of civil suit that is available to the victim of police misconduct under the Federal Civil Rights Act.

The most frequently invoked criminal provision of the Federal Civil Rights Act is that portion (U.S. Code, Title 18, § 242) which reads as follows:

> Whoever, under color of any law, statute, ordinance, regulation or custom, willfully subjects any inhabitant of any State, Territory, or District to the deprivation of any rights, privileges, or immunities secured or protected by the Constitution or laws of the United States, or to different punishments, pains, or penalties, on account of such inhabitant being an alien, or by reason of his color, or race, than are prescribed for the punishment of citizens, shall be fined not more than $1,000 or imprisoned not more than one year, or both; and if death results shall be subject to imprisonment for any term of years or for life.

Examples

1. A police officer who tries to beat a confession out of a suspect.
2. A police officer who unlawfully searches an apartment without a warrant and without grounds for a search incident to an arrest.
3. A police officer who prohibits an individual from passing out religious pamphlets in a reasonable manner.

The Citizen's Legal Actions Against the Police

4. A police officer who, in making an arrest, uses excessive force because the arrested individual is a member of a minority group disliked by the police officer.

In all the above situations the officer has violated the Federal Civil Rights Act.

Criminal prosecution, like civil liability, under the Federal Civil Rights Act is limited to state, county, municipal, and other law enforcement officers. Federal law enforcement officers are excluded from criminal prosecution under the Act, with one exception: District of Columbia police officers, although not civilly liable under the Act, are subject to criminal prosecution.

Another Federal Civil Rights Act criminal provision (Title 18, § 241) that is often invoked reads as follows:

> If two or more persons conspire to injure, oppress, threaten, or intimidate any citizen in the free exercise or enjoyment of any right or privilege secured to him by the Constitution or laws of the United States, or because of his having so exercised the same; or
> If two or more persons go in disguise on the highway, or on the premises of another, with intent to prevent or hinder his free exercise or enjoyment of any right or privilege so secured—
> They shall be fined not more than $10,000 or imprisoned not more than ten years, or both; and if death results, they shall be subject to imprisonment for any term of years or for life.

All persons, including police officers, are subject to prosecution under this provision.

Still another section of the Civil Rights Act provides for criminal prosecutions for conspiracy. Police officers, as well as private persons who conspire with them, are subject to prosecution under this provision.

Example

A citizen loaned money at a high rate of interest and received a note as evidence of the loan. When the note was not paid on time, the citizen hired a police officer to collect the amount owed. The police officer, in uniform, visited the borrower, threatened arrest, and beat the borrower in order to collect the money owed to the citizen. Both the citizen and the police officer are subject to prosecution under the Civil Rights Act.

There are a number of provisions in the federal criminal code, of course, under which federal officers may be prosecuted for criminal conduct.

Federal Civil Liability of Police

Since the landmark decision of the United States Supreme Court in 1961 (*Monroe v. Pape*), the Federal Civil Rights Act has been used with increased frequency by private citizens seeking to recover damages against police officers for alleged wrongs received during the course of police performance. The provision of the Federal Civil Rights Act that is most frequently invoked in these cases reads as follows:

> Every person who, under color of any statute, ordinance, regulation, custom, or usage, of any State or Territory, subjects, or causes to be subjected, any citizen of the United States or other person within the jurisdiction thereof to the deprivation of any rights, privileges, or immunities secured by the Constitution and laws, shall be liable to the party injured in an action at law, suit in equity, or other proper proceedings for redress.

The Federal Civil Rights Act may be invoked against a state, county, municipal, or other local police official. It may not be invoked, however, against a federal law enforcement officer.

Example
A federal narcotics officer and a state police officer made a narcotics raid together. During the narcotics raid, they performed an unreasonable search and seizure and also beat the person in whose apartment the raid occurred. The state police officer can be sued, but the federal narcotics officer is immune from prosecution under the Federal Civil Rights Act.

Despite the fact that a federal officer may not be sued under the Federal Civil Rights Act, he (a) may be sued civilly in a state court, and (b) under a 1971 decision of the Supreme Court he may be sued in a federal court on a *tort* (civil wrong) theory based upon a constitutional right violation.

In order for suit to occur under the Federal Civil Rights Act, the conduct that is the subject of the lawsuit must have been performed by a police officer "under color of" his official position. That means that if the police officer performs a wrong in the conduct of his duties as an officer, even though his conduct is beyond the scope of his proper duties or is prohibited by his department, he may be liable under the Federal Civil Rights Act. But when a police officer is clearly acting as a private citizen, he may not be sued under the Federal Civil Rights Act.

Example
On his night off, Officer Jones goes to a tavern, drinks too much, engages Citizen Al in a fight and breaks Al's jaw. The next day, while on duty and irritated by the effects of the previous night, Officer Jones uses excessive force in arresting Citizen Bob. Citizen

Bob, who did not provoke Officer Jones in any manner, receives a broken jaw. Citizen Bob may invoke the Federal Civil Rights Act; Citizen Al may not. When Officer Jones struck Citizen Bob, he was acting in his official capacity; Citizen Al, however, was struck while Jones was acting as a private citizen. Citizen Al, of course, can still sue Officer Jones as a private citizen in a tort action.

Although the Federal Civil Rights Act may be invoked to collect damages for violation of "rights, privileges, or immunities secured by the [Federal] constitution and laws," it does not provide for redress for a violation by a police officer of a state constitution or a local law.

Example

Officer Brown arrests Citizen Kane. A state statute provides that upon making an arrest an officer must bring the arrested person before a magistrate within a two-hour period. Officer Brown delays three hours before bringing Kane before a magistrate. During that period, Kane is not interrogated by the police, nor is any other unlawful conduct performed. Kane may not sue Officer Brown under the Federal Civil Rights Act. Officer Brown deprived Kane of a right secured under a state statute, not under federal law or the United States Constitution.

The Federal Civil Rights Act provides for every type of relief available under the law, which means that the relief need not be limited to money damages.

Example

Fred Burns owns and operates a book store. The local ladies' club thinks that he sells dirty books. The police have examined the books that Burns sells and determined that they are not legally obscene. However, the president of the ladies' club is married to Officer White, who is assigned to the police district where Burns' book store is located. Every morning Officer White, influenced by his wife, goes to Burns' store, searches for dirty books, and seizes the books which his wife has told him about. Burns may file a Federal Civil Rights Act complaint against Officer White and, in addition to collecting money damages, may enjoin Officer White from coming into the book store and harassing him.

Although there is no legitimate reason why citizens should be deprived of a right to compensation for harm caused by unwarranted police conduct, there is no justification whatsoever to using civil suits or criminal complaints against the police merely for harassment or other ulterior motives.

PROSECUTORIAL IMMUNITY

Although the police are subject to civil suits for their errors and abuses, either under state statutes or ordinary tort law concepts, under the Federal Civil Rights Act, or on the theory of a constitutional right violation, prosecuting attorneys and judges have absolute immunity from civil suits. The rationale for this—however unappealing and unsatisfying it may be to police and laymen—is that there is a grave danger to the cause of the administration of justice if those officials, with the wide, unstructured discretion they must exercise, were to be held accountable for their actions. The law to this effect stems from several important Supreme Court decisions, the latest one, as regards prosecutorial immunity, having been rendered in 1976.

Appendix

Provisions of the Constitution of the United States, and certain Amendments thereto, of particular significance in the administration of criminal justice:

Preamble

We the People of the United States, in Order to form a more perfect Union, establish Justice, insure domestic Tranquility, provide for the common defense, promote the general Welfare, and secure the Blessings of Liberty to ourselves and our Posterity, do ordain and establish this Constitution for the United States of America.

Article I

. . .

Section 8. The Congress shall have Power To lay and collect Taxes, Duties, Imposts and Excises, to pay the Debts and provide for the common Defence and general Welfare of the United States; but all Duties, Imposts and Excises shall be uniform throughout the United States; . . .

To regulate Commerce with foreign Nations, and among the several States and with the Indian Tribes; . . .

To provide for the Punishment of counterfeiting the Securities and current Coin of the United States; . . .

To constitute Tribunals inferior to the supreme Court;

To define and punish Piracies and Felonies committed on the high Seas, and Offences against the Law of Nations;

To declare War . . . and make Rules concerning Captures on Land and Water; . . .

To make Rules for the Government and Regulation of the land and naval forces;

To provide for the calling forth the Militia to execute the Laws of the Union, suppress Insurrections and repel Invasions;

To provide for organizing, arming, and disciplining, the Militia, and for governing such Part of them as may be employed in the Service of the United States, reserving to the States respectively, the Appointment of the Officers, and the Authority of training the Militia according to the discipline prescribed by Congress;

To exercise exclusive Legislation in all Cases whatsoever, over such District (not exceeding ten Miles square) as may, by Cession of particular States, and the Acceptance of Congress, become the Seat of the Government of the United States, and to exercise like Authority over all Places purchased by the Consent of the Legislature of the State in which the Same shall be, for the Erection of Forts, Magazines, Arsenals, dock-Yards, and other needful Buildings;—And

To make all Laws which shall be necessary and proper for carrying into Execution the foregoing Powers, and all other Powers vested by this Constitution in the Government of the United States, or in any Department or Officer thereof.

Section 9.

. . .

No Bill of Attainder or ex post facto Law shall be passed.

Article III

Section 1. The judicial Power of the United States, shall be vested in one supreme Court, and in such inferior Courts as the Congress may from time to time ordain and establish. The Judges, both of the supreme and inferior Courts, shall hold their Offices during good Behaviour, and shall, at stated Times, receive for their Services, a Compensation, which shall not be diminished during their Continuance in Office.

Section 2.

. . . the supreme Court shall have appellate Jurisdiction, both as to Law and Fact, with such Exceptions, and under such Regulations as the Congress shall make.

The Trial of all Crimes, except in Cases of Impeachment, shall be by Jury; and such Trial shall be held in the State where the said Crimes shall have been committed; but when not committed within any State, the Trial shall be at such Place or Places as the Congress may by Law have directed.

Section 3. Treason against the United States, shall consist only in levying War against them, or in adhering to their Enemies, giving them Aid and Comfort. No Person shall be convicted of Treason unless on the Testimony of two Witnesses to the same overt Act, or on Confession in open Court.

The Congress shall have Power to declare the Punishment of Treason, but no Attainder of Treason shall work Corruption of Blood, or Forfeiture except during the Life of the Person attainted.

Article VI

. . .

This Constitution, and the Laws of the United States which shall be made in Pursuance thereof; and all Treaties made, or which shall be made, under

Appendix

the Authority of the United States, shall be the supreme Law of the Land; and the Judges in every State shall be bound thereby, any Thing in the Constitution or Laws of any State to the Contrary notwithstanding.

. . .

Amendments

Amendment I

Congress shall make no law respecting an establishment of religion, or prohibiting the free exercise thereof; or abridging the freedom of speech, or of the press; or the right of the people peaceably to assemble, and to petition the Government for a redress of grievances.

Amendment II

A well regulated militia, being necessary to the security of a free State, the right of the people to keep and bear arms, shall not be infringed.

Amendment III

No Soldier shall, in time of peace be quartered in any house, without the consent of the owner, nor in time of war, but in a manner to be prescribed by law.

Amendment IV

The right of the people to be secure in their persons, houses, papers, and effects, against unreasonable searches and seizures, shall not be violated, and no warrants shall issue, but upon probable cause, supported by oath or affirmation, and particularly describing the place to be searched, and the persons or things to be seized.

Amendment V

No person shall be held to answer for a capital, or otherwise infamous crime, unless on a presentment or indictment of a Grand Jury, except in cases arising in the land or naval forces, or in the militia, when in actual service in time of war or public danger; nor shall any person be subject for the same offence to be twice put in jeopardy of life or limb; nor shall be compelled in any criminal case to be a witness against himself, nor be deprived of life, liberty, or property, without due process of law; nor shall private property be taken for public use, without just compensation.

Amendment VI

In all criminal prosecutions, the accused shall enjoy the right to a speedy and public trial, by an impartial jury of the State and district wherein the crime shall have been committed, which district shall have been previously ascertained by law, and to be informed of the nature and cause of the accusation; to be confronted with the witnesses against him; to have compulsory process for obtaining witnesses in his favor, and to have the assistance of Counsel for his defence.

Amendment VII

In Suits at common law, where the value in controversy shall exceed twenty dollars, the right of trial by jury shall be preserved, and no fact tried by a jury, shall be otherwise re-examined in any Court of the United States, than according to the rules of the common law.

Amendment VIII

Excessive bail shall not be required, nor excessive fines imposed, nor cruel and unusual punishments inflicted.

Amendment IX

The enumeration in the Constitution, of certain rights, shall not be construed to deny or disparage others retained by the people.

Amendment X

The powers not delegated to the United States by the Constitution, nor prohibited by it to the States, are reserved to the States respectively, or to the people.

. . .

Amendment XIII

Section 1. Neither slavery nor involuntary servitude, except as a punishment for crime whereof the party shall have been duly convicted, shall exist within the United States, or any place subject to their jurisdiction.

Section 2. Congress shall have power to enforce this article by appropriate legislation.

Amendment XIV

Section 1. All persons born or naturalized in the United States, and subject to the jurisdiction thereof, are citizens of the United States and of the State wherein they reside. No State shall make or enforce any law which shall abridge the privileges or immunities of citizens of the United States; nor shall any State deprive any person of life, liberty, or property, without due process of law; nor deny to any person within its jurisdiction the equal protection of laws. . . .

Section 5. The Congress shall have power to enforce, by appropriate legislation, the provisions of this article.

Amendment XV

Section 1. The right of citizens of the United States to vote shall not be denied or abridged by the United States or by any State on account of race, color, or previous condition of servitude.

Section 2. The Congress shall have power to enforce this article by appropriate legislation.

Amendment XVI

The Congress shall have power to lay and collect taxes on incomes, from whatever source derived, without apportionment among the several States, and without regard to any census or enumeration. . . .

Glossary

(The glossary does not include the most common offenses or criminal procedures discussed in the text; references to these appear in the Index.)

Arraignment—the appearance of a person before a court in order that the court may inform him of the accusation(s) against him and so that he may enter a plea.

Arrest—taking a person into custody by authority of law for the purpose of charging him with a criminal offense or for the purpose of initiating juvenile proceedings, terminating with the recording of a specific offense.

Arrest warrant—a document issued by a court authorizing the police to arrest a person for the commission of an offense.

Attainder, bill of—an act of a legislature, now rendered impermissible in the US Constitution, which penalized criminally certain named or described persons.

Attorney—a person trained in the law, admitted to practice before the courts of a particular jurisdiction, and authorized to advise, represent, and act for persons in legal proceedings.

Bill of Rights—the first eight Amendments to the U.S. Constitution.

Booking—a police administrative action officially recording an arrest and identifying the person, the place, the time, the authority, and the reason for the arrest.

Charge—an accusation contained in a criminal complaint, an indictment by a grand jury, or in an information filed by a prosecuting attorney.

Counsel—a synonym for attorney.

Complaint—a written accusation made for the purpose of initiating some form of legal action. It may emanate from a private citizen, a police officer, or a prosecutor.

Conviction—a judgment of a court, based either upon the verdict of a jury or a judicial officer or upon the guilty plea of the defendant, that the defendant is guilty of the offense(s) with which he was charged.

Court—an agency of the judicial branch of government authorized to decide controversies in law and disputed matters of fact presented to it. The word also is used to refer to the judge himself.

Delinquent—a juvenile whose wrongful conduct is less than that ordinarily defined as criminal, or who is in a status requiring court action for rectification.

Directed verdict—an order by the judge (based upon an essential weakness of the prosecution's case) that the jury must find that the defendant was not proved guilty beyond a reasonable doubt.

Diversion—the official halting or suspension of formal criminal or juvenile justice proceedings against an alleged offender, and the referral of that person to a treatment or care program administered by a non-criminal justice agency, or a private agency, or perhaps without any referral at all. Such actions are usually termed diversionary programs.

Double jeopardy—a constitutional concept that prohibits the trial of an accused person twice for the same offense.

Ex post facto—a term usually applied to a law making an act an offense "after the fact" of its commission; prohibited by the Fifth Amendment.

Felony—a serious offense for which the penalty is usually either capital punishment or incarceration in a penitentiary for one year or more.

Grand jury—a panel of citizens selected by a court to investigate crimes and to determine whether or not there is probable cause (reasonable grounds) for a suspect to be tried for a felony.

Hearing—a proceeding in which arguments and witnesses are heard by a judicial officer, grand jury, or other governmental unit.

Immunity, grant of—a judicially sanctioned agreement that an individual's testimony will not be used against him, or that he will not be prosecuted for the offense(s) about which he is questioned, usually in exchange for his testimony against an accomplice or other offender.

Indictment—a document voted and filed by a grand jury charging a person with, and requiring that he stand trial for, the commission of a felony. Also called a true bill.

Information—a document prepared by the prosecutor charging a person with, and requiring that he stand trial for, the commission of a misdemeanor, or, in some jurisdictions and under certain circumstances, for a felony.

Infraction—an offense punishable by fine or other penalty, but not by incarceration, e.g., a minor traffic violation.

Inmate—a person in a confinement facility.

Jail—a confinement facility, usually administered by a local law enforcement agency, intended for adults but sometimes also containing juveniles, which holds persons who are detained for pending charges or who have received sentences of less than one year.

Judgment—the decision of a court that the defendant is convicted of the offense(s) charged.

Jurisdiction—the territory, subject matter, or person over which lawful authority may be exercised.

Juvenile—a person subject to juvenile court proceedings because a statutorily

defined event was alleged to have occurred while his age was below a specified one (e.g., 17).
Jury (*petit jury, trial jury*)—a panel of citizens selected by court process to determine whether the evidence offered at trial proves the accused guilty beyond a reasonable doubt.
Lawyer—a synonym for attorney.
Misdemeanor—an offense for which the penalty is usually either a fine or incarceration in a jail for less than a year.
Motion—a request, made either in writing or orally, that the court rule on a particular legal issue.
Nolo contendere—a plea which has the same effect as a plea of guilty, except that it cannot be regarded as an admission of guilt in any civil trial.
Ordinance—legislation enacted by a political subdivision of a state (city or county). Violations, sometimes referred to as infractions, are punishable by monetary fines.
Offense (*crime*)—a violation of a state statute for which a penalty is prescribed.
Parole—a conditional release before the completion of a sentence of incarceration.
Plea bargaining—the exchange of prosecutorial and/or judicial concessions, usually in the form of either a reduction in penalty or to a lesser charge, in return for a guilty plea.
Preliminary hearing—a court proceeding to determine whether or not there is sufficient evidence against the accused to take the case to the grand jury or for him to stand trial. Known within the federal system as arraignment.
Presentence report—a document resulting from an investigation by a probation agency of convicted persons and their background in order to assist the judge in determining the appropriate sentence or whether he should release that person on probation.
Prison—a confinement facility having custodial authority over adults sentenced to confinement for a year or more.
Probation—the conditional freedom granted by a judicial officer to a convicted person in lieu of confinement in jail or penitentiary.
Probationer—a convicted person who has been granted conditional freedom (probation) in lieu of confinement in jail or penitentiary.
Pro se—a term signifying that an accused or convicted person acts as his own attorney.
Prosecutor—an attorney who is either elected or appointed to represent the people (state, district, county, or city) in matters involving criminal accusations. He may be known in some states by alternative titles such as district attorney, states attorney, or commonwealth attorney. In the federal system he is called a United States attorney.
Public defender—an attorney employed by a governmental agency to represent accused persons who are unable to hire private attorneys.
Quashing of indictment—an order by the judge that the formal written document charging the accused with a felony is defective.
Search warrant—a document issued by a court authorizing the police to search a place or person (usually for evidence of an offense).

Subpoena—an order of a court or grand jury for a named person to appear and give testimony.

Subpoena duces tecum—a subpoena to present to a court or grand jury documents or other tangible material.

Substantive offense—the specific, basic crime, as distinguished from an auxiliary one, such as a conspiracy to commit the offense itself.

Summons—a written order issued by a judicial officer requiring a person to appear at a certain time and place to answer charges or questions relating to a matter before the issuing authority.

Suppression of evidence—an order by the judge refusing to permit certain evidence against the defendant to be considered.

Tort—a civil wrong to a person that can be compensated by money damages but ordinarily not punishable criminally.

True bill—a synonym for indictment.

Venue—the place or court where a trial is to be held.

Index

Abortion: constitutionality of prohibitory laws, 47; as "victimless" crime, 55–56
Accessory, criminal responsibility of, 93–94
Accomplice, criminal responsibility of, 93
Addicts. *See* Narcotics
Adultery, 31
Aircraft, crimes connected with, 76–77
Alcoholics, public intoxication of, 62
Annoying conduct: anonymous telephone calls, 34; disorderly conduct, 62; disturbing the peace, 62; public intoxication, 62; sexual exhibitionism, 33; window peeping, 33–34
Antitrust activities, 67. *See also* "White collar" crimes
Appeals: from conviction, 174; from pretrial court orders, 174; from pretrial suppression orders, 129; from sentence, 173; "reversed and remanded," 174
Appellate courts, functions and procedures of, 12, 15
Arraignment, 147–148

Arrest: arrestee's right to early court presentation, 141; citizen duty in assisting, 113; citizen powers of, 112, 113; definition of, 106; by federal officers, 110–112; of fugitive, 112; geographic boundaries for police, 112; "hot pursuit," 112; invalid arrest consequences, 108; legal alternatives to, 114; merchants' precaution in making, 28; permissible delay before arraignment, 132; permissible force in, 113; post-arrest obligations, 113–114; obtaining warrant for, 109; requirements of probable cause (reasonable grounds), 106, 108–109; upon court warrant, 108–109; without court warrant, 106
Arrest warrant: conditions when not required, 122; for disregarding summons, 114; federal court process for, 15; invalid, consequences of, 110; invalid, protection of arrester from liability for, 111; minor errors inconsequential in, 110; requirements for issuance of, 109, 110

201

Arson, 42–43
Assault: aggravated, 30; criminal offense by police, 185; definition of, 29
Assembly, unlawful, 62
Attempt, crime of, 89–90
Attorney general: federal, 9; state, 8
Attorneys. See Lawyers, federal; Lawyers, local

Bail: constitutional right to, 145; criteria in setting, 145; denial of, 145; lockup situations, 17; recognizance bond, 145; types of satisfactions, 145–146; uses of, 142, 144–145
Battery: aggravated, 29; child abuse, 29; definition of, 29; by police, 185
Best evidence rule, 156
Bigamy, 31
Boats, crimes on, of U.S. registry, 76
Breach of the peace, window peeping as, 33–34
Bribery, criminal offense by police, 186. See also Public official corruption
Bugging. See Eavesdropping
Burglary, 22, 39

Capital punishment, 25; insane person not subject to, 98
Certiorari, writ of, 16, 174
Child abuse, 29
CIA, 6
Citizen crime commissions, value of, 71
Citizen's remedies against police: federal civic actions, 189–191; federal criminal actions, 188–189; state civil actions, 187–188; state criminal actions, 184–187
Civil rights violations: election frauds, 61; federal and state, 60–61
Clayton Act, antitrust activities, 67
Closing arguments, 163
Collateral attack, 175

Common law: definition and nature of, 19–20; federal system devoid of, 20; murder within, 21
Commutations, 170–171
Complaint: as basis for arrest warrant, 110; initiation of prosecution upon, 144
Compounding a crime, 43, 81
Compulsion, defense of, 96
Computers, and criminal investigation, 4–5
Confessions. See Interrogations and confessions
Confidence games, 37–38
Conflict of interest, 60
Con man. See "White collar" crimes
Conspiracy, crime of, 91–92
Contempt of court, 87
Continuance, 142
Controlled dangerous substances. See Narcotics
Coroner's inquest, 142–143
Corruption. See Public official corruption
Counsel, right to: constitutional guarantee of, 141; distinguished from *Miranda* warning, 141; under eye-witness identification procedures, 115; at police interrogations, 134; waiver of, 115
Counterfeiting laws: Secret Service jurisdiction, 74; violations of, 74–75
County attorney, 7
Court orders: disobedience of, 87; for procurement of physical evidence, 128; for suppression of evidence, appeals from, 129
Courtroom, consequences of disruptive behavior in, 86, 88
Courts, federal: courts of appeal, 15; district courts, 14–15; magistrate courts, 14; Supreme Court, 15
Courts, local and state: appellate courts, 12; juvenile courts, 12; major trial courts, 12; minor trial courts, 11

Index

Credit card offenses, 42
Crimes, categories of, 19
Cruel and unusual punishment, and narcotic addiction, 49–50
Customs agents, 5

Dangerous conduct potential: looting, 63; mob action, 62; protest marches and parades, 63–64; rioting, 62; unlawful assembly, 62
Defendant's evidence, 162
Defense counsel: appointed, 9; constitutional right to, 9; military, 10; public defenders, 9; retained, 10
Defense intelligence agents, 6
Destruction of property. See Property damage
Detention facilities: federal, 18; local and state, 17–18
Disorderly conduct, 62
District attorneys, 7
Disturbing the peace, 62
Diversionary programs. See Pretrial diversionary programs
Double jeopardy: protection against, 129; prohibition against, 163
Due process, 130

Eavesdropping: federal law on, 34–35; legislative authorization of, 70; by police, 185; state law on, 34–35
Election frauds, 61
Electronic surveillance, by police, 185. See also Eavesdropping
Embezzlement, 37
Entrapment, defense of, 97
Environmental protection, and state's attorney general, 9
Espionage, crime of, 75
Ethics. See Rules of ethics
Evidence: admissibility of, 151–152; circumstantial, 162; confessions inadmissible as, 130–131; of conspiracy, 91–92; defendant's, forms of, 162; "derivatively obtained," 129; direct, 162; hearsay, 107, 126 (see also Hearsay rule); illegally

Evidence: (cont'd)
seized, 129; law of, 151–158; laying a foundation, 152; motion to suppress, 129; objections to, 152; physical, 128, 136; prosecutor's evidence, forms of, 162; rejection of, 129; rules of, 152–153; tampering with, 81; testimonial, 136; test of competence, 152; test of materiality, 153; test of relevance, 152–153; test of voluntariness in confessions, 130; weight of, 152. See also Exclusionary rule
Exclusionary rule: applicability to confessions, 132; effect on firearms cases, 57; history of, 120–121; and illegal arrest, 108; and illegally seized evidence, 154; and illegal stop-and-frisk, 118; purpose of, 120, 129
Excusable homicide, 21
Exhibitionism, 33
Extortion, 59, 184
Eye-witness identification, procedures of, 115–116

False pretenses, 37–38
Federal Bureau of Investigation (FBI), 4–5
Federal Civil Rights Act: federal civil prosecution under, 189–190; federal criminal prosecution under, 188–189; federal officers exempted, 189–190; *Monroe v. Pope* decision, 189; police civil and criminal liability under, 188
Federal officers. See Police
Felony: definition of, 19; preliminary hearing in case of, 142; requirement of grand jury indictment, 144
Felony-murder, 22
Fingerprints: court orders for, 128; FBI file of, 5; obtaining by compulsion, 101
Firearms: controls on, 56–58; illegal seizure of, 57

Flight to avoid or hamper prosecution, 82
Forgery, 41
Fornication, 31
Fraudulent schemes, 65–66
Free speech, and protest marches, 64
Friend of court briefs, 16
Fugitives: arrest of, 112; flight of, 83; harboring, 83

Gambling, 50–54; charitable institution games, 52–53; conspiracy to commit, 92; contracts unenforceable, 54; federal laws against, 53–54; forfeiture of funds for, 54; forfeiture of liquor license for, 53; legalization consequences, 54; lotteries, 51–52; nuisance offense, 53; state operated, 52, 54; syndicated, 52; things excluded from definition of, 50–51; as "victimless crime," 55–56. *See also* Organized crime
Gambling devices: interstate transportation of, 53–54; possession, sale, etc., of, 53; seizure of, 54
Glue sniffing, 49
Grand jury: abolition of, in some states, 143; composition and function of, 102, 143, 182; investigative efforts of, 102; power of subpoena, 102–103, 129; state's attorney's use of, 9; "true bills" or indictments by, 143; types of, 182–183
Guns. *See* Firearms

Habeas corpus writ: federal, 15, 175; nature and purpose of, 142, 175; petition for, 175
Health and safety inspectors, searches and seizures by, 128
Hearsay evidence: as basis for warrant, 126; definition of, 107
Hearsay rule: 154, 156; "dying declaration" and other exceptions to, 156

Hijacking, 40
Hobbs Act, 59
Homicide: definition of, 21; federal law on, 24; legislation on criminal, 24–25; in self-defense, types of, 21–24; window peepers as targets of, 34
Homosexual conduct, 32, 56

Immigration: agents, 6; violation of laws on, 73
Immunity: consequences of failure to testify after grant of, 103; contempt of court finding after grant of, 88; grant of, issued by judge, 104; grant of, to compel testimony, 60, 103; judges' and prosecutors', from civil suits, 191; pros and cons of granting, 103; prosecution considerations in deciding upon grants of, 104
Impeachment, of federal judges, 14
Incest, 31
Incompetence, test of, 98
Indian reservation police, 6
Indictment: grand jury return of, 102; required for federal criminal prosecutions, 143
Information, initiation of prosecution upon, 142, 144
Informers' tips: as basis for arrest, 107; as basis for warrant, 126
Insanity: defense of, 98; tests of, 98
Insurance, burning property to obtain, 43
Intelligence agents, military and national, 6
Intent, requirement of: in obscenity cases, 45–47; in tax law prosecutions, 72; in theft cases, 36–37, 39
Internal Revenue Service (IRS) agents, 5
Interrogations and confessions: admissibility of, 130–131; and delay in arraignment, 132; general guideline for interrogators, 134; *Miranda* requirements, 132–134;

Index

Interrogations: (cont'd)
and promise of immunity or leniency, 130, 131; right to counsel during, 134
Interstate commerce, as basis for federal jurisdiction, 40, 59
Intoxication: defense of, 96; public, 62

Jails, 17, 18
Judges, federal, 13–14; immunity from civil suits, 191
Jurors: commuting with, 84; disqualification of, 182; persons excused or exempted from serving, 182; selection of, 160–161, 182; sequestering of, 183
Jury: challenges for cause in selection of, 160; composition of, 160; deliberation by, 163; foreman, function of, 163; function of, 159; grounds for disqualification of, 182; "hung," 164; instructions by the court to, 163; peremptory challenges in selection of, 160; polling of, 164; questioning of (*voir dire* examination), 160, 161; right to trial by, 159; selection of, 160, 161, 182; sequestering of, 183
Jury trial: function of judge in, 159; function of jury in, 159; right to, 159
Justifiable homicide, defense of, 21
Juveniles: constitutional rights of, 12; detention facilities for, 18; federal court dispositions, 12

Kickbacks, 66. See also Public official corruption
Kidnapping: definition of, 26; as federal offense, 27; killing in commission of, 22; unlawful restraint distinction, 28

Laboratories, scientific crime detection, 5

Larceny, 36–37
Lawyers, federal: attorney general, 9; defense counsel, 10; military attorneys, 10; organized crime strike-force attorneys, 10, 70; solicitor general, 10; United States attorneys, 10
Lawyers, local: commonwealth attorneys, 8; county attorneys, 7; defense attorneys, 9; district attorneys, 7; municipal, 7; prosecuting attorneys, 8; public defenders, 9
Loan-sharking, 92
Lockups, police, 17
Looting, 63
Lotteries, 51–52

Mafia. See Organized crime
Mails: fraudulent use of, 59, 74; interference with, 74; Postal Inspection Service function, 6; protective agents, 6; Travel Act violations and, 77
Malicious mischief, 42
"Mann Act," 33
Manslaughter: definition of, 22; involuntary, 23; modern legislation on, 24; voluntary, 23. See also Homicide
Marijuana: and criminality issue, 48; nature and effect of, 48; use of, as "victimless" crime, 56
Marshal, federal, 5
Mayhem. See Battery
Mental responsibility: and compulsion defense, 96; and entrapment defense, 97; "evil-meaning" mind requirement, 95; and incompetency to stand trial, 98; and infancy defense, 96; and insanity defense, 98; and intoxication defense, 96; and necessity defense, 96
Military: attorneys, 10; courts, 16; judges, 78; police, 6; trials of personnel and their dependents, 78, 79

Miranda decision, 132–134; erosions of, 133; nullification attempt by Congress, 133
Misdemeanor, definition of, 19
Misprision of felony, 43, 81
Mistake, as defense, 95
Mob action, 62
Morals, public, offenses against, 44
Motions: change of venue, 148; pretrial, 148–149; to quash an indictment, 148; to quash a warrant of arrest, 110; to suppress evidence, 110, 129, 149
Motor vehicle killings, 24
Murder: arson death, 43; definition of, 21; degrees of, 22; felony, 22, 43; modern legislation on, 24

Narcotics: abandoned, seizure of, 123; addiction, as "victimless crime," 55; addicts, prosecution of, 48–50; conspiracy to violate laws on, 92; federal investigative agents, 5; federal jurisdiction over, 48; free issuance of, to addicts, 55; glue sniffing and sales, 49; heroin, kinds and sources of, 69; history of, 47; hypodermic, possession of, 49; importation of, 48; methadone treatment of addicts, 50; penalties for law violations, 48; possession of, 49; prescription restrictions, 49; types of, 48, 49, 69; use of, as "victimless crime," 55–56
National Security Agency, 6
Necessity, defense of, 96
Nolo contendere plea, 148
Notice to appear, as alternative to arrest, 114

Obscenity: motion pictures and, 46–48; offense of, 44; protection of children from, 47; search warrant requirements, 126; tests of, 44–47; as "victimless crime," 55–56
Opening statements, 161–162

Opinion rule: admissibility exception, 157–158; inadmissible as evidence in witness testimony, 157
Ordinances, definition and nature of, 19
Organized crime: combating, 69; congressional statutes for fight against, 70; electronic eavesdropping against, 70; federal strike force attorneys, 10, 70; and gambling, 52, 68–69; immunity grants for testimony against, 60, 103; "juice" loans, 68–69; labor union infiltration by, 69–70; legitimate business infiltration by, 68–69; loan-sharking and, 68–69; mafia, as misnomer of, 68; narcotic traffic by, 68–69; nature of, 68; prosecutor's investigative effort against, 102; and prostitution, 68; public education in fight against, 71; public official corruption and, 69; Travel Act violations and, 77; and "victimless crime" issue, 56

Pardons and commutations, 170–171
Parole: board of, 170; definition and conditions for grant of, 170; officers, 4
Penitentiary system, 18, 173
Perjury: offense of, 85–86; by police, 186; subornation of, 86
Petition: postconviction, seeking collateral remedies, 175; for writ of certiorari, 174; for writ of habeas corpus, 175
Picketing. *See* Dangerous conduct potential
Pickpocketing, 39
Piracy, 76; skyjacking, 76
Plea bargaining, 149–150
Police: arrests by federal, 110–112; assaults upon federal, 81; citizens' legal actions against, 184–191; Federal agents, types

Index

Police: (cont'd)
of, 4–6; giving false information to, 81; interfering with, 80; local officers, types of, 3–4; prosecutorial immunity of, 191

Police crimes: assault, 185; battery, 185; bribery, 186; carrying unauthorized deadly weapons, 185; coercion to obtain confession, 185; electronic surveillance, 185; extortion, 184–185; failure to report a bribe, 186; false arrest and imprisonment, 187; federal, civil, 188–189; federal, criminal, 189–191; harassment of witnesses or jurors, 186; indemnification of officers, 188; injury through ordinary negligence, 187; intimidation, 184; malicious prosecution, 187; official misconduct, 186; perjury and subornation of perjury, 186; state, civil, 187–188; state, criminal, 184–187; tampering with public records, 186; violating rights of accused, 187

Pornography, display and sale of, as "victimless crime," 5. See also Obscenity

Postal Inspection Service, 6

Post-conviction remedies: collateral, 175; habeas corpus writ, 175

Preliminary hearing, 141–142

Press, freedom of, and obscenity issue, 44–47

Pretrial diversionary programs: administration of, 147; nature and purpose of, 146; station adjustment, 146–147; supervision, 147, 167; use of, in drunk-driving cases, 147

Prisons, 18, 173

Privacy, right to, in abortion cases, 47

Privileged communications, 157

Probable cause, requirement of: for arrest, 106, 108–109; for seizure of evidence, 106

Probation, 168

Probation officers, 4

Property, stolen. See Theft and related offenses

Process service, obstructing, 81

Property damage: arson, 42–43; malicious mischief, 42; at schools, 43

Property intrusions: trespass, 43; window peeping, 34

Prosecuting attorneys: federal, types of, 9–10; local, types of, 7–8. See also Prosecutors

Prosecutions: time limit on initiating, 158–159; statute of limitation, 159

Prosecutorial discretion, 146

Prosecutors: immunity from civil suits, 191; investigative efforts of, 102; power of, 146. See also Prosecuting attorneys

Prosecutor's evidence, 162

Prostitution: and organized crime, 68; and the "victimless crime" issue, 56

Protest marches and parades: and constitutional rights, 64; controls on, 63–64

Public defenders, 9

Public official corruption: as basis for federal prosecution of state officials, 59; bribery, 59; conflict of interest, 60; conspiracies, 92; defrauding citizens of faithful public services, 60; extortion, 59, 184; Hobbs Act, 59; immunity grants in prosecution of, 60, 104; mail fraud, 59; need for laws to discourage, 58; and organized crime, 71; police crimes, 184–191; prosecutor's investigative effort, 102; Travel Act violations, 77

Racketeer Influenced and Corrupt Organization (RICO) statute, 70–71

Racketeering. See Organized Crime

Rape, 30–31

Reasonable doubt, requirement for proof of guilt beyond, 107
Reasonable grounds, requirement of: for arrest, 106; for seizure of evidence, 106
Receiving stolen property, 38
Rehabilitation concept, rejection of, 172
Restraint, unlawful, 28
Rioting, 62
Robbery, 22, 39. See also Theft and related offenses
Rules of ethics: ABA standards, 164; ethical restrictions, 165; for criminal law practitioners, 164

Sabotage, 75
Search and seizure: of abandoned property, 123; by administrative agencies, 128; at border, 124; by consent, 122; of contraband in plain view, 123; due process violations in course of, 124; emergency, 123, 124; incidental to arrest, 120–122; independent of arrest, 122–125; inventory search in police facility, 121, 122; in obscenity cases, 126, 127; of physical evidence on suspects, 128; plain view, 123; shocking search, 124; of vehicle, 122, 124; with warrant, 125–128; without warrant, 121–125, 128
Search warrant: execution of, 127; form of, 127; form of complaint for, 125; grounds for issuance of, 125; independent of arrest, 125; issuance of, 127; objects subject to seizure, 125; particularization of, 126; undercover agent's information as basis for, 126
Secret Service Agency, 5
Self-defense: justifiable, 21; and paramour killings, 23
Self-incrimination privilege: history and policy of, 135; immunity

Self-incrimination privilege: (cont'd) grant as substitute for, 60, 103; inapplicable to eye-witness identification procedures, 114; inapplicable to procurement of physical evidence, 101, 136; investigative level protection, 101; limitations upon, 136; and *Miranda* warnings, 133; and physical evidence obtainable by compulsion, 136; and privacy protection, 157; protections offered by, 136; restricted to testimonial evidence, 101; testimonial evidence, protected, 136
Sentence: appeals for commutation of, 173; determinate, 167–168, 172; fine, 167; flat time, 172; indeterminate, 167–168, 172; jail and penitentiary confinement, 167; by judge after guilty verdict, 163; mandatory, 173; reasons for imposition of, 166–167; standardization of, 172; supervision, defined, 167; types of, 167–168
Sex offenses: adultery, 31; anonymous telephone calls, 34; bigamy, 31; contributing to child delinquency, 31; deviate sexual conduct, 32; exhibitionism, 33; fornication, 31; homosexual conduct, 32, 56; incest, 31; indecent liberties with children, 31; "Mann Act," 33; narcotic addicts as offenders, 48; rape, 30; statutory rape, 31; "White Slave" Act, 32, 33; window-peeping, 33–34
Sheriff, county, 4
Sherman Act, antitrust activities, 67
Shoplifting: arrests for, 28; detention of suspects, 28; intent requirement, 36
Skyjacking, 76
Smuggling: offense of, 73; Treasury agency function, 5
Solicitation, offense of, 90–91

Index

Speech, freedom of, 44; and obscenity issue, 44–47
Spies, diplomatic niceties regarding foreign embassy, 75
Statutes of limitation, 159
Stop-and-frisk: legal guidelines and limitations on, 117–118; permissible force in, 119; statutes authorizing, 119
Street crimes, 21–30, 39
Summons, alternative to, 114
Suspects, obtaining physical evidence from, 128
Swindler. See "White collar" crimes

Tax law violations, 72–73; IRS agents and, 5
Telephone offenses: anonymous calls, 34; in criminal activities, 65, 77; tapping, 34–35
Theft and related offenses: burglary, 22, 39; commission by deception, 65; confidence games, 37–38; credit card crimes, 42; Dyer Act violations, 40; embezzlement, 37; false pretenses, 37–38; federal law violations, 40; federal property stolen, 41; forgery, 41; hijacking of vehicle, 40; intent, problem of, 36–37, 39; larceny by bailee, 37; larceny, grand and petit, 36, 38; modern legislation on, 38; pickpocketing, 39; receiving stolen property, 38; robbery, 22, 39, shoplifting, 28. See also "White collar" crimes
Threatening communications, 78
Traffic violations: alternatives to arrest for, 114; lack of intent as no defense for, 95; release on bail for, 144
Travel Act, violations of, 77
Treasury agents, 5
Trespass. See Property intrusions
Trial: bench trial, 154, 159; by jury, right to, 159; right to speedy trial, 158; stages of, 151–165

United States attorneys, 10

Venue, motion for change of, 148
Verdict by jury: of acquittal, 162, 163; double-jeopardy prohibition, 163; of guilty, 163; motion for new trial, 164; unanimity requirement, 160–161, 164
Veterans Administration Benefits, false applications for, 67
"Victimless" crimes: civil enforcement alternative in, 56; issue of, pros and cons, 34, 55–56; offender as source of tips, 56; percentage of, in law enforcement, 56; types of, 55–56
Voir dire examinations, 160–161

Waiver: of right to counsel, 115; of right to object to evidence, 151, 152; of trial by jury, 159
Warrant. See Arrest warrant; Search warrant
"White collar" crimes: con man crimes, 65; definition of, 65; false statements, 66; fraudulent schemes, 65–66; kinds of, 65–68
"White Slave" Act, 32–33
Witnesses: harassment of, 84; national protection program for, 5; objections to questions in examination of, 180; refusal to testify, 87; rules of conduct for, 179–182; tampering with, 84–85
Window peeping, 33–34
Wiretapping. See Eavesdropping
Work-release programs, 168
Writ of certiorari, 174; Supreme Court function in, 16
Writ of habeas corpus. See Habeas corpus writ